JOURNAL OF THE AMERICAN ACADEMY OF RELIGION
September 2002, Volume 70, Issue 3

LIBRARY

EDITOR:
Glenn Yocum, *Whittier College*

BOOK REVIEW EDITOR:
Sheila Greeve Davaney, *Iliff School of Theology*

ASSOCIATE EDITORS:
Gary Laderman, *Emory University*
Joseph L. Price, *Whittier College*

PRODUCTION EDITOR:
Elizabeth Gardner, *Oxford University Press*

AMERICAN ACADEMY OF RELIGION

The *Journal of the American Academy of Religion* is an official publication of the American Academy of Religion. The *Journal* may be received by either subscription or by membership in the Academy. Membership in the Academy is open to those engaged in research and/or instruction in the field of religious studies. Individuals interested in membership may write to: American Academy of Religion, 825 Houston Mill Road, Atlanta, GA 30333-4211, USA.

The Academy maintains executive offices on the campus of Emory University, Atlanta, GA 30329-4025, telephone (404) 727-7920, under the direction of Barbara DeConcini, Executive Director. For more information about the American Academy of Religion, please visit the web site at www.aarweb.org.

KU-997-619

JOURNAL OF THE AMERICAN ACADEMY OF RELIGION

September 2002
Volume 70
Number 3

BOOKS RECEIVED

Beyond the Founding Fratricidal Conflict: A Tale of Three Cities

Rebecca S. Chopp

The dominant structure of bureaucratic differentiation in higher education, created through boundaries and divisions of epistemological differentiation that preclude active engagement with the public, is changing. Higher education is now more like a global city with flexible boundaries and multiple networks than like a rigidly structured metropolis. Scholars of religion can shape the university in this time of rapid change and in so doing can shape the contours of the study of religion in higher education to have a new engagement with the public.

IN THE AFTERMATH of the events that befell the United States and the world on 11 September 2001, the American Academy of Religion Board, under the guidance of our executive director, discussed whether or not we should issue a statement. Like the rest of the world, we wanted to protest against the terror; to express solidarity with the victims, their families and friends, and others; and to caution prudence as gongs of war and sirens of profiling were sounding. We wanted to *do* something. In the end

Rebecca S. Chopp is the president and a professor of religion at Colgate University, Hamilton, NY 13346.

I wish to express appreciation to Ted Smith of Emory University, who served as my research assistant for this project, and to Elaine Robinson, who also helped me with research and read many drafts of this address. Steven Tipton helped me a great deal with ideas and suggestions for the bibliography, and I am deeply grateful for his help. Finally, I thank Miroslav Volf for responding to an early draft of this address and for engaging me in conversation on its implications.

Journal of the American Academy of Religion September 2002, Vol. 70, No. 3, pp. 461–474.

we decided that we, the members of the board, had to issue a statement to our members urging them to contact the press offices in their universities and to find other ways to serve as resources for educating the public. We decided to make this surprising suggestion to our members: that they actively engage as citizens of the university in the broader public precisely as teachers and researchers. After expressing horror at the terrorist attacks of 11 September, we stated:

> We grieve with our members, their colleagues, and students who have lost loved ones in this tragedy. As the major professional association of scholars and teachers in the field of religion, we feel a special responsibility in this time of crisis. We therefore urge our members to find appropriate educational responses to these events and their aftermath in our classes, our colleges and universities, and our communities, and to serve as resources in the national conversation on a range of issues that have been foregrounded by this tragedy: suffering and evil, human rights and religious liberties, international order and justice, democracy and the common good. The AAR Board especially wishes to urge members to encourage conversation on campuses and in communities about the dangers of religious and ethnic harassment and discrimination. Such educational engagements are appropriate to the Academy's mission to foster reflection upon and understanding of religious traditions, issues, questions, and values by bringing the teaching and scholarship of our members to bear on the public understanding of religion and religions. (AAR Board Statement 2002)

I believe it was the good and right thing to do. It certainly did not feel like much, but what could in relation to the enormity of the tragedy? Yet it made me, serving in this ephemeral and illusive role as president, ask myself: How *can* we speak to the public? Are there ways we can organize our lives together so that we can serve the public good in and through our profession as scholars?

And this is, in sum, my question: Can our universities serve the public, and can academic guilds such as the AAR help our profession serve the public? I am not asking if we ought to give ourselves permission as individual scholars to write on popular topics, or to appear on talk shows now and again, or even, among the theological types, to be active in some kind of organized religious group. My question is simpler than those, perhaps even more preliminary: I want to know how it is that we can structure our universities and our guilds to serve the public. (I use the term *public* but recognize that *public* today rightly includes multiple publics.) In other words, I want to understand the material conditions for citizenship of the academy itself. I want to move the discussion away from individual intention in relation to the public toward one of institutional structures that intertwine in some fashion with public institutions and forces. The topic of exploring higher education and its role as a moral institution of and in the public was my chosen topic long before 11 September occurred, but the topic has an urgency now far more pressing than that suggested in my initial abstract ponderings.

The history of western education casts its rationale in serving the public through the interrelated, yet distinguishable, goals of shaping future citizens and producing knowledge. Yale University's charter, secured in 1745 and similar to the charters of many universities, speaks of training worthy persons "for the service of God as well as the state." Various Christian denominations migrated across this country to establish colleges and universities under the assumption that the formation of citizenship and formation for church had the same characteristics. Even Jefferson's insistence on the nonsectarian nature of the University of Virginia was an attempt to preserve and protect the paideia, or character formation, function of education by sheltering it from the threat of rigid dogmatism and narrow sectarianism. With the Morrill Act of 1862 and the establishment of truly "public" universities, this notion of education serving the public good was open to various classes and cultures and, though not universal at first, races and sexes.

Education, as Maxine Greene has noted, drawing on Hannah Arendt and John Dewey, is about "futuring"; that is to say, education serves the public by ensuring that the future, as well as the present, is created, preserved, and protected. And because of this link to the future as well as to the present and the past, education has as its horizon an imagined public alongside the existent public. To serve the future and the present, education cannot simply concern itself with ideas but must also address practices and disciplines that form the future citizen. Though it is popular in this post-postmodern and cultural studies–dominated era to talk about the "materiality" of ideas, education is rarely examined in terms of its own social practices and social disciplines. Here, we will explore the material structures, the practices and disciplines, that shape our universities. To do this, we will need to find a trope to help us "see" the university in a new, yet familiar, way. In our resistance to considering the practices and disciplines that shape our lives as educators, we tend to assume, with Bill Readings, that the university is in ruins. A new way of seeing is needed.

As Augustine used the analogy of the city to explore the mystical allegiance and ordering of love of the citizens of earth and eternity, so we can use the metaphor of the city to explore the material order, the social practices and disciplines, of higher education. In the West, university education has been linked to the city since medieval times, but education for citizenship defined the city long before the existence of universities. Citizens, after all, must live in or near the city so that, as members of the city, they may gather, discuss and debate, invent knowledge, perform the arts, and rule the city. I think most of us agree that the materiality—the structures, infrastructures, cultures, identities, organizing patterns, and even geography—shapes a city, and so the civic metaphor may help us attend to the material conditions of education in relation to the public. And, sadly, given the events of 11 September, the iconic imagery of the city is painfully important for us to remember. Not all cities are the same, of course. How we think of "city" as public may well help us conceive of higher education in new ways.

Thomas Bender, a historian of education, reminds us that educational institutions, like cities, have different structures. The institutional structure provides the material conditions for the ideas that exist in a particular era, just as the ideas set the frame for particular structures. How an educational institution is structured, the way its culture is expressed, and how faculty understand their identity combine to make a particular type of university as city.

I will suggest that our current academy and our recent history include three basic forms of educational institutions that we can identify as three quite different kinds of cities. The first form of education as a city is that of village: organic, civic, having a consensus of values and cultural images, with the public formed as the village commons, in which educated citizens engage in civic debate. The second form of education as the city is the metropolis: highly differentiated and compartmentalized in space, function, and identity. The public is the realm of technical experts and professional politicians, and the private is enlarged to contain individual arenas such as religion. The third city, one just emerging, is about networks and strategy, blurred boundaries and tactical projects, constructed identities, and a public that is at best clamorous dialogue and at worst postmodern mayhem. By exploring these three cities/universities, I want to suggest (1) that structures matter; (2) that the very structure, the social forces and disciplines, of higher education in the second city prevents engagement with the public; and (3) that a new structure of educational institution is emerging that seems, in some sense, to serve the public in a more engaged fashion than the university as metropolis. I want to challenge us to think of the AAR as a space to imagine how emerging shapes of higher education can engage us more directly with our public or publics both in training citizens—perhaps, as Martha Nussbaum calls them, world citizens—and in producing new knowledge.

In the remainder of my introduction I will sketch, briefly, our first city: the university as the village city, an image dominating much of our history and still present today in small liberal arts colleges. In the village city, the university relates quite organically with the public. Bender, in his book entitled *Intellect and Public Life*, observes:

The advancement of learning in eighteenth- and early nineteenth-century American cities was a civic role, and the substantive meaning of this culture was improvement, personal and social. The educated and powerful worked to establish a cluster of urban institutions that nourished cultural life: libraries and philosophical societies, mechanics and agricultural associations, historical societies, colleges, and small, informal discussion groups devoted to mutual education. Culture and learning had a distinctive and from our perspective notably preindustrial quality. Instead of the language of scholarly productivity and the creation of knowledge, phrases so common in the age of the university, we find in earlier diaries and correspondence such key words as cultivation, pleasure, and improvement. (33)

The structure and culture of the institution intertwined with the identity of faculty members to train leading citizens. College functioned more as an organic whole than as a set of additive departments, the prevailing culture cultivated the well-rounded person for both student and faculty, and the identity of a faculty member was one of the intellectual involved with civic organizations as well as with the college. The faculty member belonged to the school in this town, and this town, in turn, engaged and respected the faculty member as an important participant in the present and future. The public was that of day-to-day engagement in the public affairs of the city, the village, in which the town was located.

THE FOUNDING FRATRICIDAL CONFLICT: THE SECOND CITY

In the last decades of the nineteenth century, education underwent enormous changes in its structures, its culture, and the identity of faculty. Rapid expansion in the numbers of students and institutions (between 1870 and 1940, the U.S. population tripled, and the number of college students increased thirty times) meant greater room for specialization and the development of well-defined departments and professional schools. Greater differentiation among departments and programs of study replaced the earlier organic unity of the school as village. As Thomas Bender and other historians of U.S. higher education have noted, massive changes in higher education occurred (Bender and Schorske; Veysey). Research funding, much of it from the federal government, replaced the role of city funds and wealthy patrons to support higher education. Along with the funding came new standards of professionalism, building on the professional culture of the expanding middle class and making the profession of the scholar that of disciplinary researcher instead of civic intellectual. Students, soon to be young professionals, became trained not as civic leaders for broader social good but as white-collar profession-als who could apply their mastery of narrow knowledge to a discipline. Faculty members no longer participated in civic associations, and universities, bowing to pressure that they become more engaged in their local communities, established offices of university–community partnerships. The public entered in, narrowly and discretely, for funded research, and universities reached out to the public to provide "continuing education."

For faculty members, validation in the community of scholars was not derived through involvement in civic associations but, rather, came from peers now gathered in professional associations and learned societies, such as the AAR, which were formed to bring together professional experts in increasingly narrow subspecialties. The shape of knowledge came to be characterized more and more through the mounting specialization and differentiation in the discipline itself. The pressures of outside funding and the need for private fund-raising, the professionalization of scholarship, and the growing community of validation in nonlocalized spaces such as the AAR intermingled to make the matter of dividing disciplines along methodological lines of self-definition crucial to identification of scholarly excellence. Material conditions and intellectual assumptions merged together to shape disciplines such as religion through principles and practices of securing mastery through the establishment of structural and intellectual boundaries or trenches.

Because this is the city in which, I imagine, current faculty members have been trained, an analogy may be helpful, especially as it relates to the AAR. One analogy to this, our second city, is the city known as Rome, founded through the inscription and continual reinscription of its origi-nating fratricidal conflict: the slaying of Remus by Romulus. We will pick up the story as the two brothers established their own city. Perhaps they wanted to return to the land of their childhood, or, as the text says, "perhaps it was necessary now that they had so many slaves and fugitives around them"; whatever the reason, a new space (the AAR?) had to be created. But as they began to plot out the city, Remus and Romulus quar-reled about its location. Mediation was agreed on, but Romulus lied in the midst of the trusted act of settling their dissension. When Remus learned of his brother's deceit, he went to where Romulus was building the city to ridicule and obstruct the work. Remus leaped across the trench, and Romulus killed him. And then Romulus went on to mark the bound-aries, digging deep trenches that shall forever mark the founding of this city in conflict. Plutarch describes the result of this crime in the founding of the city:

And the founder, having shod a plough with a brazen ploughshare, and having yoked it to a bull and a cow, himself drove a deep furrow around the boundary lines, while those who followed after him had to turn the clods, which the plough threw up, inwards toward the city, and suffer no clod to lie turned outwards. With this line they mark out the course of the wall, and it is called, by contraction, "pomerium," that is "post murum," *behind* or *next the* wall. And where they proposed to put in a gate, there they took the share out of the ground, lifted the plough over, and left a vacant space. And this is the reason why they regard all the wall as sacred except the gates; but if they held the gates sacred, it would not be possible, without religious scruples, to bring into and send out of the city things which are necessary, and yet unclean. (119–120)

In this city fratricidal conflict is the founding discourse, and this crime of origin continues to haunt the deep trenches and narrow gates of its purity. This is an apt analogy for the metropolis university and for academic guilds such as the AAR: The discourses are turned inward, and the disciplinary boundaries are plowed and replowed to maintain them, whereas the gates that might let in other disciplines are left small and unplowed. Numerous analogies between Rome and the metropolis university or the AAR could be made. At certain moments we might be interested to explore the analogy between Rome and the university, with the AAR as a kind of asylum. Some might want to explore the early suckling of Remus and Romulus by a she-wolf and a woodpecker (sacred animals) as a need for child care or even nurturing for graduate students in the job market "fair." But I will keep with this basic point: A city established through fratricide is haunted by this founding; or, to say it differently, to conceive of our discipline as constituted by the trench between two brothers, religious studies and theology (fact and value, descriptive and constructive), is to turn the discourse inward and narrow the gates of our questions, our topics, and our engagement.

Previous presidential addresses of the AAR illustrate why the founding fratricidal conflict is an apt metaphor for the academy. Nearly every presidential speech of the last twenty years, for instance, has addressed the trenchant boundary between theological studies and religious studies as a founding conflict. What I mean by "founding fratricidal conflict" is the social organization of the study of religion, produced and reproduced by theology and religious studies and by the attempts to overcome this split. What is important in analyzing this conflict is not only the problematic violence directed toward the other side but also the way the conflict itself forces an epistemological debate to the foreground so to ignore and hide other important realities, such as the social organization of knowledge and what lies outside the gate: an imagined public with questions that cannot be addressed within the walls of epistemological conflict. Many of the AAR presidential addresses attempt to overcome this founding fratricidal conflict through either a proclamation of our essential unity or an invitation to welcome a bit more into our city through the narrow gates.

Some of the AAR addresses attack the founding conflict directly: Robert Neville's 1993 address, entitled "Religious Studies and Theological Studies," identifies a crisis of identity for the AAR and offers eight theses that seek to provide a broad, inclusive vision. Neville's theses are filled with goodwill and striking vision, but the fact/value, descriptive/constructive conflict is reinscribed even as he longs to move beyond it. And Neville's must be considered perhaps the clearest statement of what others' speeches insist on time and time again. Langdon Gilkey comes quite close to my own assessment of the conflict as fratricidal when he suggests in his 1979 address, "My point is that it is time this hostile, well-nigh cannibalistic struggle cease. If what I have said is sound, both sides have been in error about the menace to their own work which the other side represented" (18). Martin Marty, in the 1988 address, speaks of committing the study of religion in public to encouraging, in the language of our analogy, individual scholars of goodwill to go back and forth through the gates of the city. And finally, in his talk of 1996, Larry Sullivan, in one of the dearest embraces of the gates and the public outside the boundaries of our city, asks us to come to our senses and, in acts of individual goodwill, address such topics as the sense of freedom, the sense of pain, the senses quickened in the arts, and sensory experience as seen through the neurosciences (11). But even when we commit ourselves or locate interesting questions, the gates remain narrow and unplowed because the structures, the social forces and disciplines of the academy, will not bend—or should I say, will not even be bridged.

To structure—both materially and intellectually—a discipline through a founding conflict is to privilege a process of boundary formation, in this case often through epistemological claims, and to ignore or to relegate other material at the gates as unclean. Founding conflicts haunt the ongoing life of the discipline. Augustine, in *Concerning the City of God against the Pagans*, calls this first founding of the city "the archetype of crime" and notes that it riddles Rome's history (600). To lay fratricidal conflict as the foundation of the city, guild, or even the discipline means that the founding conflict cannot be easily escaped. So long as we are defined by this conflict, which produces and reproduces bureaucratic structures and frameworks of discursive identity, it will define and haunt us. And so long as we plow and replow the trenches of this founding conflict, the public will be imagined as "outside and other" and, as such, both belittled and impure, only allowed to enter on occasion through narrow gates.

BEHOLD: A NEW CITY

Contemporary urban geography suggests that just as the village city gave way to the metropolis, the metropolis is giving way to a new configuration of the city that Saskia Sassen has termed "global city." These new global cities, such as Los Angeles, Tokyo, and New York, emerge through a combination of ideas, identities, economics, material structures, and new patterns of immigration. Global cities are not a more complex form of the bureaucratic city of the metropolis but, rather, a different structure, identity, and frame for this term *city*. Sassen employs the phrase "strategic site" to speak of global cities, and I think that this may well be an apt metaphor for new forms of university life that are emerging.

Observers of higher education have noted shifts that are comparable to the ones Sassen and other thinkers have recognized in cities. Universities, once considered nearly self-contained, as illustrated by the truth in the caricature "Ivory Tower," now seek partners endlessly: with one another, with neighborhoods, with science parks and biotech incubators, with international cities, and with nonprofit and community-based organizations. Much the same driving forces in global cities—technology, interdisciplinarity, internationalism—cause universities to enlarge the gates of the city and, in so doing, to reduce the depth of the trenches. Clyde Barrow traces the economic and policy forces that push what he calls "multiuniversities" (global cities) to four interrelated structural reforms: "(1) a shift from institutional emulation to differentiation, (2) a shift from basic research to applied research and development, (3) a shift toward multidisciplinary and interdisciplinary studies, and (4) a shift from department-based research activities toward organized research units as centers and institutes" (464). In the literature on higher education as well as in many of our universities, we can observe the same realities of permeable boundaries, partnerships, strategic sites, contextual and multitraditioned/multidisciplinary identities, and an intensification of resources in these sites as compared to the bureaucratized differentiation of resources. Fratricidal conflict seems to give way to a new rhetoric of partnership, boundary crossing, and collaboration. The spotlight on subspecializations with deeply ploughed, "entrenched" methods begins to fade as scholarly interest, and accompanying fiscal resources, pours into multidisciplinary collaborations. In sum, new institutional structures are emerging, and these structures, along with changing intellectual assumptions, may challenge us to imagine the public as an engaging space for scholarship.

Two aspects that Sassen identifies in the global city particularly interest me as analogous to the emergence of the new university city: (1) a shift to organizational structure as defined through permeable boundaries and shifting processes and (2) a change in frame from one in which culture *represents* an expression of the essence of the nation, particular culture, or tradition to one in which culture is the *production* of identity in a multi-cultured, multitraditioned, multilocated fashion (xxx–xxxiv). In global cities the rules of structure become fluid and fast changing, while the practices of identity become multitraditioned, multicultured, and negotiated rather than fixed or lost, as in the metropolis. Let me elaborate a bit on these two important aspects of the university as global city. I base my comments on the increasing body of literature in higher education on these changes; several institutional studies of my former institution, Emory University, in partnership with the Office of Institutional Research and Planning and with the assistance of Ted Smith; and observations at Yale, my current institutional home, and other universities.

Sites and centers, by definition, are structured with permeable boundaries and shifting processes. A preponderance of the following characteristics identifies a site or center: external funding; faculty and professional staff researchers; separation from academic departments; a high level of integration within the university; an interdisciplinary and multidisciplinary focus; and a relative emphasis on applied, engaged, or discovery-based research (Stahler and Tash: 541). In a way quite similar to what Sassen describes in the global city, foundations and philanthropists play a major role in "partnering" in order to concentrate resources that will bring diverse groups of scholars together to work on topics that will have broad public impact. The fiscal resources provided by foundations allow faculty time to be purchased away from teaching for research as well as provide monies to support seminars, conferences, and workshops. Simply by being new in the organizational design of a university, from a fiscal point of view, they do not have to pay the accruements of years and years of faculty hires, student scholarships, and so on. In a day of fiscal cutbacks in higher education the traditional bureaucratized departments or schools simply no longer have funds for special programs. The sites and centers are spaces where fiscal, physical, intellectual, and cultural resources can be found, and these concentrated resources, though not luxurious, are often sufficient to mark these sites out as "special."

The sites and centers operate as a network or multilaned highway across a boxed-in, departmentalized structure; they are, to use Sassen's language, "strategic" rather than bureaucratic. Such sites and centers become places for faculty to connect with other scholars on topics relevant to research. In such spaces there is no "university" business to be conducted as in routine faculty meetings, and there is no enduring commitment of any group of faculty to work together forever even when topics get stale! In terms of the topics or foci of research, the centers do not refute the departments and metropolis organization of knowledge: They simply ignore the fratricidal conflict so determinate of the organization of knowledge in the second city. The gate of the city, the place through which the unclean enter and exit in the city of Rome, is enlarged, multiplied, and made flexible as highways and networks. The gates, in a sense, become the primary physical space and play the role of letting the public in rather than keeping it out. In a day when insiders and outsiders of the academy are tired of fossilized methods, this type of research feels relevant, broad, engaged, fast paced, and interesting.

The second parallel I wish to draw with a global city has to do with the identity of the scholar and the resulting scholarship produced: or, to use my earlier language, identity as unmoored from a historical situatedness in which culture *represents* an expression of the essence of the nation, particular culture, or tradition and relocated to one in which culture is the *production* of identity in a multicultured, multitraditioned, multilocated fashion (Sassen). In the global city diversity of all sorts gets nestled in, and identity is "negotiated" and produced in new forms and styles. It is much the same in the sites and centers we are considering, if we take identity as both the scholars' identity and the scholarship produced. The sites are project based and populated by scholars from different fields and disciplines. Though there is more consistency in some sites than in others, most of the faculty participants change on a fairly frequent basis. A loosening of the relationship between space and identity occurs in a way quite similar to the way it occurs in the global city: One scholar talks about him- or herself as a scholar in multiple ways or, we might even say, as multicultured—historian, theologian, with the sciences, and so forth. Another scholar speaks of "boundary persons" such as him- or herself who work across various institutional partnerships as well as academic disciplines. These scholars are quite aware of a more "public" aspect to their work as compared with the work found in the discipline-bound research of some of their colleagues.

If one believes as I do that scholarly identities are formed as much as given, this complex identity is quite fascinating as a new type of scholar. Many of these scholars become gifted at such entrepreneurial activity, which stands in stark contrast to the bureaucratic administration of a department. The identity is—I need to emphasize—a "both/and" of living in the sites with this density of resources as well as in traditional bureaucratized structures. (And, I must add, faculty members are quite aware that their work in centers and sites is both valorized and resented by departmentally based faculty as well as by deans and department chairs.)

The presence of the public in our global city is, as in the village city, quite apparent within the university. But the existent public and the imagined public are not so much a kind of organic harmony as they are a series of networks, connections, opportunities, and issues. The university is neither as bounded as the second city nor as whole as the first city. The gates are multiplying and enlarging, while the city itself is less compartmentalized and more fluid. As a field, religion is vital in new and interesting ways but is no longer confined to either theology or religion departments. One striking observation is that while the first city expresses its organic link to the public through education and the second city, through limited research foci, the third city seems to expand the gates of research while leaving the paideia function in either small liberal arts colleges or the narrow teaching fields found in the second city. The public, in our new city, is engaged through research on topics often of interest to foundations, corporations, or other partnership institutions. Will the new global city of the university attempt to shape the public, as did our foreparents in the progressive education movement? Whose interest will the strategic pulses of these centers serve? It is not yet clear whether the university serves the public in a highly instrumentalist way—serving the requirements of the pharmaceuticals industry and private money—or stands in some kind of partnership model based on advocacy.

THE TALE OF THREE CITIES

I have told, at least by implication, a tale of three cities, and all three exist among us, though the first is what Raymond Williams might call a residual; the second, a dominant; and the third, new city, an emerging. Our first city, the one described by Thomas Bender, is like a village in which scholars stand in an organic community of town and gown, reinforced through discourses of cultivation and formation, and participate in civic republican values. Our second city is like the metropolis, structured through a bureaucracy of additive parts, produced through discourses of disciplinary identity, and skilled at a single method and approach. Our third city, the emergent, focuses on the project and is flexible and fluid in structure, as practices, discourses, and culture exist within ever changing boundary zones.

Academic guilds, certainly the AAR, have been born and have flourished almost exclusively in the second city. Academic guilds once functioned to protect and extend the specialization of disciplines and subdisciplines and served as the ground for annual reenactments of the founding conflict in fields such as religion. Serving the interests of professionalization, the AAR provided a space of valorization for professionals who were no longer serving the public directly and were experiencing a decline of respect in their local communities. I mean no criticism: The actual work of the guilds has simply been phenomenal in the extension of the disciplines and the professionalization of scholars. But the question I want to pose at the end of this address is, How do we imagine our academic guilds serving the university shaped like a global city? At the outset, I must say, it should be possible: The AAR (and other academic guilds) functions as a scholarly society to serve the interests of its members. But as the interests of its members change, how does the AAR change? In recent years the AAR has included topics on teaching, independent scholars of religion, the public role of religion, and a multiplicity of "religion and . . . " topics. As the third city emerges into more and more prominence, we will need to give new directions to the AAR's mission and purpose. Should we start meeting with a variety of other guilds? Should we actively solicit scholars who do not teach in religious studies or theology schools? Should we start experimenting with program structures, moving away from traditional divisions and allowing more projects to be created and shaped? Can we see the academic guilds as engaged in practical reason, assisting scholars and universities as agents to participate in the university as a moral institution? Might we play the helpful critic in the new organizing structures of the university? Can we help our universities think creatively about new structures, new kinds of relationship to the public, and new identities for scholars?

CONCLUSION

How the university is structured matters. Such structure creates, shapes, disciplines, and produces us as scholars. I have tried to suggest that the dominant structure of bureaucratic differentiation, which I have termed the "metropolis," is changing. This structure was created through boundaries and divisions of epistemological differentiation that preclude active engagement with the public. I have termed this the "founding fratricidal conflict" of our discipline. Rather than oppose it, for I am not sure that intellectual opposition is effective against it, I suggest that we see a new structure as emergent and, as such, still able to be shaped. I invite the reader to be about the task of imagining fundamental changes in the world of intellect and the organization of knowledge.

REFERENCES

AAR Board Statement 2002   Available at http://www.aarweb.org/news/pressrelease/ 20010919BoardStatement.asp. Accessed 1 November.

Augustine 1984   *Concerning the City of God against the Pagans.* Trans. by Henry Betternson. New York: Penguin.

Barrow, Clyde W.
1996
"The Strategy of Selective Excellence: Redesigning Higher Education for Global Competition in a Postindustrial Society." *Higher Education* 41: 447–469.

Bender, Thomas
1993
Intellect and Public Life: Essays on the Social History of Academic Intellectuals in the United States. Baltimore: Johns Hopkins University Press.

Bender, Thomas, and Carl E. Schorske, eds.
1987
American Academic Culture in Transformation: Fifty Years, Four Disciplines. Princeton: Princeton University Press.

Gilkey, Langdon
1979
"The AAR and the Anxiety of Nonbeing: An Analysis of Our Present Cultural Situation." *Journal of the American Academy of Religion* 48/1: 5–18.

Greene, Maxine
1995
Releasing the Imagination: Essays on Education, the Arts and Social Change. San Francisco: Jossey-Bass.

Marty, Martin
1988
"Committing the Study of Religion in Public." *Journal of the American Academy of Religion* 67/1: 1–22.

Neville, Robert Cummings
1993
"Religious Studies and Theological Studies." *Journal of the American Academy of Religion* 61/2: 185–200.

Nussbaum, Martha
1997
Cultivating Humanity: A Classical Defense of Reform in Liberal Education. Cambridge, MA: Harvard University Press.

Plutarch
1982
Plutarch's Lives, vol. 1. Trans. by Bernadotte Perrin. Cambridge, MA: Harvard University Press.

Readings, Bill
1998
The University in Ruins. Cambridge, MA: Harvard University Press.

Sassen, Saskia
1998
Globalization and Its Discontents: Essays on the New Mobility of People and Money. New York: New Press.

Stahler, Gerald J., and William R. Tash
1994
"Centers and Institutes in the Research University: Issues, Problems, and Prospects." *Journal of Higher Education* 65/5: 40–554.

Sullivan, Lawrence
1996
"Coming to Our Senses: Religious Studies in the Academy." *Journal of the American Academy of Religion* 66/1: 1–11.

Veysey, Laurence R.
1965
The Emergence of the American University. Chicago: University of Chicago Press.

Williams, Raymond
1977
Marxism and Literature. Oxford: Oxford University Press.

 ARTICLES

Assaulting the Border: Kabbalistic Traces in the Margins of Derrida

Elliot R. Wolfson

This study explores the thought of Jacques Derrida in relation to the eso-teric wisdom of the traditional kabbalah, a comparison suggested by Derrida himself, who on occasion utilizes kabbalistic symbols to elucidate central tenets of deconstruction. This relationship should be construed as conver-gence rather than direct influence. In particular, two elements of the world-view of kabbalists bear close resemblance to Derrida: the belief that the materiality of being is textual and the special role assigned to the Tetragram-maton, the ineffable name, in illumining the double bind of language, the unsaying that makes each saying (im)possible. It is especially in Derrida's analysis of the gift and secrecy that the resemblance to kabbalistic herme-neutics is most conspicuous: Just as the gifting of the gift is annulled in the giving of the gift, so the secret can be a secret only if it is disclosed as the secret that is hidden. In a manner consonant with kabbalists, moreover, the rite of circumcision is affirmed by Derrida as the figurative instantiation of the nexus that links language, secrecy, and the gift. For all of these simi-larities, however, there remains a fundamental difference between the ontological orientation of kabbalists and the heterological perspective of Derrida, a difference best illustrated in their respective understandings of the trace. For kabbalists the trace is a demarcation of the negative presence

Elliot R. Wolfson is the Abraham Lieberman Professor of Hebrew and Judaic Studies at New York University, New York, NY 10012-1075.

Journal of the American Academy of Religion September 2002, Vol. 70, No. 3, pp. 475–514.

of absence, whereas for Derrida it is the sign of the wholly other that is neither a presence nor an absence.

> We dance around in a ring and suppose,
> But the secret sits in the middle and knows.
>
> —Robert Frost

PERHAPS THE MOST expedient way to discuss the relationship of Derrida and Jewish mysticism is to remain silent. This reticence is due neither to the traditional paradox of negative theology—how to speak of the unspeakable transcendence of God—nor to the contemporary challenge of deconstruction—how to speak at all when the meaning of words can never be rendered unambiguously clear.[1] The difficulty I face is far more prosaic: With all his literary accomplishments, and they are considerable, Derrida has not overtly professed expertise in any area of Judaic studies, let alone an area that is limited to a handful of specialists spread about several continents.[2] To be sure, in at least one context, Derrida delineates the three major components of kabbalah as "negativity in God," "exile as writing," and the "life of the letter" (Derrida 1974: 74; see Kilcher: 354–357). Elsewhere Derrida utilizes various kabbalistic motifs, including the image of the ungraspable column of air from zoharic literature, which he relates more generally to the depiction of the *sefirot* as a column of numerations; the Lurianic symbol of the "pneumatic layer" (*tehiru*) in which the contraction (*tsimtsum*) occurs, to which Derrida refers as the dramatic crisis of self-determination within God; and the notion of the messianic Torah of invisible letters written in white fire upon black fire, a theme that he associates especially with the Hasidic master, Levi Isaac of Berditchev, to articulate the polysemous nature of the text (Derrida 1981a: 342–345).[3] In that context, Derrida offers an alternative taxonomic account of the Jewish occult tradition: "The Kabbalah is not only summoned up here under the rubric of arithmosophy or the science of literal permutations . . . it also cooperates with an Orphic explanation of the earth" (1981a: 342).[4] In an-

---

[1] For discussion of Derrida and negative theology, see Foshay 1992a; Klemm; Srajek: 214–233, 255–257; Taylor: 33–39, 46–50; Devries; Caputo 1997: 26–57; and Marion 1999, which includes a brief response from Derrida.

[2] For a critical assessment of the Jewish dimension of Derrida's philosophical writings, see Ofrat 2001. The possible influence of kabbalah is noted on 13–14.

[3] See Wright: 114. In the conference "Interpreting the Sacred Word: Jewish Hermeneutics in the European Context," held at the Herzog August Bibliothek in Wolfenbüttel, Germany, 11–13 December 2000, Moshe Idel presented a paper in which he mentioned this text of Derrida and, correctly in my opinion, identified his source as the description of Levi Isaac of Berditchev in Scholem: 81–82. See below, n. 24.

[4] Idel (1986: 149) suggests that reflected in the words of Derrida is Abulafia's technical understanding of letter combination, which is a cornerstone of his prophetic kabbalah. Idel's suggestion

other essay, Derrida summons the lore of kabbalah, reflected especially through the interpretative prism of Gershom Scholem, to articulate the view that the "power of language" is

> an enveloped virtuality, a potentiality that can be brought or not to actuality; it is hidden, buried, dormant. . . . This is indeed an explicit motif in certain trends of the Kabbalah. The magical power of the name produces effects said to be real and over which we are not in command. The name hidden in its potency possesses a power of manifestation and of occultation, of revelation and encrypting [*crypte*]. What does it hide? Precisely the abyss that is enclosed within it. To open a name is to find in it not something but rather something like an abyss, the abyss as the thing itself. (Derrida 2002: 213–214)[5]

In the autobiographical *Circonfession*, Derrida refers somewhat enigmatically to the acronym of *Pardes*, first used by medieval kabbalists to name the four levels of meaning in Scripture,[6] *peshat*, "literality denuded like a glans"; *remez*, "crypt, allegory, secret, diverted word"; *derash*, "morality, homily, persuasive and pulpit eloquence"; and *sod*, "profound, cabbalistic" meaning. After delineating the four levels, which he tellingly labels the "quaternary model of a paradisiac discourse of Jewish 'rationality,'" Derrida remarks:

---

is accepted by Ofrat (2001: 14). This is certainly a plausible explanation, but it is necessary to emphasize that Derrida utilizes this definition in a broader context that engages technical theosophic symbols derived, at least in part, from zoharic literature.

[5] Here it is of significance to note Derrida's ruminations on the *tallit*, the traditional Jewish prayer shawl, in Cixous and Derrida: 21–108. Although Derrida does not refer explicitly to kabbalistic literature, he embraces the fundamental paradox of concealing and revealing in his account of the fringe garment that hides nothing but that nevertheless calls forth to memory the obligation to heed the command, the un/showing that fosters envisioning the sign of the covenantal law that must be appropriated by the individual person through the gaze because it can never be owned by another, the paradox that marks the way of dissimulation, the doubling of the secret in the withholding of the bestowal: "It veils or hides nothing, it shows or announces no Thing, it promises the intuition of nothing. Before seeing or knowing [*le voir ou le savoir*], before fore-seeing or fore-knowing, it is worn in memory of the Law. You still have to see it in another way for that, have it to yourself, have oneself [*s'avoir*] that skin, and see it indeed. . . . So there would be, on sight, *your* sight ('see,' 'look'), an appropriation ('to you,' 'you will have,' 'for you'), a taking possession. But this is the property (the fore-self) that at bottom does not belong and is there only to recall the Commandments. . . . As if everyone discovered his own shawl to his own sight, and right on his own body, but only with a view to hearing and recalling the law, of *recalling* oneself to it or of *recalling* it to oneself. And so to do more or something different, through memory, than 'seeing.' Each time is signed the absolute secret of a shawl—which can of course, at time for prayer, say the precepts, be lent, but not exchanged, and especially not become the property of someone else. The secret of the shawl envelops one single body. One might think that it is woven for *this* one body proper, or even by it, from which it seems to emanate, like an intimate secretion, but this is less through having engendered it thus right up close to oneself than through having already opened it or given it birth into the divine word that will have preceded it. For a secretion, as is well known, is also what separates, discerns, dissociates, dissolves the bond, holds to the secret" (43–44).

[6] Idel 1995; Scholem: 53–61.

Although I've got the PaRDeS of this partition "in my blood," it does not correspond exactly to the one imposing itself on me, some laborious translation of it is not forbidden. . . . it was the last time, the mirror on my right, her left, sudden terror faced with the secret to be kept, of no longer being able to form the letters and words, fear of absolute inhibition through fear of betraying oneself. . . . it was like a beehive sponge of secrets, the buzzing rumor, the mixed-up noises of each bee, and yet the cells near to bursting, infinite number of walls, internal telephone. (Bennington and Derrida 1993: 110–111)[7]

In both contexts, Derrida turns to the kabbalistic tradition to elicit support for the notion of an amorphous text, that is, a text whose language is no longer broken conventionally into discrete words, a fore-text, we might say, that serves as the hermeneutical basis for polysemy, the "white fire" of the primordial Torah, according to kabbalists, which is infinite and thus not fixed in any form,[8] the "text written in letters that are still invisible" (Derrida 1981a: 343). In the second passage, this idea is linked more specifically to the notion of secrecy, a theme to which I shall return, but suffice it here to note that Derrida does consciously relate his conception of the secret as a text without discernible parameters to the kabbalah.

Notwithstanding these occasional asides, which assuredly are not marginal or inconsequential, Derrida hitherto has neither offered a sustained analysis of Jewish mysticism in any of his writings nor has he intimated that a grasp of this material is critical for an understanding of his philosophic orientation. It is not even obvious that we should refer to Derrida as a Jewish writer or as someone who writes primarily about themes of Jewish concern. Surely, Derrida struggles with aspects of his Jewish heritage, but he does not position himself primarily as a thinker trying to determine his place within Judaism. On the contrary, he has expressed the view that if he is to be considered inside the tradition, it is by being outside it, that for him the covenant, *alliance*, is a cut that has cut both ways, tearing him apart from the very thing to which he is bound.[9] As he instructs himself in the entry of

---

[7] In a second passage from this work, Derrida utilizes the kabbalistic acronym again: "A circumcision is my size, it takes my body, it turns round me to envelop me in its blade strokes, they pull upward, a spiral raises and hardens me, I am erect in my circumcision for centuries like the petrified memory . . . we have just enough breath left to ask for pardon, for the Great Pardon, in the languages of the PaRDeS, for all the evil that my writing is drawn, withdrawn and drawn out from, an eternal skin above not you, but me dreaming of him who dreams of the place of God" (Bennington and Derrida 1993: 242–243, see also 246, 247–248, 252, 312).

[8] Idel 1986: 141–157; Scholem: 48–49.

[9] Smith astutely comments on this aspect of Derrida's thought when he notes, "What cuts also closes; what closes also cuts. It cuts both ways. The *annulment* creates the circle of '*anneau*,' the ring" (78). The degree of Derrida's alienation from Jewish tradition may be determined from his reflection on the childhood trauma in Algiers of being thrown out of school together with other Jewish children: "From that moment—how can I say it—I felt as displaced in a Jewish community,

30 December 1976, in *Circonfession*, "leave nothing, if possible, in the dark of what related me to Judaism, alliance broken (*Karet*) in every aspect, with perhaps a gluttonous interiorization, and in heterogeneous modes: last of the Jews, what am I . . . the circumcised is the proper" (Bennington and Derrida 1993: 154).

It is significant that Derrida glossed the comment about the broken covenant with the Hebrew *karet*, for in ancient Israel this term referred to the gravest of punishments, being permanently cut off from the community of Israelites, a reversal, one might say, of the rite of circumcision by which males were attached to the community. Inverting and subverting the meaning of the traditional idiom, Derrida understands circumcision as the cut that loosens him from rather than binds him to the Abrahamic community into which he was born, but, of course, in being cut off he somehow remains bound, indeed being bound for him consists in being cut off.[10] "Circumcision is a determining cut. It permits cutting but, at the same time and in the same stroke [*du même coup*], remaining attached to the cut" (Derrida 1986: 41). In virtue of this cut that binds, Derrida identifies himself as the "last of the Jews," *le dernier des Juifs* (Bennington and Derrida 1991: 145), not as someone who is no longer a Jew whether through assimilation or conversion, and not even as a modern day Marrano, inwardly Jewish but outwardly not.

---

closed unto itself, as I would in the other (which they used to call 'the Catholics'). . . . Symmetrically, oftentimes, I felt an impatient distance with regard to various Jewish communities, when I have the impression that they close in upon themselves, when they pose themselves as such. From all of which comes a feeling of non-belonging that I have doubtless transposed" (Wood and Bernasconi: 75). Derrida's alienation from Judaism is also attested in the comment he made in an oral conversation about prayer recorded in Shapiro, Govrin, and Derrida: "And I was, of course, rebelling when I was a young Jewish boy in Algeria, and they forced me to pray in a language which was totally unintelligible to me. But, I think that at that moment, I understood something essential of the prayer. One can pray without understanding the words. . . . For me Hebrew is this. And it has to do with the book too. Because, of course, for the same reason pure prayer should be improvised" (59). On Derrida's sense of alienation from French, which he identifies as his "only mother tongue," see Derrida and Ferraris: 38. Derrida's relationship to Judaism is one particular instantiation of a larger sense of belonging-by-not-belonging that has informed his way of being in the world. See Derrida and Ferraris where the matter is depicted in terms of the characterization of the place of philosophy as *unheimlich*: "Philosophy has a way of being at home with itself [*chez elle*] that consists in not being at home with itself, whence this double bind with respect to the philosophical" (55). The title of the volume, *A Taste for the Secret*, is related directly to this sense of not-belonging (see Derrida and Ferraris: 59). On the essential nonbelonging of the secret, "the *Unheimlichkeit* of the *Geheimnis*," see Derrida: "It is perhaps there that we find the secret of secrecy, namely, that it is not a matter of knowing and that it is for no-one. A secret doesn't belong, it can never be said to be at home or in its place [*chez soi*]" (1995a: 92). An important source for Derrida's observations on the phenomenon of *Unheimlichkeit* is Freud. For example, see Derrida 1994b: 172–174.

[10] For discussion of circumcision in Derrida, culminating in the observation that circumcision is "another name for deconstruction," see Caputo 1997: 250–263.

What he is, by his own classification, is the last of the Jews, and as the last of the Jews, he is still a Jew, albeit a Jew whose Jewish identity is problematic because he does not envision the possibility of meaningfully perpetuating the tradition:[11]

> I am perhaps not what remains of Judaism, and I would have no trouble agreeing with that, if at least people really wanted to prove it . . . but after all what else am I in truth, who am I if I am not what I inhabit and where I take place . . . today in what remains of Judaism to this world . . . and in this remainder I am only someone to whom there remains so little that at bottom, already dead as son with the widow, I expect the resurrection of Elijah, and to sort out the interminably preliminary question of knowing how they, the Jews and the others, can interpret circumfession, i.e. that I here am inhabiting what remains of Judaism, there are so few of us and we are so divided. (Bennington and Derrida 1993: 302–303)

The messianic resonance here cannot be missed unless one is utterly tone-deaf. What is particularly noteworthy is that death surrounds the messianic hope, for Derrida describes himself "already dead as son with the widow," expecting the resurrection of Elijah, a name that traditionally denotes the prophet who heralds the coming of the messiah and the imaginal form present at each circumcision, but it is also the author's Hebrew name.[12]

Lest there be any misunderstanding, let me state unequivocally that I am not suggesting that Derrida affirms traditional Jewish messianism, whatever the contours of that phenomenon might be. The intent of his eschatological leanings and the portrait of the apocalyptic ideal are formulated lucidly in *Specters of Marx*, published originally in 1993:

> Well, what remains irreducible to any deconstruction, what remains as undeconstructible as the possibility itself of deconstruction is, perhaps, a certain experience of the emancipatory promise; it is perhaps even the formality of a structural messianism, a messianism without religion, even a messianic without messianism, an idea of justice—which we distinguish

---

[11] In evaluating the remarks about Jews scattered in Derrida's writings, one must also consider the fact that Judaism can stand metaphorically for something broader than an ethnic, cultural, or religious identity. For example, see Derrida: "What is called the 'mother' tongue is already 'the other's language.' If we are saying here that language is the native land, namely, what exiles, foreigners, all the wandering Jews in the world, carry away on the soles of their shoes, it is not to evoke a monstrous body, an impossible body, a body whose mouth and tongue would drag the feet along, and even drag about under the feet. It is because this is about the *step*, once again, of progression, aggression, transgression, digression" (2000b: 89). Clearly, in this context, the epithet "wandering Jews" does not apply exclusively to those born or converted into Judaism. It is of interest to note that Derrida ends this lecture with an exegesis of Genesis 19:1–9 and Judges 19:23–30 in an effort to elucidate the possibility of placing the law of hospitality above morality or ethics (2000b: 151–155). This does not, however, have any bearing on the question of the author's ethnic identity.

[12] The double role of Elijah as the messianic prophet and as the one who holds the infant at the rite of circumcision is duly noted in Derrida 1994a: 62.

from law or right and even from human rights—and an idea of democracy—which we distinguish from its current concept and from its determined predicates today. (Derrida 1994b: 59)

In the essay "Faith and Knowledge: The Two Sources of 'Religion' at the Limits of Reason Alone," written in April 1995, Derrida elaborated this notion of "messianicity without messianism," that is, a messianic aspiration that entails the "opening to the future or to the coming of the other as the advent of justice, but without horizon of expectation and without prophetic prefiguration. . . . Possibilities that both open and can always interrupt history, or at least the ordinary course of history" (Derrida and Vattimo: 17).[13]

Messianicity, which implies the hope of what is to come without expectation and the possibility of repetition without indebtedness to heritage, is "older than all religion, more originary than all messianism" (Derrida and Vattimo: 47). The very prospect of religion endures in the "space and time of a spectralizing messianicity beyond all messianism" (Derrida and Vattimo: 51). In a lecture honoring Levinas delivered in Paris on 7 December 1996, Derrida refers to his view as a "structural or *a priori* messianicity," which is not an "ahistorical messianicity, but one that belongs to a historicity without a particular and empirically determinable incarnation. Without revelation or without the dating of a given revelation" (1999a: 67). From these passages, and undoubtedly others that could have been cited, we see how far removed is Derrida's eschatological stance from traditional forms of Jewish messianism. Nevertheless, he does retain something of the sanctioned rhetoric. Derrida has grasped the paradoxical implication of the conventional Jewish, messianic belief: The possibility of the messiah's coming is predicated on the impossibility of the messiah's arrival.[14] "There has to be the possibility of someone's still arriving, there has to be an *arrivant*

---

[13] See Derrida: "Not to-come without some sort of messianic memory and promise, of a messianicity older than all religion, more originary than all messianism" (1997a: 326). On the "double bind" of the messianic posture, which embraces the concomitant belief in the coming and deferral of the future, see Derrida 1997b: 173–174. A more comprehensive assessment of the messianic dimension of Derrida's thought would require a detailed analysis of other twentieth-century Jewish thinkers influenced by and responding to modes of philosophical eschatology. For a representative study, see Gibbs. On the messianic implications of Derrida's thought as they relate to his quest for a "God beyond God," that is, the wholly other liberated from the ontological chain, see Wallace.

[14] One thinks of the provocative insight of Kafka: "The messiah will come only when he is no longer necessary; he will come only on the day after his arrival; he will come, not on the last day, but on the very last" (81). Kafka's remark resonates with the traditional messianic hope harbored by Jews through the generations, which is based on the belief in the future coming of the messiah, a coming that is possible only as long as the messiah has not come. An interesting formulation of this dialectic is found in the teachings of Nahman of Bratslav, especially in the tale of the seven beggars. According to the Bratslav tradition, the footless beggar, the last of the seven, who does not come to the wedding symbolically represents the messiah. See Wolfson 2002b: 121.

... someone absolutely indeterminate ... who may be called the Messiah" (Derrida and Ferraris: 31). In the distinctive language of Derrida's style, messianicity involves the constant advent of what is to come (*l'avenir*),[15] a present perpetually deferred to the future, a givenness always yet to be given, the wholly other (*tout autre*) that refuses incorporation into any category of the same.[16] The messianic figure is ghostlike according to the following depiction offered by Derrida: "But one has to realize the ghost is there, be it in the opening of the promise or the expectation, *before its first apparition*: the latter had announced itself, from the first it will have come second. *Two times at the same time*, originary iterability, irreducible virtuality of this space and this time. That is why one must think otherwise the 'time' or the date of an event" (1994b: 163). Derrida's messianicity is a doctrine of "hauntology," the haunting "apparition of the inapparent," that disrupts ontology (1994b: 161). What appears from the first is second; at the beginning is repetition of the same that is always different.

The extent to which Derrida feels detached and estranged from the patrimony of his youth may be gauged from another rather dark and brutally honest comment in his notebooks, "and the last of the Jews that I still am is doing nothing here other than destroying the world on the pretext of making truth" (Bennington and Derrida 1993: 190–191). Derrida returned to the question of his Jewish upbringing in *Monolingualism of the Other or The Prosthesis of Origin* (1999b), a study originally published in 1996 based on an oral presentation from April 1992. At one point he candidly comments, "Such, in any event, would have been the radical lack of culture from which I undoubtedly never completely emerged. From which I emerge without emerging from it, by emerging from it completely without my having ever emerged from it" (1999b: 53). In the continuation of this passage, Derrida admits that he was not capable of breathing new life into an ossified and necrotized Judaism because he carried the "negative heritage" of an "amnesia," which he never had the courage, strength, or means to resist, and because he did not feel he was qualified to do the original work of the historian. Significantly, Derrida tacitly admits that historical scholarship in the study of Judaism, which is based on the philological competence that has eluded his grasp, could have redemptive or restorative value. In an astonishing moment of self-disclosure, Derrida acknowledges that he has been influenced by "an insidious Christian contamination: the respectful belief in inwardness, the preference for intention, the heart, the mind, mis-

---

[15] See, for example, Derrida: "The affirmation of the future to come: this is not a positive thesis. It is nothing other than the affirmation itself, the 'yes,' insofar as it is the condition of all promises or of all hope, of all awaiting, of all performativity, of all opening toward the future, whatever it may be, for science or for religion" (1996: 68).

[16] Caputo 1997: 69–87, especially 77–81, and 117–159, especially 147–151; 1999: 199–200.

trust with respect for literalness or to an objective action given to the mechanicity of the body, in short, a denunciation, so conventional, of Pharisaism" (1999b: 54). To his credit, it must be recalled that in a number of his discussions about circumcision, he does emphasize that the notion of an inward circumcision of the heart is expressed by the prophet Jeremiah and thus has textual roots in Judaism independent of Christianity (Cixous and Derrida: 75–76; Derrida 1994a: 64). Nevertheless, he concedes that his attitude toward Judaism reflects a bias against Pharisaic literalism well attested in the history of Christian polemic with Judaism.

This stark self-portrait of one who depicts the specific behavioral patterns of Judaism as parochial would seem to leave little room to consider Derrida in any meaningful way a living link in the chain of Jewish mysticism, which has steadfastly affirmed the central and unwavering significance of ritual behavior even if the latter must be abrogated to be fulfilled. Indeed, the very notion of considering kabbalah as an influence on Derrida strikes me as embracing the impossible, the jarring realization that the moment the matter is uttered its truth rests on being false and its falsity on being true. Yet it is precisely the impossibility of appropriation that yields the possibility of writing. As Derrida confides to us about his own autobiographical praxis, "only write here what is impossible, that ought to be the impossible-rule" (Bennington and Derrida 1993: 194).

To grasp the intent of this comment, one must bear in mind that, for Derrida, inscription more generally, and not simply autobiographical writing, constitutes the signature of being that "remains an other whose law demands the impossible. It does not demand this thing or that, something which could turn out to be impossible. No, it demands the impossible, and demands it because it is impossible, and because this very impossibility is the condition of the possibility of demand" (1984: 14–15). To write I must confront "the thing that would be other, the other thing" (*la chose serait donc l'autre, l'autre-chose*) that

> gives me an order or addresses an impossible, intransigent, insatiable demand to me, without an exchange and without a transaction, without a possible contract. Without a word, without speaking to me, it addresses itself to me, to me alone in my irreplaceable singularity, in my solitude as well. I owe to the thing an absolute respect which no general law would mediate (*un respect absolu que ne médiatise aucune loi générale*): the law of the thing is singularity and difference as well. An infinite debt ties me to it, a duty without funds or foundation. I shall never acquit myself of it. Thus the thing is not an object; it cannot become one. (Derrida 1984:14–15)

The "rule of the impossible," *la régle-impossible* (Bennington and Derrida 1991: 181), hinges on the fact that the writer is indebted to bear through verbal discourse the other that addresses one without speaking, the thing that can never become object, the presence that cannot be represented except as the absence of the presence that it could not presently be. In a profoundly tragic and ironic turn, Derrida observes that inscription requires "the muteness of the thing" (*le mutisme de la chose*), for the thing that must be written is an "insatiable *thou must*" (*tu dois insatiable*) that "remains beyond exchange and priceless" (1984: 14–17). The thing imposes itself as that which must be written, but it offers no specific direction or content; it demands to be heard from the depth of its muteness. Had the other spoken, there would be an exchange and an ensuing contract binding writer and what is written, but in its muteness, there is asymmetry that defies exchange, the indebtedness of the gift that cannot be negotiated contractually. Of the gift and the impossibility of representation I will have more to say at a later stage of this analysis. For the time being, suffice it to note that in writing this article I have found it impossible not to follow the rule of the impossible, which cannot be followed unless it be broken, for writing the impossible, the only writing that is possible, indeed the impossibility that facilitates the possibility of writing, is a rule about breaking rules, a law fulfilled when abrogated.

What sense, then, can we ascribe to the admittedly impossible task that marks our path? Is there an advantage to speak of Derrida, deconstruction, and Jewish mysticism in one breath? Can we think this triad together in a manner that provokes thoughtfulness? A key here will lie in understanding Jewish mysticism primarily in semiological terms, with particular emphasis on the mystical experience of contemplative envisioning, which rests on the ontic presumption regarding the textualization of reality, that is, the idea that reality is a text, for the most basic stuff of existence consists of twenty-two letters of the Hebrew alphabet, and these twenty-two letters are comprised in the four letters of the name *YHWH*, the mystical core of Torah. The divine being, and by implication all beings of the worlds contained therein, is circumscribed in the book that is signified by the proper name par excellence. The proper name, which may also be envisioned as the prism of *sefirot* variously configured, signifies what lies beyond signification, the dimension of divine being that is without name, even beyond signification by any of the letters. The name, itself a curious phenomenon insofar as it is ineffable, its articulation through the cloak of the epithet, leads one to the nameless, in/significant other that demarcates all that is signified, inaudible voice that differentiates all that is articulated. This portrait of YHWH, which may be elicited from medieval kabbalistic literature, bears comparison with some views expressed by Derrida, a point to which I shall return. However, at this juncture, it is important to stress that addressing the question of Derrida and Jewish mysticism from a strictly historiographical or textological point of view is not terribly productive. On the contrary, as I have noted, it is easy to dismiss the matter when cast in this way, for there is no definitive proof that Derrida has been influenced by Jewish mystical sources directly and only scanty evidence for a secondary influence.[17]

In an essay published in 1982, "Derrida, Jabès, Levinas: Sign-Theory as Ethical Discourse," Shira Wolosky argues that in the studies on Jabès and Levinas included in *L'Ecriture et la différance*, which appeared in 1967, Derrida acknowledged the relationship between his grammatological scheme and the theory of language found in kabbalistic writings. I will not investigate each of the passages to which she refers as support of her argument, but let me say that the gist of my concern is that it is not obvious that Derrida's exegetical remarks on either Jabès or Levinas are meant to be taken as statements of his own views. Let me offer one example of the methodological problem. After citing Derrida's remark, "Jabès is conscious of the Cabalistic resonances of his book" (Derrida 1978: 74), Wolosky comments on "a consciousness which Derrida shares, and which can be applied to his own work as well. Jabès' path, which Derrida also follows, leads into the kabbalistic world of linguistic mysticism, where claims for grammatological primacy open into an extensive and radical system" (1982: 292). There is nothing in Derrida's remarks that would necessarily substantiate this claim. It is conjectural, at best, to assert that the kabbalistic resonances of the poetic fragments of Jabès apply equally well to Derrida, for Derrida's observations are a commentary to Jabès, a commentary that surely is written on the basis of attentive reading—attunement to the voice of the other resonating in the written text—but as commentary there is distance between text and interpreter, a distance that can never be entirely overcome in the hermeneutical act no matter how astute one's interpretative prowess. As Derrida himself puts it in this very essay on Jabès, writing is a "tearing of the self toward the other within a confession of infinite separation" (1978: 75). To assume unequivocally, as Wolosky does, that Derrida's comments about Jabès can be transferred to him without disruption, one would have to efface all difference between reader and text, an effacement that would fly in the face of the deconstructionist hermeneutic affirmed by Derrida.

---

[17] Here it is important to emphasize that Derrida 1995b: 25–26 insists that the notion of the secret in which he is interested is not mystical in nature, related either to the negative theology in Christian tradition or to an esoteric doctrine in the Pythagorean, Platonic, or Neoplatonic community. It does not seem imprudent to assume that the secrets promulgated by kabbalists would also be rejected by Derrida.

I am prepared to grant that Derrida is correct in ascribing kabbalistic import to the views of Jabès expressed in *Le Livre des Questions*.[18] What is at stake, however, is how to interpret this affinity as it relates to Derrida's own views. It is not at all certain that his explication of Jabès is meant to be read as an account of Derrida's opinions. Support for this position, however, may be culled from the passages in Derrida's writings that are suggestive of the influence of traditional kabbalistic symbolism, or at the very least the convergence of that symbolism and his own thought, particularly some of the technical tropes in sixteenth-century Lurianic kabbalah such as the notion of the trace (*reshimu*) in primordial space (*tehiru*) that results from contraction (*tsimtsum*) of the infinite from itself unto itself.[19] The point has not gone unnoticed in scholarly literature. Harold Bloom, for instance, proposed an influence of kabbalistic hermeneutics on Derrida's critical notion of *différance*: "Though he nowhere says so, it may be that Derrida is substituting *davhar* for *logos*, thus correcting Plato by a Hebraic equating of the writing-act and the mark of articulation with the word itself. Much of Derrida is in the spirit of the great Kabbalist interpreters of Torah, interpreters who create baroque mythologies out of those elements in Scripture that appear least homogeneous in the sacred text" (1975a: 43). In another context, Bloom compared the kabbalistic notion of "writing before writing," articulated especially in Lurianic theosophy, and the Derridean notion of the trace. Bloom casts kabbalah as a "theory of *writing*" akin to this brand of French criticism, emphasizing, in particular, the denial of an absolute distinction between writing and speech shared by both. Yet he is mindful to draw the following contrast: "Kabbalah too thinks in ways not permitted by Western metaphysics, since its God is at once *Ein-Sof* and *ayin*, total presence and total absence, and all its interiors contain exteriors, while all of its effects determine its causes. But Kabbalah stops the movement of Derrida's 'trace,' since it has a *point* of the primordial, where presence and absence co-exist by continuous interplay" (1975b: 52–53). In a third study, Bloom reiterates the affinity between the "overdetermined" conception of language as a "magical absolute" in kabbalistic tradition and the "*absolute* randomness" of language in the "linguistic nihilism" advocated in deconstruction (1979: 4).

On balance, it strikes me that the scales of judgment regarding the relationship of Derrida to Jewish esotericism should be tipped in the direction of convergence rather than influence, but even presuming the

---

[18] For an elaboration of Derrida's claim, see Mole: 87, 116–117. On the resemblance between Jabès and kabbalistic notions of textuality and writing, see also my brief remarks in Wolfson 2002c: 138–139.

[19] See above, n. 3.

former is not without problems. To illustrate this point let me note that in the lengthy essay "How to Avoid Speaking: Denials," which was delivered as a lecture in Jerusalem, Derrida discusses negative theology as it has been formulated in the history of Christian mysticism, focusing most notably on Pseudo-Dionysus and Meister Eckhart, but he does not mention a word about kabbalah or Jewish mysticism. Lest one protest that this observation is trivial, I remind such a person that Derrida himself makes a point of noting that in the address he cannot treat negative theology "in a tradition of thought that is neither Greek or Christian," that is, in Jewish and Islamic thought (Derrida 1992c: 100). With respect to these traditions, Derrida must perform the gesture of disavowal or *dénégation*,[20] speaking by unspeaking, which is appropriate to the subject at hand. Thus, in a second passage from this composition, Derrida interrupts his discussion of the relationship of avoidance that pertains to Heidegger and the apophasis of Dionysius the Areopagite and Meister Eckhart with the comment, "*To say nothing*, once again, of the mysticism or theologies in the Jewish, Islamic, or other traditions" (1992c: 124). To say nothing—not for the first time but *once again*—the saying of nonsaying must be reiterated because what is spoken in this speaking is unspoken.[21]

To appreciate the importance of this parenthetical musing, we must recall that in this lecture Derrida displayed that he was keenly aware of the geographical locale in which he gave his talk; indeed, he grappled with the philosophical intent of what it meant to be in Jerusalem. There is, Derrida reminds us, a certain impossibility of being in this place, an impossibility that he associates with the traditional formula uttered at the end of the Passover seder, "Next year in Jerusalem," that is, Jerusalem, symbolically, is the place to which one must always be going, deferring of the pledge and postponing of the promise, indefinitely, an experiential feature of the structure of the messianic architectonic.[22] Precisely in the place where one cannot be except by anticipating being there is it most suitable to speak of what cannot be spoken. Interestingly, Derrida referred to this lecture

> as the most autobiographical speech I have ever risked. . . . It is necessary to surround with precautions the hypothesis of a self-presentation passing through a speech on the negative theology of others. But if one day I had to tell my story, nothing in this narrative would start to speak of the thing itself if I did not come up against this fact; for lack of capacity, competence, or self-authorization, I have never yet been able to speak of what

---

[20] For discussion of this Derridean theme, see Foshay 1992a; Taylor: 36–37.
[21] Taylor: 53.
[22] Consider the interpretation of Jerusalem in Derrida 1999a: 101–114.

my birth .... should have made closest to me: the Jew, the Arab. (1992c: 135 n. 13)

Bracketing the important issues of cultural and linguistic identity that emerge from this revealing note, and especially the somewhat perplexing tag of ethnicity, "the Jew, the Arab,"[23] let me reiterate the main point for the purposes of this study: Derrida shies away from comporting himself as someone who can discourse about Jewish mysticism even in the lecture on apophasis delivered in Jerusalem, a site that would have naturally facilitated a discussion of this matter in Jewish and/or Islamic mysticism.[24] This comment must give pause to all those involved in the effort to discern Derrida's relationship to Jewish mysticism, not to mention Judaism more generally. One cannot simply ignore the fact that Derrida has not taken upon himself the responsibility of discussing this matter because he does not feel at ease and in control of the relevant material that would have to be deconstructed.[25] The more engaging question, then, is how the study of Derrida and the study of kabbalah can mutually illumine one another.

To assess this question properly, we must again raise the issue of the compatibility of Derrida's enterprise and theories of interpretation that have been operative in various forms of Jewish textual practice, for I think

---

[23] The hybrid cultural identification is illumined by the following remark Derrida made about his youth in an interview from April 1989 conducted by Derek Attridge: "Racism was everywhere in Algeria at that time, it was running wild in all directions. Being Jewish and a victim of anti-semitism didn't spare one the anti-Arab racism I felt everywhere around me, in manifest or latent form" (Derrida 1992a: 39). Perhaps the thread linking Jew and Arab in Derrida's mind is the shared sense of being persecuted. See also Derrida's musing on the memory of being blessed on Yom Kippur, the "Day of Atonement," in Cixous and Derrida: "I can still see this father, but I could not see him, by definition, by situation, he blessed his two sons one day bigger than he, lifting with both arms his tallith stretched above the two heads. Bigger than he, and one bigger than the other, the sons are stifling a little under the solemn protection, under the roof of that temple so close, during the interminable prayer, in what was called the 'great temple,' an old mosque right in the middle of an Arab district, anciently judeo-arab, a mosque in the Spanish style since become a mosque again" (45). For an extended discussion of this destabilizing cultural marker of self-identity, see Gil Anidjar, "Introduction: 'Once More, Once More:' Derrida, the Arab, the Jew," in Derrida 2002: 1–39.

[24] In this connection, it is of interest to recall the comment in Derrida: "Whatever the translations, analogies, transpositions, transferences, metaphors, never has any discourse expressly given itself this title (negative theology, apophatic method, *via negativa*) in the thoughts of Jewish, Muslim, Buddhist culture" (1995b: 63). It is possible to contest Derrida's claim on historical and textual grounds, but what is important for the purpose of this analysis is his assumption that negative theology shows exclusive affinity with Christian philosophy.

[25] For a different interpretation of Derrida's statement in "How to Avoid Speaking," see Foshay 1992b: 84. According to Foshay, Derrida's silence regarding apophasis in Jewish and Islamic thought "is an inherent function of the need to avoid speaking of essences, identities and 'things in themselves.' In other words, Derrida can allow himself to speak of the Platonic and Neoplatonic heritage of negative theology, but not of the Jewish or Islamic, which are closest to him and, as it were, identical with him. He cannot altogether avoid speaking of the analogy and isomorphism of apophaticism and deconstruction, but he can defer mere personal and 'attitudinal' questions of identity" (1992b: 84).

this is the appropriate context within which to place kabbalah. To approach the relationship of Derrida to Jewish mysticism without getting a handle on Derrida and Judaism would amount to what Alfred North Whitehead called the "fallacy of misplaced concreteness," that is, mistaking the part for the whole. If there is an efficacious way to think about Derrida in terms of Jewish mysticism, then it will have to be approached from within the broader context of his relationship to the religious and intellectual culture of the Jews.

In her book published in 1982, *The Slayers of Moses: The Emergence of Rabbinic Interpretation in Modern Literary Theory*, Susan Handelman argued that Derrida's deconstructive method could be viewed as a form of "Jewish heretic hermeneutics" (163). It is, more accurately, in Derrida's notion of writing as *différance*, the dissemination of the word through the infinite play of signification occasioned by the rejection of a transcendental signifier, that Handelman finds a coalescence of the main themes of this hermeneutic, to wit, castration or mutilation of the phallus, which is linked to circumcision, rebellion, irrevocable loss, displacement, and breaking the covenant (165). On the basis of a passage in *Glas*, Handelman suggested that Derrida's choice of writing, and by implication the notion of text, to oppose the logocentrism of western thought is related to the veiled Torah scroll that is unveiled from behind the curtain at a dramatic moment in the Jewish liturgical service (165–166). I note, parenthetically, that Wolosky independently cited the same text as proof that Derrida's life experience as a Jew provided the "stance for a radical re-vision of Hellenic assumptions" (290–291). Subsequently, I shall return to the image of unveiling the veiled as it is revealed in kabbalistic hermeneutics, paying special attention to the convergence of the themes of writing, circumcision, and exposition of secrets. For the moment, what is worthy of note is that there is something compelling to the argument that the primacy accorded the written text over the spoken word, the affirmation of the grammatological as opposed to the logocentric, may have, at least in part, been informed by Derrida's visceral familiarity with Jewish ritual experience.

The crucial question, however, is, Should the deconstructionist hermeneutic be compared theoretically to rabbinic claims regarding the polysemous nature of Torah as the originary script decoded in the displacements and contraversions of midrashic reading, a textual strategy greatly expanded and embellished in medieval kabbalah? Can we accept the further suggestion of Handelman, following Bloom, that Derrida's notion of the trace, the "elusive originating-nonoriginating mark of meaning," is similar to the kabbalistic conception of the divine name (described by Scholem) as the meaningless, primordial language, encoded in the text of Torah, which assumes meaning only through the mediation of multivalent interpretations (1982:205–206, 1987: 118–122)? There are, as we have seen, passages in Derrida that would corroborate this claim. We should bear in mind as well that Derrida himself makes explicit the connection between the Greek privileging of logos as spoken word and the Johannine notion of the word become flesh (Wolosky: 285–287). Of the many examples that illustrate the point, consider the following remark in *Of Grammatology*: "The difference between signified and signifier belongs in a profound and implicit way to the totality of the great epoch covered by the history of metaphysics, and in a more explicit and more systematically articulated way to the narrower epoch of Christian creationism and infinitism when these appropriate the resources of Greek conceptuality" (Derrida 1976: 13). In semiotic terms, the son is the phonic sign of the father, who would be identified as the transcendental signified. Conventional sign theory, with its privileging of the spoken word over the written text, derives from the ontological scheme of Greek metaphysics reinforced by the Christological doctrine of incarnation. Are we justified in assuming that the emphasis placed on writing as the primary act of God's creativity and the consequent notion that being may be compared to a book, which derives from ancient Hebraic wisdom, provides an alternative to the ontotheology that has prevailed in Hellenistic culture?

That Judaism came to play a vital role in Derrida's depiction of the deconstructionist process can be asserted with confidence. Perhaps this is enunciated most explicitly in his lengthy study "Violence and Metaphysics: An Essay on the Thought of Emmanuel Levinas." The ruminations of Levinas, Derrida tells the reader, "make us tremble," for by attempting to think Judaism and Greek philosophy together, a subversive role is assigned to the former, particularly in terms of a challenge to the dominant ontology or metaphysics of presence that underlies the logocentric orientation.[26] "At the heart of the desert, in the growing wasteland, this thought, which fundamentally no longer seeks to be a thought of Being and phenomenality, makes us dream of an inconceivable process of dismantling and dispossession" (Derrida 1978: 82). The ethical relationship to the other as infinitely other is the one experience that is "capable of opening the space of transcendence and of liberating metaphysics. . . . It is opening itself, the opening of opening, that which can be enclosed within no category

---

[26] On the relationship of "Greek" and "Jewish" in the philosophy of Levinas, see the extensive discussion in Levy: 156–178. Levy deals specifically with Derrida's perspective on this question on 170–171. See also the recent discussion of Derrida's essay, with special focus on the hybrid terms *jewgreek* and *greekjew*, in Llewelyn: 143–155. For an alternative approach, see Bennington. In an attempt to go beyond the jewgreek identity, with its cultural roots respectively in Jerusalem and Athens, Bennington suggests that Egypt is symbolically the "place" of deconstruction, a surmise that is based primarily on Derrida's own admitted fascination with Egyptian hieroglyphics.

or totality" (Derrida 1978: 83). In the end of the essay, Derrida raises several questions aimed at destabilizing the dichotomy between Hebraism and Hellenism implied in the citation by Matthew Arnold placed at the beginning of the essay, ending with words of James Joyce that affirm the coincidence of the presumed opposites:

> Are we Jews? Are we Greeks? We live in the difference between the Jew and the Greek, which is perhaps the unity of what is called history. We live in and of difference, that is, in hypocrisy.... Are we Greeks? Are we Jews? But who, we? Are we (not a chronological, but a pre-logical question) first Jews or first Greeks? ... And what is the legitimacy, what is the meaning of the copula in this proposition from perhaps the most Hegelian of modern novelists: "Jewgreek is greekjew. Extremes meet"? (Derrida 1978: 153)

We cannot say with certitude whether or not Derrida thinks of himself as the unique hybrid, the mongrel who is jewgreek by being greekjew. A position akin to this has been proffered by John Caputo in *The Prayers and Tears of Jacques Derrida: Religion without Religion* (1997). To be more precise, Caputo is of the opinion that although Derrida does not write in the name of a Jew, his work is nonetheless "driven by a Jewish passion." His compositions constitute his own diaspora in which the "dispersion and dissemination of his psyche are the very substance of his Jewishness" (Caputo 1997: 230). Caputo has offered us a helpful opening on our path even though he does not concern himself with the specific question of Derrida's relation to Jewish mysticism. For Derrida, Judaism functions as an interruption or disruption causing a breach in the edifice of western philosophy, the *différance*, the incessant not-saying of what it is that one is saying.

Here it is instructive to consider Derrida's criticism of Heidegger toward the conclusion of "Faith and Knowledge": "Ontotheology encrypts faith and destines it to the condition of a sort of Spanish Marrano who would have lost—in truth, dispersed, multiplied—everything up to and including the memory of his unique secret. Emblem of a still life: an opened pomegranate, one Passover evening, on a tray" (Derrida and Vattimo: 66). The pomegranate, we are told in the same context, denotes the "granulated, grainy, disseminated, aphoristic, discontinuous, juxtapositional, dogmatic, indicative or virtual, economic; in a word, more than ever telegraphic" (Derrida and Vattimo: 66) articulation of meaning. Surely it is not insignificant that the symbol that Derrida chooses for the deconstructionist method, which provides a way beyond the ontotheological obstruction of faith, is a Jewish ritual object linked to Passover, the festival that commemorates the past liberation and anticipates the future redemption. This passage lends support to Caputo's suggestion that the nomadic play that is basic to deconstruction reflects the ontic condition of the Jew as other, the uprooted, displaced wanderer who lives in the hope of a promise that, paradoxically, is fulfilled only to the extent that it is continually postponed. Derrida notes that the itinerant quality of the Jew is portrayed by the symbol of the tabernacle, the necessarily impermanent place wherein the divine glory is disclosed as the presence that cannot be iconically represented, the arcanum in and through which the infinite is envisioned as the invisible nothing that defies imaginary depiction:

> The tabernacle gives its name and its place to the Jewish family dwelling. That establishes the Jewish nation. The Jewish nation settles in the tabernacle, adores therein the sign of God and his covenant. . . . Now the tabernacle . . . remains a signifier without signified. The Jewish hearth forms an empty house, certainly, sensible to the absence of all sensible form, the Jews have tried to produce an object that gave in some way rise, place, and figure to the infinite. But this place and this figure have a singular structure: the structure encloses its void within itself, shelters only its own proper interiorized desert, opens onto nothing, confines nothing, contains as its treasure only nothingness: a hole, an empty spacing, a death. . . . No center, no heart, an empty space, nothing. One undoes the bands, displaces the tissues, pulls off the veils, parts [*écarte*] the curtains: nothing but a black hole or a deep regard, without color, form, and life. . . . The Jewish *Geheimnis*, the hearth in which one looks for the center under a sensible cover [*enveloppe*]—the tent of the tabernacle, the stone of the temple, a robe that clothes the text of the covenant—is finally discovered as an empty room, is not uncovered, never ends being uncovered, as it has nothing to show. (Derrida 1986: 49–50)

In the above passage, there is much that is said about what cannot be spoken, the text of the covenant that is continually un/covered because there is nothing visible that demands to be re/covered. How do we apply this image of nothing at the center but empty space to a text or, more specifically, to the stone tablets upon which were inscribed the ten commandments? Is the "text of the covenant" not a concrete form that renders the image of "nothing to show" inappropriate? For Derrida, it appears, even these stones may be construed as "nothing but a black hole" inasmuch as the medium on which a text is written is the white space that is as critical to the determination of significance as the black letters of text.[27]

---

[27] This is precisely how Derrida interprets the dictum of Levi Isaac of Berditchev concerning the messianic Torah composed of the white spaces in which the letters are invisible: "The blanks will never be anything but provisionally filled in, one surface or square always remaining empty, open to the play of permutations, blanks barely glimpsed as blanks, (almost) pure spacing, going on forever and not in the expectation of any Messianic fulfillment. It is a spacing that is merely attended. For there exists a whole interpretation of spacing, of textual generation and polysemy, of course, revolving around the Torah. Polysemy is the possibility of a 'new Torah' capable of arising out of the other ('Torah will issue out of me')" (1981a: 344–345).

Alternatively expressed, meaning is never fixed by authorial intent; on the contrary, the deconstructionist method is predicated on a presumably unbridgeable gap—the hole in the middle—between the intention of the writer and the interpretation posited by the reader. With regard to the hermeneutical question, the author cannot claim privileged status, for sense can only be articulated through multiple voices engaged in an endless play of dissemination:

> Dissemination endlessly opens up a *snag* in writing that can no longer be mended, a spot where neither meaning, however plural, nor *any form of presence* can pin/pen down [*agrapher*] the trace. Dissemination treats— doctors—that *point* where the movement of signification would regularly come to *tie down* the play of the trace, thus producing (a) history. The security of each point arrested in the name of the law is hence blown up. It is—at least—at the risk of such a blowup that dissemination has been broached/breached. With a detour through/of writing one cannot get over. (Derrida 1981a: 26)

The notion of secrecy is employed by Derrida to characterize the polysemy of signification enacted in the *différance* wrought by dissemination. That is, by "secret" Derrida does not refer to either the unknowable transcendence (the *hyperousios* of negative theology) or to an irretrievable hidden truth (the *mysterium* of esoteric gnosis); the secret, in his mind, relates to the fact that meaning can never be determined with absolute certainty and thus we cannot speak of immutable content in isolation from the event of reading.[28] The inherent secretive nature of language is that there is always a surplus of signification to be determined through a multivocality of voices. Consider, for example, the following account of the "apophatic aspect" of the secret: "The apophatic is not here necessarily dependent on negative theology, even if it makes it possible, too. And what we are attempting to put to the test is the possibility, in truth the impossibility, for any testimony to guarantee itself by expressing itself in the following form and grammar: 'Let us testify that . . .' We testify to a secret that is without content, without a content separable from its performative experience, from its performative tracing" (Derrida 1995b: 24). The Jewish stricture against representing the deity visually within the inner sanctum of the tabernacle and temple is interpreted by Derrida as an allusion to the hermeneutical dynamic that partakes of the structure of secrecy: The text veiled behind the curtain can never cease being uncovered inasmuch as the meaning discovered in the text is what comes to light by being re/covered.

Above all else, the Jew as other functions symbolically as bearing the character of writer, for writing, *écriture*, is not a return to origin but a

---

[28] On the secret in Derrida's deconstruction, see Caputo 1997: 101–112.

recurrent retracing of one's steps to the text that is the homeland where one has never been, a marking of absence, a delimiting of the limitless, the saying of something without saying it, inscription under erasure. It is for this reason that Derrida returns on a number of occasions in his compositions to circumcision, the primordial cut that traditionally binds the Jewish male to the covenantal community, the differentiating mark, the mark of difference, the inscription of singularity, the proper name that can be pronounced only once, in a moment that is unique, the present that is always to come for it has always already been, a presence that cannot be represented even as absence. For Derrida, the cut of circumcision signifies autobiographical self-representation,[29] for it is the ring of double affirmation, the circle of return wherein the same recurs because it is different. And it is exactly here that one finds, in my judgment, the element of Derrida's thinking that can be applied most fruitfully to kabbalistic symbolism, the nexus between circumcision, inscription, and obliteration, the re/marking of the mark occluded in its demarcation.

As I have suggested in a number of studies, the primary site of contemplative envisioning in kabbalistic praxis is the circumcised phallus, which must be veiled in its exposure (Wolfson 1987, 1994: 330–331, 342–343, 357–358). The link between circumcision and secrecy in the esoteric teaching can be viewed as an elaboration of the rabbinic emphasis on the need to conceal the *membrum virile*, an aspect of the etiquette of modesty (*tseniʿut*) required of the Jewish male (Stern 1994: 229–231). In kabbalistic lore, the concealment of the penis on pietistic/moral grounds served as the ritual foundation for the symbolic interpretation of circumcision as embodying the hermeneutical play of secrecy, that which is hidden (*tseniʿutaʾ*) is divulged exclusively to those who are humble (*tsenuʿin*), for they know the art of concealing the concealment in disclosing the disclosure (Wolfson 1999: 135–148). Circumcision, therefore, may be viewed as the sacrament through which the Jew enacts the role of dissimulation by cutting away the foreskin to inscribe the covenantal sign, *ʾot berit*, the "letter of the covenant," the "sign (or simulacrum) of castration" (Derrida 1986: 42),[30] a sacrificial marking that is imprinted by taking away, the presence re/presented through its own absence. The paradox is fully expressed in the repeated insistence on the part of kabbalists that it is forbidden to gaze on the phallus (or, more specifically, the corona) that is laid bare (Wolfson

---

[29] Smith: 41–42, 77–78, 82–83.

[30] Derrida 1986: 41 refers to circumcision as the "symbolic castration." By contrast, see Derrida 1996: 42, where Derrida emphasizes the irreducibility of circumcision to castration in opposition to the Freudian view that circumcision is a symbolic substitute of the castration of the son by the primitive father. The change in Derrida's perspective has been noted by Caputo (1997: 234, 240, 259, 262, 306–307).

1994: 336–345). Inscripting the sign occasions erasure of the name that cannot be written. This claim rests on the assumption that what is revealed of the secret is unveiled in its concealment and what is concealed is hidden in its unveiling.

In a manner consonant with kabbalists, Derrida proposes that the literal cut of circumcision is the cutting of the letter in the flesh.[31] The ritual thus assumes a figurative meaning without diminishing its concrete sense; indeed, somatic concreteness is transformed in a manner akin to what one finds in the Jewish mystical orientation. The nature of corporeality must be conceived semiotically as body is constituted by letters. To be even more specific, for the kabbalists, the twenty-two letters of the Hebrew alphabet, the basic stuff of reality, are all comprised in the four letters of the most sacred of divine names in the Jewish tradition, YHWH, also identified as the inner essence of Torah. In contrast to the christological doctrine of incarnation, which is predicated on the identification of a particular historical figure as the embodiment of God's word, the Jewish esoteric tradition is based on the notion of divine body as scriptural text, which is the name.

Needless to say, Derrida does not embrace the kabbalistic idea in all of its symbolic complexity, eschewing, as he does, any metaphysical, let alone theosophic, conception of transcendence. Nevertheless, he does affirm two of the main elements of the worldview of kabbalists. First, it is axiomatic for Derrida's deconstruction that the materiality of being is textual. Consider this formulation:

> The nonquestion of which we are speaking is the unpenetrated certainty that Being is a Grammar; and that the world is in all its parts a cryptogram to be constituted or reconstituted through poetic inscription or deciphering; that the book is original, that everything *belongs to the book* before being and in order to come into the world; that any thing can be born only by *approaching* the book, can die only by failing *in sight of* the book; and that always the impassible shore of the book is *first*. (Derrida 1978: 76–77)

---

[31] The nexus between circumcision and writing in Derrida's thought implicates him in a phallocentrism that is characteristic of the kabbalistic sources as well. This is somewhat ironic for Derrida himself challenged the phallocentric nature of the logocentrism of western metaphysics, insisting on the need to attend seriously to the problematic of sexual difference, which entails assigning to the woman a genuine role as the other rather than subsume her under the dominance of the masculine. The matter is cast as the difference between the phallogocentrism of hermeneutical anxiety and the feminine displacement of reading in Derrida 1995c: 96. See Cornell: 194–197; Spivak: 60–68. Relevant to this discussion is the parenthetical remark in Derrida 1992a: 58 that no text "completely escapes" the rubric of phallocentricism. Although no mention is made in that context of circumcision, it seems reasonable to make this connection when pondering Derrida's utilization of circumcision as a rhetorical trope to characterize writing and reading.

To place the book at the beginning is not to lapse back into a logocentric positing of an origin or transcendental signified, for there is no book that is not composed by traces of another book, and so on in an endless chain of significations. The book is first, at the beginning, but the beginning, paradoxically, cannot begin and remain the beginning because to be the beginning it must have already begun.[32] The beginning, then, must be conceived as a breaking-point, an interruption, interference, a rupture of the "discontinuous series of instants and *attractions*" (1998: 580). If, however, the book at the beginning, which is the beginning of the book, has no beginning, then writing the book has no end, and, consequently, meaning cannot be fixed in any resolute fashion. "To risk meaning nothing is to start to play, and first to enter into the play of *différance* which prevents any word, any concept, any major enunciation from coming to summarize and to govern from the theological presence of a center the movement and textual spacing of differences" (Derrida 1981b: 14). To commence with a book, therefore, is to mandate interpretation as the incipient evocation: "The necessity of commentary, like poetic necessity, is the very form of exiled speech. In the beginning is hermeneutics" (Derrida 1978: 67).[33]

The second similarity to traditional kabbalah relates to the special role that Derrida ascribes to YHWH in illumining the language of secrecy and the secrecy of language. From the biblical narrative of the Tower of Babel, Derrida adduces that this name simultaneously "imposes and forbids translation. . . . Translation then becomes necessary and impossible, like the effect of a struggle for the appropriation of the name, necessary and forbidden in the interval between two absolutely proper names" (Derrida

---

[32] It is this logical conundrum that underlies Derrida's notion of "iterability," which presumes a convergence of sameness and difference such that there is genuine reiteration of the "wholly other," *tout autre*, in every moment. The distinctiveness of each moment necessitates that what is experienced in the present is utterly new, but the present can be new only to the extent that it is old. Innovation is possible against the backdrop of replication. See, for example, Derrida's remark in Derrida and Ferraris: "Every time I write something, I have the impression of making a beginning— but in fact that which is the same in texture is ceaselessly exposed to a singularity which is that of the other (another text, someone else, another word of the language). Everything appears anew: which means newness and repetition together. . . . In the actual writing, of course, I'm well aware of the fact that at bottom it all unfolds according to the same law that commands these always different things. . . . I can only hope that what I say about philosophy, literature, the event, the signature, the iterability (altering-altered repetition) is consistent with our encountering this ever renewed singularity" (47).

For a similar description of prayer in terms of the paradox of being concurrently old and new, see the comments of Derrida in Shapiro, Govrin, and Derrida: 65–67. Also relevant is the following comment of Derrida: "What I write resembles, by my account, a dotted outline of a book to be written, in what I call—at least for me—the 'old new language,' the most archaic and the newest, unheard of, and thereby at present unreadable. You know that the oldest synagogue in Prague is called the Old-New?" (Wood and Bernasconi: 73–74).

[33] On the symbolic nexus of exile and writing, which includes a brief discussion of Derrida, see Ofrat 2000: 160–164.

1985: 170). The Tetragrammaton, therefore, is designated the "translatable-untranslatable name" (Derrida 1985: 174), that is, on the one hand, translatable inasmuch as it is ineffable and hence cannot be voiced except through cognomens, yet, on the other, untranslatable insofar as it names the wholly other and absolute singularity[34] that cannot be named.[35] From the specific case of YHWH, "the proper name which is never proper,"[36] we can extrapolate about the concomitant necessity and impossibility of translating every proper name, a double bind that is indicative of language more generally.[37] YHWH paradigmatically exemplifies the role of *dénomination*—"at the same time to name and to unname"[38]—implicit in every linguistic utterance, the unsaying that makes each saying (im)possible: "God's name would then be the hyperbolic effect of that negativity or all negativity that is consistent in its discourse. God's name would suit everything that may not be broached, approached, or designated, except in an indirect and negative manner. Every negative sentence would already be haunted by God or by the name of God, the distinction between God and God's name opening up the very space of the enigma" (Derrida 1992c: 76).

If the reader may indulge me, I would like to cite the beginning of an essay I wrote in 1993, but which was not published until 1996. I refer to this passage because it underscores what I still consider to be the greatest affinity between Derrida's grammatology and kabbalistic hermeneutics:

> The following tradition is reported by the Hasidic master, R. Zadoq ha-Kohen of Lublin: *we-khakh qibbalti ki ha-'olam kulo hu sefer she-'asah ha-shem yitbarakh we-she-ha-torah hu perush she-'asah we-hibber 'al 'oto ha-sefer*, "Thus I have received that the world in its entirety is a book that God, blessed be He, made, and the Torah is the commentary that He composed on that book." . . . The Hasidic tradition articulated by R. Zadoq is rooted deeply in the Jewish idea that God's creative act is essentially linguistic, in fact that divine creativity is an act of written composition. The first book that God writes is the world and the second the Torah. This statement implies, in a quintessentially Jewish manner, that God's first book, the text of the cosmos, requires a commentary, Scripture, and that commentary, we can well imagine, engenders other commentaries that not God but human beings create in a seemingly endless effort to reveal the hidden depths concealed in the original traces of God's writ-

---

[34] On the link among "alterity," "singularity," and an "essential and abyssal equivocality" that cannot be rendered in translation, see Derrida 1995a: 87–88.

[35] On the "double bind" that the name *YHWH* imposes on the recipient as something that necessarily must be translated but which it is impossible to translate, see Derrida 1988: 102–103, 1992d: 26.

[36] This formulation is used by Derrida in Marion 1999: 45.

[37] On the depiction of deconstruction in terms of the conditions of the translatability and untranslatability of language, see Caputo 1997: 53.

[38] Derrida's language in Marion 1999: 44.

ing that make up the universe. R. Zadoq's comment, while perhaps not consciously intended in this manner, subverts any hermeneutical theory that posits a final truth, a foundation that ends all play of meaning. In perfectly good Derridean fashion we may say that the way back leads not to an original truth, but rather to an origin that is a text that needs to be interpreted by another text. In the beginning there is interpretation. The necessity of commentary thus constitutes the very texture of existence from the vantage point of the Jew. There is nothing that is not inscribed within the book and therefore open to interpretation, not even God's being. One is here reminded of the provocative observation of Jacques Derrida, "there is nothing outside of the text." All transcendence is reduced to textuality. (Wolfson 1996: 145)

The textualization of body is related by Derrida, as it is by numerous kabbalists over the centuries, to circumcision, for the latter is the act by means of which the flesh is engraved and the individual receives a proper name. Derrida provides a way to get beyond the "great war between Judaism and Christianity," as he put it in *Archive Fever*, that is, the debate regarding the literal versus the figurative interpretation of the ritual of circumcision, excision of flesh, on the one hand, and immersion in baptismal water, on the other. The sign of circumcision, like the phylacteries, which Derrida describes as "archives of skin or parchment covered with writing," is "right on the body . . . but with a being-right-on that this time does not exclude the detachment and the untying of the ligament, of the substance, and of the text simultaneously" (1996: 42). The text of the inscribed body for Derrida yields the body of the scripted text, and just as the former arises as a consequence of an ostensibly violent infringement upon the flesh, so the latter is written in the disrupting rupture of eruption. The Jewish rite is (hyper)literally preserved by Derrida, for the mark of circumcision is the primal cut of discernment that differentiates one from the other and renders the other inaccessible in its otherness, a mark that is "at once both endowed with and deprived of singularity" (1994a: 59). Circumcision thus functions as a figure of speech for the method of deconstruction because the latter is analogously understood as a cut, a tearing off and taking apart, a setting of boundaries traversed by rendering the inside outside and the outside inside.[39] In an extraordinary entry in *Circonfession*, Derrida relates the main themes of his writings, some of whose titles are specified by name, to the ancient Jewish rite of passage: "*Circumcision, that's all I have ever talked about, consider the discourse on the limit, margins, marks, marches, etc., the closure, the ring (al-*

---

[39] See Caputo 1997: 233.

liance and gift), the sacrifice, the writing of the body, the pharmakos *excluded or cut off, the cutting/sewing of* Glas, *the blow and the sewing back up . . . yes but I have been, I am and I always will be me and not another, circumcised"* (Bennington and Derrida 1993: 70–71).

The link between circumcision and writing is treated more fully by Derrida in his study "Shibboleth for Paul Celan," published in 1986. The main thesis is summed up in the statement, "There must be circumcision, circumcision of the word, writing, and it must take place once, precisely, each time one time, the one time only" (1994a: 68). The choice of the Hebrew term *shibbolet* is based on the use of this sign in the testing of the Ephraimites by the men of Gilead in Judges 12:6. The indication that one was from Ephraim was his inability to pronounce *shibbolet*, saying instead "sibbolet." The *shibbolet*, therefore, as Derrida expresses the matter in another essay, is a "solid barrier of a social division" (1992c: 93), for the way of speaking serves as an idiomatic mark to distinguish between those who belong and do not belong to a particular speech community. According to Derrida, therefore, *shibbolet* has a double edge for it cuts two ways, that is, the tear it makes in the fabric of being facilitates entry to those who belong by turning away those who are alien. Predictably, the double edge is related to circumcision, which is concomitantly a "mark of belonging and of exclusion" (Derrida 1994a: 67). By virtue of circumcision the Jew becomes other, the embodiment of difference, otherness, estrangement, homelessness, inscrutability. "The Jew is also the other, myself and the other; I am Jewish in saying: the Jew is the other who has no essence, who has nothing of his own or whose own essence is not to have one. Thus, *at one and the same time*, both the alleged universality of Jewish witnessing . . . and the incommunicable secret of the Judaic idiom, the singularity of 'his name, his unpronounceable name'" (Derrida 1994a: 54). Derrida's reflections seem to be rooted in the fact that it is customary to name the Jewish infant at the time of circumcision. I suggest this ritual lies behind his comment, "But does one ever circumcise without circumcising a word? a name? And how can one ever circumcise a name without doing something to the body? First of all to the body of the name which finds itself recalled by the wound to its condition as word, then as carnal mark, written, spaced, and inscribed in a network of other marks, at once both endowed with and deprived of singularity" (Derrida 1994a: 59).

The understanding of literal circumcision as a circumcision of the word allows Derrida to identify the Jew as poet. In support of this claim, Derrida cites the comment of Marina Tsvetayeva, "All poets are Jews," which brings to mind the statement of Blake in "The Marriage of Heaven and Hell" that the people of Israel "taught that the Poetic Genius . . . was the first principle and all the others merely derivative" (1982: 39).[40] It is in this sense that the poet/writer participates in the "enigma of circumcision," which is described further as "an incision in the body of language," the opening of the word to the other, the door that "opens history and the poem and philosophy and hermeneutics and religion. Of all that calls itself—of the name and the blessing of the name, of yes and of no, it sets turning the ring, to affirm or to annul" (Derrida 1994a: 68).

Here a note of caution is in order, for if it is Derrida's opinion that all poets are Jews, it is not the case that all Jews are poets. In his essay on Jabès to which I have already referred, Derrida differentiates between the rabbi and the poet. Although both agree about the necessity of exegesis, they reflect two distinct interpretative stances, the rabbi representing heteronomous allegiance to law and the poet autonomous independence from law. "Between the fragments of the broken Tables," Derrida writes, "the poem grows and the right to speech takes root" (1978: 67). Although both types are legitimate responses to the "original opening of interpretation," it is the poetic that justifies the characterization of the writer as Jew. Poetic autonomy presupposes the shattering of the tablets of law, but this freedom is not absolute, for even the outlaw remains bound to law—if there were no law, how could one be out of the law and hence an outlaw? For the poet, the lawful breaching of law is intricately connected to language. "The poet, in the very experience of his freedom, finds himself both bound to language and delivered from it by a speech whose master, nonetheless, he himself is" (1978: 64–65).

In my judgment, this insight corresponds to what I have called the "hypernomian" tendency in kabbalistic literature, which can be expressed concisely as the insight that law is fulfilled most perfectly in its abrogation.[41] In a gesticulation of mind even closer to Derrida, kabbalists have discerned that the lawful repudiation of law is intertwined with the presumption that in his utter otherness God is unrepresentable but still the measure of all that is representable, a measure that is meted in the ordinance prohibiting representation. From this peculiar Jewish-inspired exegesis, law, more generally, is delineated as the measure that puts things in place by circumscribing them in the limit that must be trespassed. In face of what cannot be represented, all representation of the other is trans-

---

[40] Although Derrida does not mention the comment of Blake, it is of interest to note that he does observe that "Blake's *Jerusalem*, that great poem of circumcision, regularly associates these three turns of speech, these three revolutions: *circumcision, circumscription,* and *circumference*" (1994a: 63).

[41] See Wolfson 2002a. A fuller version of this essay will appear in Elliot R. Wolfson, *Venturing Beyond—Law of Limits and Limits of Law: Engendering a Kabbalistic Ethos* (forthcoming). See also Wolfson 2000: 36–37.

gressive, but without representation of the other there would be no law to follow.[42] Transgression thus lies in the womb of law, for trespassing the law determines the boundaries of law.[43] Moreover, for kabbalists, as for Derrida, the issue of law and its overcoming is related to the problem of language and its transcendence.[44] Just as the path to overcome the law is by way of undergoing the law, the unsayable can be heeded merely by way of what is spoken, albeit spoken as the unspoken, a paradox that is ritually instantiated in the custom to vocalize the ineffable name by its circumlocution.

The transgressive element, and particularly the connection that Derrida makes between it and linguistic representation, is also helpful in ascertaining the nexus between secrecy and illicit sexual relations that figures prominently in the kabbalistic tradition and whose trace is discernible in Derrida's thinking. More specifically, Derrida asserts that transgression discloses an essential link between the gift and secrecy, a theme found in an ancient mythical fragment preserved in *Sefer ha-Bahir*, considered by scholars to be one of the oldest works of kabbalah. I have had the opportunity to examine this passage elsewhere, utilizing Derrida's reflections, so in this context I will only briefly recapitulate the main points.[45]

In an effort to explain the first word of Torah, *be-re'shit*, "in the beginning," the bahiric text offers a parable about a king who gives his daughter as a gift in marriage to his son. What in the nature of this bestowal necessitates its being characterized as a giving of a gift? Indeed, according to rabbinic law, which is upheld in the *Bahir*, marriage is a contractual arrangement, and thus it would be superfluous to speak of a woman betrothed to a man as being offered as a gift. The clue is provided in the concluding remark of the king to the prince, "Do with her as you wish." To appreciate the intent of this comment, it would be useful to recall Derrida's reflection on the nature of the gift as that which opens the circle of economy, the circular exchange of goods, so as to defy reciprocity or

---

[42] Derrida reiterates this point in a number of writings. For example, see Derrida 1987: 131, 1990: 137, 2000b: 81.

[43] Derrida writes: "A transgression should always know what it transgresses, which always makes the transgression impure, and compromised in advance with what it transgresses" (2002: 43).

[44] Particularly relevant is Derrida's observation that "apophatic discourse," like a "certain mysticism," "has always been suspected of atheism," a suspicion that seems at once "merited" and "insignificant." Derrida refers to the remark of Leibniz about Angelus Silesius from a letter to Paccius on 28 January 1695, cited by Heidegger, to the effect that mystical texts are full of difficult metaphors "inclining almost to Godlessness." Commenting on this, Derrida writes: "Inclining, but not going beyond incline or inclination, not even or almost (*beinahe zur Gottlosigkeit hinneigend*), and the oblique slope [*penchant*] of this *clinamen* does not seem separable from a certain boldness of language [*langue*], from a poetic or metaphoric tongue" (1995b: 36).

[45] Wolfson 1998: 156–163.

symmetry,[46] for "the *given* of the gift (*that which* one gives, *that which* is given, the gift as given thing or as act of donation) must not come back to the giving (let us not already say to the subject, to the donor). It must not circulate, it must not be exchanged, it must not in any case be exhausted, as a gift, by the process of exchange, by the movement of circulation of the circle in the form of return to the point of departure. . . . It is perhaps in this sense that the gift is the impossible" (Derrida 1995a: 7).[47]

The bahiric parable can be profitably read through the lens of Derrida's account of the gift and particularly its link to the temporization of language in the dynamic of bestowing and receiving, opening and closing. That the prince is given the princess as a gift by the king signifies that the act of giving is not a symmetrical relation: Nothing the son does can reciprocate the action of the father, for there is no exchange of commodities, no reciprocal giving and taking. Moreover, the son who receives the daughter as gift cannot donate this gift to another; the daughter belongs exclusively to the son to whom she has been given as a gift. Finally, in the absence of reciprocity, the recipient of the gift assumes complete control and mastery over that which is given; in the act of giving, the donor relinquishes all claims of ownership and possession with respect to the gift, a gesticulation that exceeds the circle of economy. In the bahiric passage, the excessive power of gifting is expressed as an entitlement with a distinctly sexual nuance—the prince is instructed by his father to do as he pleases with the princess. The symbolic import of the parable blatantly contradicts the normative strictures of biblical law, for the taboo of siblings mating (Lev. 18:9) is undermined by the relationship that is described between the son and the daughter of the king. The secret alluded to here, which later kabbalists relate to the mystery of illicit sexual relations (*sitrei 'arayot*) mentioned in the Babylonian Talmud (Hagigah 11b), is that the sexual prohibitions necessary to preserve the fabric of human society can be, indeed must be, transgressed in a symbolic manner in the divine realm (Stern 1991: 222). In that sense, the gift of wisdom is truly the impossible, that which defies the limits of temporal possibility inscribed within the parameters of law. The only time of the gift, therefore, is the present, the paradoxical instant that is an effraction in the linear circularity of time (Derrida 1995a: 9).

But there is an additional element in Derrida's analysis of the gift and secrecy that can be applied to kabbalistic hermeneutics. The gift is marked by

---

[46] It is on account of this feature of generosity, giving without any thought of return, that Cixous associates the realm of the gift with the feminine in contrast to the masculine, which is linked with the realm of the proper. See Moi: 110–113.

[47] On the analysis of gift giving in terms of sacred objects that are not exchangeable, see Godelier.

structural paradoxes, the stigmata of the impossibility. . . . So as not to take over the other, the overtaking by surprise of the pure gift should have the generosity to give nothing that surprises and appears *as* gift, *nothing that presents itself as present, nothing that is;* it should therefore be surprising enough and so thoroughly made up of a surprise that it is not even a question of getting over it, thus of a surprise surprising enough to let itself be forgotten without delay. . . . The secret of that about which one cannot speak, but which one can no longer silence. (Derrida 1992b: 147)

The paradox of the gift is that it is always "the gift of something that remains inaccessible, unpresentable, and as a consequence secret. . . . The gift is the secret itself, if the secret *itself* can be told. Secrecy is the last word of the gift which is the last word of the secret" (Derrida 1995a: 29–30). Just as the disclosure of the secret undermines its claim to being a secret, so the gifting of the gift is annulled in the giving of the gift. The "unconditional respect" of the secret, Derrida tells us, in an obvious challenge to Kantian epistemology, is that the "secret is not phenomenalizable. Neither phenomenal nor noumenal" (1995b: 25). The secret is not something that can be unveiled because it "remains inviolable even when one thinks one has revealed it." The secret is "nonprovisional, heterogeneous to all manifestation. The secret is not a reserve of potential knowing, a potential manifestation. And the language of ab-negation . . . *necessitates* doing the impossible, necessitates going there where one cannot go" (1995b: 26). To be a secret the secret must persist as secret, mute and impassive, and thus one can speak of the secret ad infinitum without disrupting its secrecy. The ineffability of the secret, paradoxically, generates a potentially unlimited sequence of attempts to articulate the secret (1995b: 26–27).[48] The duplicity of the secret as the saying of what cannot be said, the hermeneutical condition of *différance,* is illustrated by the biblical narrative of the *'aqedah,* Abraham's attempted sacrifice of Isaac (Gen. 22:1–19). Commenting on Kierkegaard's observation that Abraham both speaks and does not speak, Derrida writes that he "speaks in order not to say anything about the essential thing he must keep secret. Speaking in order not to say anything is always the best technique for keeping a secret" (1995a: 59). By speaking what cannot be spoken, the secret is preserved.

The secret for the kabbalists necessarily exemplifies this double bind as well: The secret can be a secret only if it is hidden, but the secret can be hidden only if it is revealed (Wolfson 1999, 2000: 21–38). Again, to quote Derrida, the secret is "the thing to be dissimulated, a thing that is neither shown nor said, signified perhaps but that cannot or must not first be delivered up to self-evidence" (1992d: 26). The secret is thus linked to

---

[48] On the impossibility of testifying to a secret, see Derrida 2000a: 30–31.

dénégation; that is, the secret of necessity is the negation that negates itself. In this doubling of the negative, the secret both is and is not what it is, a dissimulation that dissimulates in the concealment of disclosure. "There is a secret of denial and a denial of the secret. The secret as such, as *secret*, separates and already institutes negativity; it is a negation that denies itself. It de-negates itself. This denegation does not happen to it by accident; it is essential and originary" (1992d: 25).[49] The secret's text is woven in and from the interweave of veiling and unveiling, dissimulation and exposure. Precisely with respect to overcoming this dichotomy by occupying a space between does bestowing the gift illumine the secret. The secret can be safeguarded only if it has been divulged and thus is no longer a secret, and, similarly, the gift can be given only if it is received and thus is no longer a gift. It follows that the secret remains untold in the telling, the gift withheld in the giving (Caputo 1997: 33).

The way of withholding-bestowal elicited from examining the secret and the gift illumines Derrida's understanding of language as an encircling cut, a circum/cision, that tears the fabric to which one is bound, the opening of space that fosters the possibility of piecing together the peace of the whole that has been ruptured. In one passage, Derrida relates this process to the act of translation, "translation-proof, grace would perhaps come when the writing of the other absolves you, from time to time, from the infinite *double bind* and first of all, such is a gift's condition, absolves itself, unbinds itself from the double bind" (1992d: 26).[50] To be unbound of the double bind, opening up to receive the gift, is elsewhere referred to by Derrida in the technical term from German occult literature, *Gelassenheit*, "serenity of abandonment," "releasement," letting-go to take hold, the "rarest secret" beyond all knowledge, even knowledge of the name, unheard when spoken:[51]

---

[49] On the "negativity of the secret" and the "secret of denegation," see Derrida 1992d: 18.

[50] On the double bind of translation, see Derrida 1979: 76–79.

[51] On *Gelassenheit* see Caputo 1978: 99–100, 118–127, 173–183. Derrida's view, in my judgment, seems very close to the opinion regarding the divine name expressed by Marion: "The Name has no name in any language. No language says it or understands it. This is why the Jew never pronounces the Tetragrammaton, which he nevertheless reads. By orally substituting other titles for it, one indicates that the Name does not belong to our language but comes to it from elsewhere. The Name appears as a gift, where, in the same gesture, the unthinkable gives us a name as that in which it gives itself, but also as a gift that gives the unthinkable, which only withdraws in the distance of the gift. The name therefore delivers the unthinkable, as the unthinkable that *gives* itself; the same unthinkable also gives *itself*, and hence withdraws within the anterior distance that governs the gift of the Name. The Name delivers and steals away in one and the same movement" (2001: 142).

For a comparative analysis of Derrida and Marion, see Caputo 1999. The concomitant bestowing and withholding resonates with the dialectic of disclosure and concealment that marks the way of kabbalistic hermeneutics. See Wolfson 1999: 114–121, 2000: 27–34, 2002c: 110–115. Particularly germane is the comment in Derrida that the play of words in the expression *tout autre est tout autre* "seems to contain the very possibility of a secret that hides and reveals itself at the same time within a single sentence and, more than that, within a single language" (1995a: 87).

One can have doubts about it from the moment when the name not only is nothing, in any case is not the "thing" that it names, not the "nameable" or the renowned, but also risks to bind, to enslave or to engage the other, to link the called, to call him/her to respond even before any decision or any deliberation, even before any freedom. . . . According to a formula that haunts our tradition from Plotinus to Heidegger . . . and to Lacan . . . the gift of the name gives that which it does not have, that in which, prior to everything, may consist the essence, that is to say—beyond being—the nonessence, of the gift. (1995b: 84–85)[52]

Through the gifting of what cannot be given, the performative act of calling God by the name that cannot be uttered, the spontaneous irruption of prayer, indeed the entreaty to pray, is made possible: "So, when this break, this interruption happens in the everyday life, on the exceptional moment of prayer, we are going back to the name, to the name of the name, a nameless name, or a placeless place, and so on and so forth. We don't simply address someone, we pray to someone—God if you want, some unique one, to allow us to pray. . . . It's praying after the prayer—*prier après la prière*—which is the prayer before the prayer, the prayer for the prayer."[53]

If we are to speak of the influence of Jewish mysticism on Derrida, it would be in the decidedly apophatic sense of unbinding the double bind to facilitate the liturgical utterance of the unutterable name, the name that demarcates the "essence" that is "beyond being," *au-delà de l'être*, the "nonessence of the gift," *l'inessence du don* (Derrida 1993b: 112). Yet, it is particularly with regard to this very gesture that the critical difference between traditional kabbalah and Derridean deconstruction becomes apparent: For the kabbalist, unlike Derrida, divine alterity does not preclude an ontological presumption regarding the superessentiality of God's being. In the writings of kabbalists, therefore, the absence of God, his withdrawal from the spectrum of the visible, signifies God's presence most fully, whereas, for Derrida, absence is a genuine absence and not merely an absence of what is present even if what is present is truly absent. If there can be any faith at all, it must be predicated on the likelihood that there is nothing in which to believe, the metaphysical aporia that serves as the a/theistic premise for a "nondogmatic doublet of dogma, a philosophical and metaphysical doublet, in any case a *thinking* that 'repeats' the possibility of religion without religion" (Derrida 1995a: 49). Prayer itself is only possible to the extent that it embraces this impossibility: "If we were sure that at the other end of the prayer God would show up, and that we produce the addressee, that wouldn't be prayer. The possibility that God re-

---

[52] It is of interest to note that this paragraph does not appear in the first version of the study, which was published originally in English translation (Derrida 1992e).

[53] These comments of Derrida are taken from Shapiro, Govrin, and Derrida: 61–63.

mains eternally absent, that there might be no addressee at the other end of my prayer is the condition of the prayer. . . . So, that's why I would go so far as to say there should be a moment of atheism in the prayer."[54]

In traditional kabbalistic lore, the mystery of prayer likewise involves the invocation of the name that cannot be invoked, but such an invocation is based ultimately on the paradox of an absence that is present in its absence, a true nothing, one might say; in deconstruction, this dialectic is no mystery, for the mysterious necessitates an authentic lack, an absence that cannot be represented even as absence. To express the matter in another terminological register, the notion of an "arche-trace" is endorsed by both kabbalist and Derrida,[55] but with a critical difference: For the kabbalist the originary trace can be traced back ontologically to the infinite, the luminous darkness, exposed through its occlusion in the multiplicity of differentiated beings, a superabundance whose absence signifies the presence of a being so full that it must be empty. Derrida's critique of the notion of presence (*parousia*) in western metaphysics (including Heidegger's attempt to overcome it) applies, in my judgment, to classical kabbalah: "And yet, that which gives us to think beyond the closure cannot be simply absent. Absent, either it would give us nothing to think or it still would be a negative mode of presence" (1982: 65). For Derrida the originary trace is the heterological sign of excess that "must elude mastery" (65), the wholly other that resists reification, the mark that can in no way appear or be named, the supplementary stroke (*trait*) that retreats (*re-trait*) in the withdrawal (*retrait*) of its tracing.[56] "The trace is not a presence but is rather the simulacrum of a presence that dislocates, displaces, and refers beyond itself. The trace has, properly speaking, no place, for effacement belongs to the very structure of the trace" (1973: 156). The trace, which is "produced as its own erasure" and is thus "neither perceptible nor imperceptible" (1982: 65), is subject to an "indefinite pro-

---

[54] Shapiro, Govrin, and Derrida: 63.

[55] Derrida writes: "The concept of arche-trace . . . is in fact contradictory and not acceptable within the logic of identity. The trace is not only the disappearance of origin—within the discourse that we sustain and according to the path that we follow it means that the origin did not even disappear, that it was never constituted except reciprocally by a nonorigin, the trace, which thus becomes the origin of the origin. From then on, to wrench the concept of the trace from the classical scheme, which would derive it from a presence or from an originary nontrace and which would make of it an empirical mark, one must indeed speak of an originary trace or ache-trace. Yet we know that that concept destroys its name and that, if all begins with the trace, there is above all no originary trace" (1976: 61).

[56] The play on the words *trait*, *re-trait*, and *retrait*, is basic to the analysis in Derrida 1993a. Of particular interest to this study is the following remark: "Is it by chance that in order to speak of the trait we are falling back upon the language of negative theology or of those discourses concerned with naming the withdrawal [*retrait*] of the invisible or hidden god? The withdrawal of the One whom one must not look in the face, or represent, or adore, that is, idolize under the traits or guise of the icon? The One whom it is even dangerous to name by one or the other of his proper names? The end of iconography" (Derrida 1993a: 54).

cess of supplementarity" (1976: 163) because it cannot be retraced to any origin that is not itself also a "trace of the trace," the *différance* etched in a "mode of writing" that is from its inception "without presence and without absence" (1982: 66–67),[57] an "inscription prior to writing, a proto-writing without a present origin, without an *arche*" (1973: 146). From this vantage point all representation must be considered a "de-presentation" (1976: 203), a conclusion that conflicts with the kabbalistic tenet regarding the imaginal configuration of the formless in the form of the sefirotic emanations, a configuration that embraces the dialectic representation of the unrepresentable in the paradoxical vocalization of the ineffable.

Traditional kabbalists (in line with the apophaticism of Neoplatonic negative theology) do assume there is a reality beyond language, a super-essentiality that transcends the finite categories of reason and speech (and hence the validity of speaking about ontology), but this reality is accessible phenomenologically only through language. Insofar as kabbalists maintain that the *sefirot* are contained in the Tetragrammaton, the latter serves as the model to convey the confluence of the visual and the auditory, for just as the ineffable name is uttered in the epithet that preserves its ineffability so the invisible image is portrayed in the form that shelters its invisibility.[58] The trace, for kabbalists, likewise arises as an effacing of the trace, but in this effacing the faceless appears as the erasure of erasure and the conse-

---

[57] The full text is worthy of citation: "But at the same time, this erasure of the trace must have been traced in the metaphysical text. Presence, then, far from being, as is commonly thought, *what the sign signifies*, what a trace refers to, presence, then, is the trace of the trace, the trace of the erasure of the trace. Such is, for us, the text of metaphysics, and such is, for us, the language we speak. Only on this condition can metaphysics and our language signal in the direction of their own transgression. And this is why it is not contradictory to think *together* the *erased* and the *traced* of the trace. And also why there is no contradiction between the absolute erasure of the 'early trace' of difference and that which maintains it as trace, sheltered and visible in presence. . . . The trace of the trace which (is) difference above all could not appear or be named *as such*, that is, in its presence. It is the 'as such' which precisely, and as such, evades us forever. . . . Beyond Being and beings, this difference, ceaselessly differing and deferring (itself), would trace (itself) (by itself)—this *différance* would be the first or last trace if we still could speak, here, of origin or end. Such a *différance* would at once, again, give us to think a writing without presence and without absence, without history, without cause, without *archia*, without *telos*, a writing that absolutely upsets all dialectics, all theology, all teleology, all ontology. A writing exceeding everything that the history of metaphysics has comprehended in the form of the Aristotelian *gramme*, in its point, in its line, in its circle, in its time, and in its space" (Derrida 1982: 66–67).

This crucial articulation of Derrida's notion of trace and *différance* emerges from an engaged reading of Heidegger's reference to the "early trace" (*die frühe Spur*) of the difference between Being and beings that has been forgotten in the "oblivion of Being." See also Derrida 1973: 155–158. The key passage interpreted by Derrida occurs in Heidegger: 50–51. For a comprehensive study of "difference" in Heidegger and Derrida, see Donkel, and for discussion of the Derridean trace against the background of Heidegger's thinking, see Marrati-Guénoun: 101–204. On the notion of the trace and arche-writing, see also the nuanced discussion in Harvey: 153–181.

[58] This is not to deny that Derrida himself affirms the convergence of the ocular and verbal (see, for example, 1993a: 4), but in a manner that is quite distant from the kabbalistic understanding of synesthesia.

quent writing of the name. In marking this divergence between traditional kabbalah and Derridean deconstruction, we establish the terms necessary for a dialogical encounter between two disparate modes of discourse equally devoted to entrusting the gift of secrecy in the secret giving of the gift.

REFERENCES

Bennington, Geoffrey 1992	"Mosaic Fragment: If Derrida Were an Egyptian. . . ." In *Derrida: A Critical Reader*, 97–119. Ed. by David Wood. Oxford: Blackwell.
Bennington, Geoffrey, and Jacques Derrida 1991	*Jacques Derrida*. Mars: Éditions du Seuil.
1993	*Jacques Derrida*. Trans. by Geoffrey Bennington. Chicago: University of Chicago Press.
Blake, William 1982	*The Complete Poetry and Prose of William Blake*. Rev. ed. Ed. by David V. Erdman. Commentary by Harold Bloom. Berkeley: University of California Press.
Bloom, Harold 1975a	*A Map of Misreading*. New York: Oxford University Press.
1975b	*Kabbalah and Criticism*. New York: Seabury Press.
1979	"The Breaking of Form." In *Deconstruction and Criticism*, 1–37. Ed. by Harold Bloom. New York: Seabury Press.
Caputo, John D. 1978	*The Mystical Element in Heidegger's Thought*. Athens: Ohio University Press.
1997	*The Prayers and Tears of Jacques Derrida: Religion without Religion*. Bloomington: Indiana University Press.
1999	"Apostles of the Impossible: On God and the Gift in in Derrida and Marion." In *God, the Gift, and Postmodernism*, 185–222. Ed. by John D. Caputo and Michael J. Scanlon. Bloomington: Indiana University Press.
Cixous, Hélène, and Jacques Derrida 2001	*Veils*. Trans. by Geoffrey Bennington. Stanford: Stanford University Press.
Cornell, Drucilla 1997	"Where Love Begins: Sexual Difference and the Limit of the Masculine Symbolic." In *Derrida and Feminism: Recasting the Question of Woman*, 161–206. Ed. by Ellen K. Feder, Mary C. Rawlinson, and Emily Zakin. New York: Routledge.

Derrida, Jacques *Speech and Phenomena and Other Essays on Husserl's*
1973 *"Theory of Signs."* Trans. by David B. Allison. Evanston,
IL: Northwestern University Press.

1976 *Of Grammatology.* Trans. by Gayatri Spivak. Baltimore:
Johns Hopkins University Press.

1978 *Writing and Difference.* Trans. by Alan Bass. Chicago:
University of Chicago Press.

1979 "Living On: Border Lines." In *Deconstruction and Criticism*, 75–176. Ed. by Harold Bloom. New York: Seabury
Press.

1981a *Dissemination.* Trans. by Barbara Johnson. Chicago:
University of Chicago Press.

1981b *Positions.* Trans. by Alan Bass. Chicago: University of
Chicago Press.

1982 *Margins of Philosophy.* Trans. by Alan Bass. Chicago:
University of Chicago Press.

1984 *Signéponge/Signsponge.* Trans. by Richard Rand. New
York: Columbia University Press.

1985 "Des Tours de Babel." Trans. by Joseph F. Graham. In
Difference in Translation, 165–207. Ed. by Joseph F.
Graham. Ithaca, NY: Cornell University Press.

1986 *Glas.* Trans. by John P. Leavey Jr. and Richard Rand.
Lincoln: University of Nebraska Press.

1987 "Devant La Loi." Trans. by Avital Ronell. In *Kafka and
the Contemporary Critical Performance: Centenary Readings*, 128–149. Ed. by Alan Udoff. Bloomington: Indiana University Press.

1988 *The Ear of the Other: Otiobiography, Transference.* Ed.
by Christie McDonald. Trans. by Peggy Kamuf. Lincoln: University of Nebraska Press.

1990 "Sending: On Representation." In *Transforming the
Hermeneutic Context: From Nietzsche to Nancy*, 107–
138. Ed. by G. L. Ormiston and A. D. Schrift. Albany:
State University of New York Press.

1992a *Acts of Literature.* Ed. by Derek Attridge. London:
Routledge.

1992b *Given Time: I. Counterfeit Money.* Trans. by Peggy Kamuf.
Chicago: University of Chicago Press.

1992c   "How to Avoid Speaking: Denials." In *Derrida and Negative Theology*, 73–142. Ed. by Harold Coward and Toby Foshay. Albany: State University of New York Press.

1992d   "Of an Apocalyptic Tone Newly Adopted in Philosophy." In *Derrida and Negative Theology*, 25–71. Ed. by Harold Coward and Toby Foshay. Albany: State University of New York Press.

1992e   "Post-Scriptum: Aporias, Ways and Voices." Trans. by John Leavey Jr. In *Derrida and Negative Theology*, 283–323. Albany: State University of New York Press.

1993a   *Memories of the Blind: The Self-Portrait and Other Ruins.* Trans. by Pascale-Anne Brault and Michael Naas. Chicago: University of Chicago Press.

1993b   *Sauf le nom.* Paris: Galilée.

1994a   "Shibboleth for Paul Celan." In *Word Traces: Readings of Paul Celan*, 3–72. Ed. by Aris Fioretos. Baltimore: Johns Hopkins University Press.

1994b   *Specters of Marx: The State of the Debt, the Work of Mourning, and the New International.* Trans. by Peggy Kamuf. New York: Routledge.

1995a   *The Gift of Death.* Trans. by David Wills. Chicago: University of Chicago Press.

1995b   *On the Name.* Ed. by Thomas Dutoit. Trans. by David Wood, John P. Leavey Jr., and Ian McLeod. Stanford: Stanford University Press.

1995c   *Points . . . Interviews, 1974–1994.* Ed. by Elisabeth Weber. Trans. by Peggy Kamuf et al. Stanford: Stanford University Press.

1996   *Archive Fever: A Freudian Impression.* Trans. by Eric Prenowitz. Chicago: University of Chicago Press.

1997a   ". . . and Pomegranates." Trans. by Samuel Weber. In *Violence, Identity, and Self-Determination*, 326–344. Ed. by Hent de Vries and Samuel Weber. Stanford: Stanford University Press.

1997b   *Politics of Friendship.* Trans. by George Collins. London: Verso.

1998   "Point de folie—Maintenant l'architecture." Trans. by K. Linker. In *Architecture Theory since 1968*, 566–581. Ed. by K. Michael Hays. Cambridge: MIT Press.

1999a   *Adieu to Emmanuel Levinas.* Trans. by Pascale-Anne Brault and Michael Naas. Stanford: Stanford University Press.

1999b   *Monolingualism of the Other or The Prosthesis of Origin.* Trans. by Patrick Mensah. Stanford: Stanford University Press.

2000a   *Demeure: Fiction and Testimony.* Trans. by Elizabeth Rottenberg. Stanford: Stanford University Press.

2000b   *Of Hospitality: Ann Dufourmantelle Invites Jacques Derrida to Respond.* Trans. by Rachel Bowlby. Stanford: Stanford University Press.

2002   *Acts of Religion.* Ed. by Gil Anidjar. New York: Routledge.

Derrida, Jacques, and Maurizio Ferraris 2001   *A Taste for the Secret.* Ed. by Giacomo Donis and David Webb. Trans. by Giacomo Donis. Cambridge: Polity Press.

Derrida, Jacques, and Gianni Vattimo 1998   *Religion.* Stanford: Stanford University Press.

Devries, Hent 2000   "The Theology of Sign and the Sign of Theology: The Apophatics of Deconstruction." In *Flight of the Gods: Philosophical Perspectives on Negative Theology*, 166–194. Ed. by Ilse N. Bulhof and Laurens ten Kate. New York: Fordham University Press.

Donkel, Douglas L. 1992   *The Understanding of Difference in Heidegger and Derrida.* New York: Peter Lang.

Foshay, Toby 1992a   "Introduction: Denegation and Resentment." In *Derrida and Negative Theology*, 1–24. Ed. by Harold Coward and Toby Foshay. Albany: State University of New York Press.

1992b   "Resentment and Apophasis: The Trace of the Other in Levinas, Derrida and Gans." In *Shadow of Spirit: Postmodernism and Religion*, 81–92. Ed. by Philippa Berry and Andrew Wernick. London: Routledge.

Gibbs, Robert 1997   "Lines, Circles, Points: Messianic Epistemology in Cohen, Rosenzweig and Benjamin." In *Toward the Millennium: Messianic Expectations from the Bible to Waco*, 363–382. Ed. by Peter Schäfer and Mark R. Cohen. Leiden: E. J. Brill.

Godelier, Maurice   *The Enigma of the Gift.* Trans. by Nora Scott. Chicago:
1999   University of Chicago Press.

Handelman, Susan   *The Slayers of Moses: The Emergence of Rabbinic Inter-*
1982   *pretation in Modern Literary Theory.* Albany: State University of New York Press.

1987   "Jacques Derrida and the Heretic Hermeneutic." In *Displacement: Derrida and After,* 98–129. Ed. by Mark Krupnick. Bloomington: Indiana University Press.

Harvey, Irene E.   *Derrida and the Economy of Différance.* Bloomington:
1986   Indiana University Press.

Heidegger, Martin   *Early Greek Thinking.* Trans. by David Farrell Krell
1975   and Frank A. Capuzzi. New York: Harper and Row Publishers.

Idel, Moshe   "Infinities of Torah in Kabbalah." In *Midrash and*
1986   *Literature,* 141–157. Ed. by Geoffrey H. Hartman and Sanford Budick. New Haven: Yale University Press.

1995   "PaRDeS: Some Reflections on Kabbalistic Hermeneutics." In *Death, Ecstasy, and Other Worldly Journeys,* 249–268. Ed. by John J. Collins and Michael Fishbane. Albany: State University of New York Press.

Kafka, Franz   *Parables and Paradoxes.* New York: Schocken Books.
1971

Kilcher, Andreas   *Die Sprachtheorie der Kabbala als Ästhetisches Para-*
1998   *digma: Die Konstruktion einer Ästhetischen Kabbala seit der Frühen Neuzeit.* Stuttgart: J. B. Metzler.

Klemm, David E.   "Open Secrets: Derrida and Negative Theology." In *Ne-*
1992   *gation and Theology,* 8–24. Ed. by Robert P. Scharlemann. Charlottesville: University Press of Virginia.

Levy, Ze'ev   *Otherness and Responsibility: A Study of Emmanuel*
1997   *Levinas' Philosophy.* Jerusalem: Magnes Press.

Llewelyn, John   *Appositions of Jacques Derrida and Emmanuel Levinas.*
2001   Bloomington: Indiana University Press.

Marion, Jean-Luc   "In the Name: How to Avoid Speaking of 'Negative
1999   Theology.'" In *God, the Gift, and Postmodernism,* 20–53. Ed. by John D. Caputo and Michael J. Scanlon. Bloomington: Indiana University Press.

2001   *The Idol and Distance: Five Studies.* Trans. by Thomas A. Carlson. New York: Fordham University Press.

Marrati-Guénoun, Paola
1998
La genèse et la trace: Derrida lecteur de Husserl et Heidegger. Dordrecht: Kluwer Academic Publishers.

Moi, Toril
1985
Sexual/Textual Politics: Feminist Literary Theory. London: Routledge.

Mole, Gary D.
1997
Lévinas, Blanchot, Jabès: Figures of Estrangement. Gainesville: University Press of Florida.

Ofrat, Gideon
2000
In Praise of Exile. Jerusalem: Karta.

2001
The Jewish Derrida. Trans. by Peretz Kidron. Syracuse, NY: Syracuse University Press.

Scholem, Gershom
1969
On the Kabbalah and Its Symbolism. Trans. by Ralph Manheim. New York: Schocken Books.

Shapiro, David, Michal Govrin, and Jacques Derrida
2001
Body of Prayer. New York: Cooper Union for the Advancement of Science and Art.

Smith, Robert
1995
Derrida and Autobiography. Cambridge: Cambridge University Press.

Spivak, Gayatri Chakravorty
2001
"Displacement and the Discourse of Woman." In *Feminist Interpretations of Jacques Derrida*, 43–71. Ed. by Nancy J. Holland. University Park: Pennsylvania State University Press.

Srajek, Martin C.
1997
In the Margins of Deconstruction: Jewish Conceptions of Ethics in Emmanuel Levinas and Jacques Derrida. Dordrecht: Kluwer Academic Publishers.

Stern, David
1991
Parables in Midrash: Narrative and Exegesis in Rabbinic Literature. Cambridge: Harvard University Press.

Stern, Sacha
1994
Jewish Identity in Early Rabbinic Writings. Leiden: E. J. Brill.

Taylor, Mark C.
1993
Nots. Chicago: University of Chicago Press.

Wallace, Mark I.
2002
"God beyond God: Derrida's Theological Self-Portraiture." In *The Unknown, Remembered Gate: Religious Experience and Hermeneutical Reflection in the Study of Religion*, 99–118. Ed. by Jeffrey J. Kripal and Elliot R. Wolfson. New York: Seven Bridges Press.

Wolfson, Elliot R.   "Circumcision, Vision of God, and Textual Interpre-
1987   tation: From Midrashic Trope to Mystical Symbol."
History of Religions 27: 189–215.

1994   *Through a Speculum That Shines: Vision and Imagination in Medieval Jewish Mysticism.* Princeton: Princeton
University Press.

1996   "From Sealed Book to Open Text: Time, Memory, and
Narrativity in Kabbalistic Hermeneutics." In *Interpret-
ing Judaism in a Postmodern Age*, 145–178. Ed. by Steven
Kepnes. New York: New York University Press.

1998   "Hebraic and Hellenic Conceptions of Wisdom in *Sefer
ha-Bahir.*" *Poetics Today* 19: 147–176.

1999   "Occultation of the Feminine and the Body of Secrecy
in Medieval Kabbalah." In *Rending the Veil: Concealment and Secrecy in the History of Religions*, 113–154.
Ed. by Elliot R. Wolfson. New York: Seven Bridges Press.

2000   *Abraham Abulafia—Kabbalist and Prophet: Hermeneutics, Theosophy, Theurgy.* Los Angeles: Cherub Press.

2002a   "Beyond Good and Evil: Hypernomianism, Trans-
morality, and Kabbalistic Ethics." In *Crossing Boundaries: Essays on the Ethical Status of Mysticism*, 103–156.
Ed. by Jeffrey J. Kripal and G. William Barnard. New
York: Seven Bridges Press.

2002b   "The Cut That Binds: Time, Memory, and the Ascetic
Impulse." In *God's Voice from the Void: Old and New
Studies in Bratslav Hasidism*, 103–154. Ed. by Shaul
Magid. Albany: State University of New York Press.

2002c   "Divine Suffering and the Hermeneutics of Reading:
Philosophical Reflections on Lurianic Mythology." In
Suffering Religion, 101–162. Ed. by Robert Gibbs and
Elliot R. Wolfson. New York: Routledge.

Wolosky, Shira   "Derrida, Jabès, Levinas: Sign-Theory as Ethical Dis-
1982   course." *Prooftexts* 2: 283–302.

Wood, David, and   *Derrida and Différance.* Evanston, IL: Northwestern Uni-
Robert Bernasconi, eds.   versity Press.
1988

Wright, T. R.   "Midrash and Intertextuality: Ancient Rabbinic Exege-
2000   sis and Postmodern Reading of the Bible." In *Divine
Aporia: Postmodern Conversations about the Other*, 97–
119. Ed. by John C. Hawley. Lewisburg, PA: Bucknell
University Press.

The Honesty of the Perplexed: Derrida and Ibn 'Arabi on "Bewilderment"

Ian Almond

In this article, I consider the positive manner in which both Ibn 'Arabi and Derrida approach the idea of perplexity (in Arabic, *hayrah*)—for Ibn 'Arabi, it is a prelude towards an encounter with the Real. If rational constructs are an obstacle toward our understanding of Allah—and if bewilderment means the disabling of our rational faculties—then bewilderment is no longer a sign of spiritual failure and disarray, but rather a possibility of truer knowledge about God. In this respect, I consider for comparison what Derrida already has written about the *tout autre*—how we only truly glimpse the Other when we are confused. For both deconstructive and Sufi alterities, the basic point remains the same: When we are confused, we see things that we miss when we think we know what we are doing. We see the difference of difference.

> I mistrust all systematizers and avoid them. The will to a system is a lack of integrity.
>
> —Nietzsche, *Twilight of the Idols*

> O Lord, increase my perplexity concerning Thee!
>
> —*Fusus al-Hikem* (Afifi: 73; Austin 1980: 79)[1]

BEWILDERMENT takes place when we realize that our rational faculties are not enough to understand what is happening. That something has taken place in a language our rational faculties do not speak. In a sense, bewilderment takes place *because* of our rationality, because we insist on

Ian Almond teaches English literature at Bosphorus University (Bogazici Üniversitesi), Istanbul, Turkey.

---

[1] "Zidnī fiyaka tahīraan."

Journal of the American Academy of Religion September 2002, Vol. 70, No. 3, pp. 515–537.

clinging to something that is blinding us to the "actual situation." What is to be examined in this study is a certain *desire* for bewilderment in both deconstructive and Sufi thought, a certain perception of bewilderment as a more honest possibility of truth. Words such as *perplexity* and *bewilderment* enable us to glimpse a similar vein of thought in both Derrida and the Sufi mystical thinker Ibn 'Arabi (1165–1240)—that is, a similar affirmation of confusion as a difficult, courageous, and desirable state.

For those unfamiliar with the Spanish Arab thirteenth-century thinker, Muhyiddin Ibn 'Arabi (commonly known as the *shaykh al-akhbar* or "The Great Shaykh") constitutes a pivotal figure in the history of Islamic thought. Although his work, a complex and highly original distillation of Neoplatonic thought and early Islamic spirituality, is made up of over several hundred titles, the voluminous *Meccan Openings* (*Futuhat al-Makkiyah*) and the much shorter and more esoteric *Bezels of Wisdom* (*Fusus al-Hikam*) are the two texts most frequently cited and translated. Often seen as an Islamic Meister Eckhart,[2] the scale of Ibn 'Arabi's influence upon the Muslim world of the centuries following his death really is closer to that of Aquinas—indeed, scholars such as Asin Palacios even have extended the Shaykh's influence as far as Dante, an idea the Turkish novelist Orhan Pamuk has satirized in his novel *The Black Book*. However, the fact remains that, like Meister Eckhart, Ibn 'Arabi's reservations concerning rational thought and reason (*'aql*) in attempting to speak about the Unspeakable do carry with them some implications that, for readers of contemporary theory, will sound surprisingly familiar.

Neither Ibn 'Arabi nor Derrida seems to be afraid of bewilderment—or, for that matter, bewildering. Whether it is the constantly "exploding semantic horizons" of the disseminating text (Derrida 1987a: 45), or the guidance that means being "guided to bewilderment" (Afifi: 200; Austin 1980: 254),[3] the "acceptance of incoherent incoherence" (Derrida 1967: 224; see Bass: 151)[4] or the God who is everywhere and nowhere, both Derrida and Ibn 'Arabi part with a philosophical and Koranic tradition that sees confusion synonymous with error, failure, untruth, and sin.

In the West, confusion almost always has been seen as the "problem" of philosophy. Wittgenstein sums this idea up the best: "The philosopher goes wild, screaming helplessly, until he gets to the heart of his confusion"

---

[2] A surprising number of western studies or translations of Ibn 'Arabi make some kind of reference to the German preacher Meister Eckhart (1260–1327). The strength and conviction behind such references vary—while some simply mention Eckhart in passing, others (such as R. W. Austin) speak of "striking resemblances," and Richard Netton goes so far as to call Ibn 'Arabi "the Meister Eckhart of the Islamic Tradition" (293).

[3] "Illa al-hayrah."

[4] "Acceptation . . . de l'incohérence incoherent."

(Kenny: 271). Whether it is Spinoza's desire to understand the nature of human actions or Descartes's project to overcome the anxiety of his own skepticism, a fear of confusion and doubt always has been the driving force behind most philosophical projects. Equally negative is the word in Islamic thought, where *confusion* is used to describe any state of mental or spiritual regression, an inability to understand the will of God—or the consequence of a reluctance to do so. It is the kind of confusion ʿAy al-Qudat Hamadani felt before finally reading Al-Ghazali: "My heart was a tumultuous sea with no shores, in it was drowned all the ends and all the beginnings" (Nasr and Leaman: 390). Ibn Tamiyah, in his *Muqaddimat al-tafsir*, insists the Prophet was sent to explain clearly (*tubayyin*) everything we need to know (Nasr and Leaman: 115). Given such a premise, confusion in Islam can only ever be negative, falling upon those who cannot or will not understand. Therefore, God may well be the Guide (*al-hadi*) for the righteous, but He also is the Misguider (*al-mudill*) of the wicked, dispersing and confounding those who reject His counsel and follow evil. The fact that Ibn ʿArabi can take such a standard Koranic (not to mention biblical) motif such as "confusion" and imbue it with a positive meaning—to the point of making bewilderment a gift from God—not only attests to the Shaykh's daring originality but also indicates how far Ibn ʿArabi is prepared radically to reinterpret familiar sections of the Koran such as the Surah on Noah (*Nuh*)—reinterpretations that, as we shall see, will call into question some of the familiar claims for an "orthodox" and "traditionalist" Ibn ʿArabi, centrally located in the mainstream of Islamic thought.[5]

DECONSTRUCTION—UNTYING KNOTS, THWARTING SYSTEMS

There is something implicitly negative about the word *deconstruction*, even though elsewhere Derrida has suggested "de-structuration" (translating Heidegger's *Destruktion*) as more accurately conveying the sense of the term (Midgley: 16). The variety of images Derrida supplies to describe the effects of *différance* and dissemination is bewildering in itself: *différance* is anarchic, it "instigates the subversion of every kingdom" (1982: 22), it "escapes . . . and disorganizes structure" (1987a: 84), it "disembeds" the text, "unsews" it (1987a: 85), "explodes the semantic horizon" of its subject (1987a: 45)—terms that illustrate the paradoxical

---

[5] Probably the main proponent of this has been Mahmoud al-Ghorab, who sees Ibn ʿArabi not only as a traditionalist (*salafi*) but also as a "Muhammedan mirror of the utmost clarity, symmetry and straightness" (see Hirtenstein and Tiernan: 224).

etymology of confusion, with its simultaneous sense of convergence and divergence. *Confusion* is a word that literally means "melting together" but that we often use in the opposite sense, to describe a situation in which many things are happening at the same time. *Différance* at once confuses and makes things simpler. It breaks down complexities, undoes complications, and dismantles structures into their various components. At the same time it makes a text difficult to read, disabling its primary sense in order to free a plethora of secondary ones, robbing the text of its semantic rudder so that it no longer can be said to sail in any particular direction.

This emphasis on *différance* as something that undoes/unsews/disrupts the text obviously makes use of the origins of the word *text* (from the Latin *textus*, cloth). The text is a cloth that *différance* forever threatens to undo. "Dissemination endlessly opens up a snag [*accroc*] in writing that can no longer be mended" (Derrida 1972: 26).[6] No work can escape this stitch, this inherent, ever-present possibility of its complete undoing. It is interesting to note that the Arabic term Ibn 'Arabi frequently uses for "belief" (*i'tiqād, 'aqida*) has as its root meaning the tying of a knot or to tie something firmly (Chittick 1989: 335). Thus, when Ibn 'Arabi says how "every group has believed something about God," what he means is that "every group has tied a certain knot about God" (Chittick 1989: 336; Yahia: I.266.15). The bewildering unthinkability of God unties every knot concerning Him, just as the unthinkable movement of *différance* undoes every text.

Despite the variety of metaphors Derrida offers for *différance* and dissemination, it should not be forgotten that Derrida, far from confusing the text, simply is showing how the text is already confused in itself. Deconstruction is a revelatory operation, not a stimulatory one. The "essential drifting of the text" (Derrida 1982: 317) precedes any theoretical intervention—texts are always already drifting. If deconstruction brings anarchy to the text, it is only by showing how these unruly elements always have been seething and brooding underneath a calm façade of unity and coherence. Confusion and instability are the a priori condition of every text, regardless of whether it has been analyzed or not. In the same way, for Ibn 'Arabi the essentially bewildering nature of God precedes every attempt, be it Asharite or Mutazilite, to talk meaningfully about Him— "God is the root of every diversity (*khilaf*) in beliefs within the cosmos" (Chittick 1989: 338; Yahia: III.465.25). In both Derrida and Ibn 'Arabi, confusion and perplexity seem to precede and underlie every attempt to form a system—a belief that inevitably imbues the desire for confusion with an element of honesty and courage (not to mention Nietzschean "in-

---

[6] "La dissémination ouvre, sans fin, cet accroc de l'écriture qui ne se laisse plus recoudre."

tegrity"), the desire to glimpse a "truer," more confused state of affairs and not succumb to the temptation of the system. In Derrida's case, this reappraisal of confusion is most clearly seen in his 1985 essay, "Des Tours de Babel."

DERRIDA ON BABEL

Derrida's essay, being itself an analysis of Benjamin's famous essay on translation "The Task of the Translator," displays its title with an obvious irony, quite apart from the ambiguity of "Des Tours" (Some tricks? Some towers? Some detours?). Derrida's essay on translation *has* to begin with Genesis 11:1–9, the destruction of the tower of Babel that is simultaneously the birth of the translator, the ethnoclastic event that makes translation possible. What is most immediately striking about "Des Tours" is the way in which Derrida reinterprets the episode of Babel using his own terms, retelling the Old Testament story like a medieval typologist, this time not Christianizing but poststructuralizing the chapter from Genesis to transform it into a deconstructive parable. Genesis 11:1–9 is no longer just a story about the pride of man thwarted by the omnipotence of God: it is also a tale about an unfinished structure, a monocultural and monolingual project (the Shemites) with universalist intentions being thwarted not by thunder or earthquakes but by language itself.

"Now the whole world had one language and a common speech" (Genesis 11:1). The Babel episode, although purporting to be a biblical explanation for the multiplicity of tongues, also marks the beginning of confusion for man in the Bible. It marks the beginning of a fragmentation of cultures, a dispersal of different tongues, and the deliberate introduction of a nefarious (and divinely delivered) multiplicity into the totalizing project of the Shemites. Not surprisingly, Derrida discerns clear parallels to deconstruction in all of this:

> In seeking to "make a name for themselves," to found at the same time a universal tongue and a unique genealogy, the Shemites want to bring the world to reason [*mettre à la raison le monde*], and this reason can signify simultaneously a colonial violence (since they would thus universalize their idiom) and a peaceful transparency of the human community [*une transparence pacifique de la communauté humaine*]. (Kamuf: 253; see also Derrida 1987b: 210)

The Shemites, no longer simply tower builders, have become system builders. They have become believers in universal truths, metaphysical construction engineers, trying to build a structure that would both symbolize and disseminate their supremacy—not only over other peoples ("colonial violence") but also over *language*. The Shemites want to take over the deistic function of eponymy and "make a name for themselves"—subdue and control language, decide what they may and may not be called, and control which signifieds get allotted to which signifiers. Apart from injecting something strangely biblical into Derrida's own deconstruction of western metaphysics (Is Derrida a modern Jeremiah, railing against the Babelian pretensions of structuralism and phenomenology, science, and sociology?), the passage emphasizes how the pride of the Shemites blinds them to the futility of their project. For this is precisely what Babel—to Derrida—represents: "an incompletion [*inachèvement*], the impossibility of finishing, of totalizing ... of completing something on the order of system ... and architectonics" (Kamuf: 244; see also Derrida 1987b: 203). Derrida has spent a life exploring this impossibility of ever putting a stop to meaning, of ever making a text say one thing, coherently and consistently, and nothing else. Thus, the futility of the Shemites' project also is the futility of Husserl's, whose Cartesian project sought to "return to the things themselves" and seek out "the foundation of objectivity" (Derrida 1967: 159); the futility of Foucault's *L'histoire de la folie*, which believes it can talk in a rational-analytical way about madness without ever succumbing to the rational/insane dualism it purports to critique; the futility of Levinas's *Totality and Infinity*, whose aim of reestablishing a "nonviolent" relationship with the wholly Other is revealed by Derrida to be nothing more than a "dream"—the "*dream* of a purely *heterological* thought" ("le rêve d'une pensée purement *hétérologique*" [Derrida 1967: 151]). In all these instances, the Shemites' mistaken conviction that their structure actually can get the better of language is replicated.

What is even more interesting than this contemporary allegorizing of biblical pride is the way Derrida sees God as a synonym for deconstruction. It is "from a *proper* name of God ... that tongues are scattered, confounded or multiplied" (Kamuf: 249; see also Derrida 1987b: 207).[7] God is the arch-deconstructor of the story—it is He who confounds the sign system of the Shemites by fissuring it, fracturing it, and causing it to double and triple until the Shemites no longer know who they are or what it is they were planning to do. For all this humbling, abasing, and confounding, however, Derrida's God is not simply an agent of deconstruction but also a God who deconstructs Himself: "And the proper name of God (given by God) is divided enough in the tongue, already, to signify also, confusedly, 'confusion.' And the war that He declares has first raged within his name [*a debord fait rage au-dedans de son nom*]: divided, bifid, ambivalent, polysemic: God deconstructs. Himself" (1987b: 207).

---

[7] "Depuis un nom propre de Dieu ... les langues se dispersent, se confondent ou se multiplient."

It is a point Derrida has made several times: Not even God escapes *différance*. Or, in more secular terms, even the deconstructive critic must fall prey to the same semantic instabilities she or he has detected in others. The pat distinction between deconstructor and deconstructed is dissolved. For Derrida, no-one or -thing, neither God nor Allah, neither Husserl's brackets nor Heidegger's *Sein* nor Lévi-Strauss's *bricoleur*, can escape the "metaphysical complicity" of language (Derrida 1967: 281). As soon as we begin to deconstruct, we already have deconstructed ourselves. When God delivers confusion and chaos upon the designs of the Shemites, He actually is inflicting Himself on them.

Just as God precedes history, confusion precedes order. Or, as Derrida might say, confusion inhabits order, pervades order, gives *meaning* to order. In Derrida's version of Genesis, no calm, transcendental deity deconstructs the tower—rather, one version of confusion gives birth to another. That is why "Des Tours de Babel" is so important for our own argument—it is one of the few places in the Derridean oeuvre where Derrida actually joins Ibn 'Arabi in using *confusion* as a divine name. What Derrida does in "Des Tours" is call into question the *simplicity* of God, criticize the standard and fairly simplistic images of deity we have, remind us of the confusing and overwhelming complexity of the thought of God. It is a theme Derrida has certainly touched on elsewhere—twenty years earlier, in his essay on Jabès (in many ways the most Kabbalistic of Derrida's essays) Derrida is comparing the "God" we can know with the "God" we cannot:

> If God opens the question in God, if he is the very opening of the Question [*s'il est l'ouverture même de la Question*], there can be no simplicity of God. And, thus, that which was unthinkable for the classical rationalists here becomes the obvious itself. Proceeding within the duplicity of his own questionability, God does not act in the simplest ways; he is not truthful, he is not sincere [*il n'est pas vérace, il n'est pas sincère*]. (1967: 68)

Like Ibn 'Arabi, Derrida is asking us to increase our perplexity concerning God. The "simplicity" of God—the belief that God acts and works in essentially clear, meaningful ways—is opposed to the distinctly unclassical complexity and confusion of God. Derrida's rejection of such "simplicity" replicates, to some extent, Ibn 'Arabi's frequent Koranic reminder that God is like "no thing" that we can know.

All of which leads to the question: what *exactly* is Derrida saying in "Des Tours" about confusion? Is it desirable or undesirable? Is it the birth of something new and positive—or an ineluctable fate that terminates every project we undertake?

Confusion, first and foremost, appears to be a punishment delivered in particular upon those who want to get rid of their own confusion. The

Shemites are guilty of this cardinal sin: "Come, let us build ourselves a city and a tower . . . / Let us make ourselves a name, / that we not be scattered over the face of all the earth" (Kamuf: 248).[8] Seeing the world not as a place to affirm but rather to control, the Shemites are unhappy with their wandering, nameless status—and it is precisely this proud dissatisfaction with their nomadic condition that provokes their punishment. There is something faintly paradoxical here—"True homelessness and confusion will only be inflicted on those who do not desire it," as if learning to love one's perplexity is the only way ever to be free of it.

Part of the Shemites' sin, it would appear, lies in the Shemites' refusal not just to wander but also to accept the multiplicity of language. The only truly "proper" (*propre*) name is that of "YHWH"; the Shemites, troubled by the fact that their name may take on different meanings for different people, yearn for a similar unambiguity. In this sense, the tower of Babel is (in the words of Richard Rorty) "an attempt to avoid relatedness . . . to speak a word which has meaning even though it has no place in a social practice" (Guignon: 352). The Shemites' sin is the desire for *meaning* itself; pure, unambiguous, repeatable meaning, not to be at the mercy of contexts or adrift in alien situations. Of course, the Shemites fail in this— and Derrida's conviction of the "impossibility of finishing" such towers only reflects the more general impossibility of *any* proper name (even that of YHWH) *ever* to mean one thing and one thing only.

Second, Derrida's essay seems to oppose confusion to violence—at least to a certain kind of violence, a "colonial violence." The Shemites' desire to "universalize their idiom" (Kamuf: 253), of making the whole world speak their tongue and subscribe to their culture, ultimately belongs to what Derrida earlier had called (paraphrasing Levinas) a thought of "the One and the Same"—in other words, a metaphysics that is "the origin . . . of all oppression in the world" (Derrida 1967: 83).[9] God's gesture, therefore, becomes "multicultural" in the most ironic sense of the term—the bewildering of the Shemites foils their imperialist intentions, confounding their architects and scattering their armies, and disempowering them physically as well as semantically. Confusion, here, means the loss of all the reasons why one would want to control and subdue somebody, the difficulty in forcing someone to conform to one *logos* when a multiplicity of them abound. If rational metaphysics is "the origin . . . of all oppression," and if confusion is precisely that which disables the will to metaphysicize, then it is not surprising to see how Derrida can discover pacific

---

[8] "Allons, bâtissons une ville et une tour. . . . Faisons—nous un nom / que nous ne soyions dispersés sur la face de toute la terre."

[9] "Origine . . . de toute oppression dans le monde."

overtones in the idea of bewilderment. Confusion, far from being that which foils justice or creates a breeding ground for injustice, actually becomes a disabler of tyranny, a dismantler of the violent totality, a paralyzing wrench thrown into the dictator's machine.

Derrida, in typical fashion, questions this idea as soon as he expresses it. The Babelian project "can signify simultaneously a colonial violence . . . and a peaceful transparency of the community" (Kamuf: 253). The divine abolition of a single tongue may well foil the aims of a "linguistic imperialism," but it also removes a form of communication. A difficult question briefly makes its appearance: Is Genesis 11:1–9 about the thwarting of an empire or the destruction of a community? Is the removal of one bigger, "colonial violence" only the beginning of a number of smaller, interethnic ones? It is a surprisingly generous phrase, given Derrida's antipathy toward words like *community* (in which he sees "as many threats as promises" [Coward and Foshay: 292]), not to mention the famous crossing of swords with Habermas and his communicative reason. The common idiom, however colonially imposed, would at least reduce the possibility of misunderstanding within the community—expressions, actions, gestures, would all be relatively "transparent." The language game of the Shemites would be colonially singular, and its rules transparently (albeit incontestably) clear. Even though Derrida seems to be saying, in "Des Tours," that God's deconstruction of the tower is an example of what Derrida has elsewhere termed "just deconstruction" (Midgley: 34), the possible "peaceful transparency" of the Shemites' community does inject a note of ambivalence into the essay.

If the Derrida of "Des Tours" appears to be reluctant to come out and declare confusion to be a truly pacific state—that is, declaring bewilderment to be the only way of nonviolently receiving the Other—we should not be surprised. As we already have seen in *Of Grammatology*, when using words like *violence* and *colonial* Derrida often is careful not to replicate Lévi-Strauss's error and fall into the trap of a tyrant/victim, wicked/innocent dualism. Even though Derrida believes no order or community to be free of a certain violence, this does not mean anarchy is some form of blissful utopia. The most we can say about Derrida's attitude toward confusion is that, when we are confused or bewildered, we are less likely to impose a single, reductive image onto the Other—just as Ibn 'Arabi's perfect gnostic, when in a state of complete *hayrah* or perplexity, is no longer willing or able to fix any image onto the Real.

Third, Derrida's words on Babel underline one consistent feature of his varied and diverse corpus: a delight in multiplicity at the expense of unity. For Derrida the divergent is infinitely preferable to the convergent, the fragments are more interesting than the whole, the Many is preferable to the One. Bewilderment is to be encouraged, not resisted. The allegations of anarchy that have been leveled at Derrida, although exaggerated in tone and mistaken in motive, are correct to some degree: they concern a thinker who is as interested in dissolution as he is in design. The "dissemination" of the Shemites ("YHWH disperses them from here over the face of all the earth / They cease to build the city" [Kamuf: 248; see also Derrida 1972: 206–207]),[10] a working metaphor for the deconstruction of every would-be system, is the very kind of confusion Derrida seeks to affirm. This profoundly anti-Neoplatonic strain in Derrida's writing, rather than seeking an impossible return to the One, affirms the dissolution of the One into the Many—if only because there never was a "pure," "unchanging" One to begin with:

> The quasi-"meaning" of dissemination is the impossible return to the rejoined, readjusted unity of meaning. . . . But is dissemination then the *loss* of that kind of truth, the *negative* prohibition of all access to such a signified? Far from presupposing that a virgin substance [*une substance vierge*] thus precedes or oversees it, dispersing or withholding itself within a negative second moment, dissemination *affirms* the always already divided generation of meaning [*la dissémination affirme la génération toujours déjà divisée du sens*]. (Derrida 1972: 300)

This denial of any original "oneness" or "wholeness" ("virgin substance") that might have preceded the multiple probably constitutes the most serious difference between Ibn 'Arabi and Derrida, whose attitudes toward rationality and bewilderment otherwise encounter so many points of similarity. It is a passage that reveals Derrida to be the most un-Neoplatonic of thinkers, surprising when one considers some of the favorites in the Derridean canon (e.g., Benjamin and Blanchot). Instead of the One, an emptiness lies at the heart of dissemination, a place where "there is no longer any depth of meaning" (Derrida 1972: 350). The "actual situation" for Derrida is an endlessly proliferating myriad of substitutions, without beginning or end, center or periphery, in the midst of which the unenlightened forever attempt to build their theories, structures, and truths unaware that their metaphysical towers rest upon interminably shifting sands.

IBN 'ARABI ON THE FLOOD

> Were He to come out of a thing, it would cease to be. And were He to be within a thing, it would cease to be.
>
> —*Futuhat*, II.661.10

---

10 "YHWH les disperse de lá sur la face de toute la terre. / Il cesset de bâtir la ville."

Near the beginning of his book on Ibn 'Arabi, William Chittick writes: "To find God is to fall into bewilderment" (1989: 3). No sentence sums up more accurately the Sufi's attitude toward confusion. Throughout both the *Futuhat* and the *Fusus*, Ibn 'Arabi uses a variety of metaphors for bewilderment: it is, we are told, a station, a gift, a divine name, a tool, a knowledge and ultimately, one suspects, an "actual situation" that underlies everything we think we know. "To realise that one cannot know [God] is to know" says Abu Bakr (Afifi: 62; Austin 1980: 65),[11] a Socratic disclaimer Ibn 'Arabi never tires of quoting, and in a sense Ibn 'Arabi's radically positive view of bewilderment stems directly from this equally radical unthinkability of God.

Therefore, when Ibn 'Arabi quotes the hadith "O Lord, increase my perplexity concerning You" (as he frequently does),[12] what he really is asking is, "O Lord, confuse and confound the simplistic limitations I have attempted to cage You within." Bewilderment becomes the best way the believer has of escaping the metaphysical trap of his own perspectiveness— not, in this case, by the proffering of some extralinguistic knowledge (a secret name or sign) but, rather, by presenting and confusing the believer with a multiplicity of different Gods, some orthodox, some heretical, some intimately immanent, others aloof and transcendental. In the alarming, disconcerting contiguity of this myriad of different images, one can truly begin to understand how "the actual situation of the Divinity does not become delimited or restricted and remains unknown" (Chittick 1989: 348; Yahia: II.211.29). For Ibn 'Arabi, a profusion of different beliefs is testimony to God's utter unthinkability.

This idea of understanding what God is through a confusion of contrasting images has a fairly long genealogy, one that goes back at least to the first negative theologians of the early Church; it shows the apophatic possibilities of Ibn 'Arabi as a negative theologian, one who becomes increasingly relevant to Derrida's own critique of the *via negativa*.

Perhaps the sixth-century Dionysius offers the most famous example in negative theology of how different constructions concerning God, once dismantled, actually can convey a better sense of God's ineffability. In certain moments of *The Mystical Theology* and *The Celestial Hierarchy*, he makes the remarkable assertion that to call God drunk or hungover is more suitable than calling God good or wise, for "incongruous dissimilarities"

---

[11] "Al-'ajz 'an dark al-idrak idrak."

[12] Afifi: 73; Austin 1980: 79: "Zidnī fiyaka tahīraan." Interestingly, an untraceable saying by all accounts—one almost suspects it came from Ibn 'Arabi himself. One also cannot help thinking here of Eckhart's "I pray God to rid me of God" [Her umbe sô bite ich got, daz er mich ledic mache gotes].

make us more aware of God's unreachable otherness than equally finite adjectives, such as *almighty* and *all-knowing* (Pseudo-Dionysius: 58). For the Areopagite, to call God at the same time "Almighty" and a "worm," "wise" and "drunk," is more accurately to address what one critic has called the "language-defeating reality of God" (Turner: 278). Dionysius self-consciously employs contradictory constructions of the divine Other to convey a more realistic sense of God's utter unthinkability. Constructing and disassembling the various inventions of God that affirmative theology supplies presents an interesting apophatic strategy. Dionysius offers an attempt to understand the imageless not through the abandonment of images but, rather, through the contiguity of conflicting ones.

Although Ibn 'Arabi goes to some lengths to show how "knowledge of God is bewilderment, and knowledge of creation is bewilderment" (Chittick 1989: 380; Yahia: IV.279.26), there certainly are moments in both the *Futuhat* and the *Fusus* where this idea of perplexity as a mystical end station on the believer's journey is called into question. "Bewilderment," far from being an essential state of things, occasionally is portrayed by the Shaykh in a different light—more as a temporary and inconvenient prelude to enlightenment (*'arif*) rather than any kind of knowledge in itself. In the middle of a discussion on the "transcendent reality," that is, at the same time, "the relative creature" (Austin 1980: 87), Ibn 'Arabi writes how "he who truly understands what we are discussing here is not confused"— which means that he who is confused has not truly understood. Thus comprehension, *not* confusion, is the last thing to be experienced before an encounter with the divine. This belief that the desire for knowledge of God ends, epistemologically, in a moment of calm rather than turbulence is underlined further by the ending to the chapter on Lot:

> The Mystery is now clear to you
>   And the matter is well explained.
> For that which is odd
>   Is enshrined within the even. (Afifi: 131; Austin 1980: 162)[13]

The dilemma emerges: Which vocabulary has the last word in Ibn 'Arabi, one that sees God as a holy, primordial, difference-dissolving state of confusion? Or one that leads the believer not to but through a confusion, toward an ineffable Something—the "mystery" (*sirr*) that Ibn 'Arabi so often refers to? Is God Perplexity itself or, rather, a Something that lies on the other side of all our bewilderment?

If the *Fusus* appears to give two different responses to this question— the chapters on Noah and Muhammad suggesting the former, the sections

---

[13] "Faqad nān laka al-sir waqad atthaha al-amr / waqad adraj fiyahī shara'a al-zā fiya huwa al-watr."

on Enoch and Hud the latter—some help comes from a later commentator of Ibn 'Arabi, the fifteenth-century 'Abd al-Rahman Jâmî.[14] Essentially, Jâmî discerns three kinds of bewilderment in the closing chapter of the *Fusus*. The first kind is the "bewilderment of the beginners" (Chittick 1982: 91). This, Jâmî says, is a "common" bewilderment, which most believers feel—the anxiety of those who seek meaning but have no belief or direction in which to travel. This first state of confusion usually is removed by "the determination of a quest" (91). For the "most part" of the people, this leads to tranquility—some, however, experience the second stage of bewilderment as they look around and see the believers who have "split up into numerous factions" about them, "so [the believer] becomes bewildered and does not know which of the beliefs is the most correct in reality." The removal of this bewilderment takes place when "no desire remains in [the believer] for the divine presence from a particular aspect or point of view" (92). Once this abandonment of -isms and perspectives takes place, we move onto the third stage—which belongs to what Jâmî calls "the people of the final bewilderment" (93). Significantly, this is a station that even "the greatest spiritual luminaries" do not exceed—"rather they ascend in it for ever and ever." Writing almost 200 years after the *Fusus*, Jâmî sees his predecessor's bewilderment as no temporary bridge to a final, clarifying solution but, rather, a strange land beyond God where true gnostics wander in all directions of their own accord. "So they enter the Trackless Desert in His contemplation, and their bewilderment is from Him, through Him and in Him" (93).

'Abd al-Rahman Jâmî's comments bring to light three important aspects of the Shaykh's "bewilderment"—aspects that, we shall see, will reflect on our comparison with Derrida. First of all, there are different kinds of confusion, different types of bewilderment to be encountered by the believer. In some cases, attempting to overcome confusion is seen to be spiritually necessary; in others, it is futile and foolish. Second, Jâmî rightly (and uncritically) discerns in Ibn 'Arabi a certain elitism—confusion is not for everyone. Apart from those rare spirits who are able to persist in perpetual bewilderment, the greater part of the faithful (Jâmî calls them the "people of the stopping places" [*ahl al-mawaqif*] [Chuttick 1982: 92]) stop short of the "final bewilderment" and take shelter in a niche of clarity. One almost discerns a hierarchy of perplexity here, made possible not

---

[14] Sometime after writing the *Fusus al-Hikam*, Ibn 'Arabi produced a second work that essentially summarizes and expounds on the main themes of the *Fusus*. Because of the importance of the *Fusus*, this secondary work (called the *Naqsh al-Fusus*—the *Pattern of the Fusus*) also received some attention in the commentary tradition—including, among others, Jâmî's own *Naqd al-nusûs fi sharh naqsh al-fusûs* (*Selected Texts in Commenting on the Naqsh al-fusus*), written in 1459. The translation is by William G. Chittick.

by knowledge but, rather, by nonknowledge. Those at the bottom are the ones with the clearest ideas, whereas those near the top are the most confused, the ones who have come closest to the secret of God's mind-numbing unthinkability. Third, the "final bewilderment," which Jâmî refers to makes us wonder if, in Ibn 'Arabi's oeuvre, the true goal is not so much confusion but a certain attitude toward confusion; whether true *hayrah* is not so much a state but, rather, the calm acceptance of a situation, perhaps even the *celebration* of such a moment. Of course, how close such a "celebration" would come toward the "Nietzschean . . . joyous affirmation of the play of the world" ("l'affirmation nietzschéenne . . . joyeuse du jeu du monde" [Derrida 1967: 427]), which we read in those famous closing passages of Derrida's "Structure, Sign and Play," remains to be seen.

Ibn 'Arabi's treatment of the seventy-first surah of the Koran on Noah (*Nuh*) is a good example of how the Shaykh bewilders the reader, by offering interpretations of well-known passages from the Koran that are almost the exact opposite of what they appear to mean. The hermeneutics of the *Fusus* are a lesson in perplexity in themselves: villains and tyrants are treated sympathetically, heroes are shown to be ignorant or misguided, condemnatory verses are reinterpreted as praise, idolaters are shown to be enlightened. As we shall see in a later chapter, Ibn 'Arabi's conviction that "the Reality of God lies in all things" is translated perfectly into his Koranic commentary; the intention of God's Holy Text lies in all possible readings, even in the most contradictory and outrageous ones. For now, we merely are interested in what Ibn 'Arabi's chapter on Noah in the *Fusus* says about bewilderment—and, ultimately, how this compares to Derrida's own thoughts on confusion.

In a way, Ibn 'Arabi's retelling of the story of Noah follows Derrida's version of Babel, insofar as both writers deal with a divinely delivered catastrophe—and both writers choose to redescribe this punishment as more of a blessing than a chastisement, more of a development or an advancement than a termination. The Koranic account of the flood does not differ greatly from that of the biblical version with regards to the ultimate significance of the event—in response to the rising corruption and sinfulness of man, God resolves to wipe out the unbelievers with a divine deluge, saving only Noah and those around him from the waters because of their righteousness. The Koran differs only insofar as it shows, in some detail, the despair of Noah as he attempts (in vain) to persuade his people to leave their idols and repent, and his request to God that none of the proud unbelievers should be spared.

In order to understand the Shaykh's radical rereading of this surah, one has to remember his persistent emphasis on God as being *simulta-*

neously immanent and transcendent. In his attempt to reach the unbelievers Noah, far from being praised as a solitary bastion of righteousness in a decadent world, is criticized only for emphasizing the transcendent without mentioning the immanent: "Had Noah uttered this kind of saying, they would have responded to him" (Afifi: 70; Austin 1980: 76).[15] Even more notoriously, Ibn 'Arabi interprets the final drowning of the unbelievers not as just punishment on the sinful but as the drowning of saints in the shoreless oceans of Allah: "they drowned in the seas of knowledge of God, which is what is meant by perplexity" (Afifi: 73; Austin 1980: 79).[16] The stubborn idolaters, with their bewildering abundance of idols (*Wadd, Suwan, Yaghuth, Ya'uq, Nasr* 71:23), suddenly became the purveyors of a spiritual *hayrah*—one that eludes Noah, a figure still clinging to a one-sided view of a transcendent God.

Ibn 'Arabi's version of Noah is important because it tells us a number of things about the Shaykh's attitude toward bewilderment; first and foremost, multiplicity is seen not as a problem but as a means toward the solution. The perplexity necessary toward spiritual advancement can be provided only by multiplicity—in this case, the multiplicity of idols that "cause confusion" among Noah's people. Only confusion can bring us nearer to God. One object of worship is not sufficient—it deludes the ignorant with an illusion of clarity, desists from complicating the thought of God, makes the believer think the holy is exclusive to the statue or painting she or he is worshiping. As soon as a multiplicity of idols appears, the locus of the holy—and thereby the nature of the Holy itself—is called into question. Distraction here becomes an antimetaphysical tool, one used to lever and prize the intellect out of a certain niche and into a freer understanding of things. The perplexity the believer experiences at this multiplication of possibilities provokes a sincerer inquiry into the nature of God, one that will lead (the Shaykh believes) to the all-important realization that *al-haqq* is present everywhere and in everything.

Here, especially, one sees how important a role infinity plays at the heart of both Derrida's and Ibn 'Arabi's thought. The forms of the Real, like the possible meanings of the deconstructive text, are infinite in number: There is no end to the "bottomless chessboard" (*échiquier sans fond*) on which *différance* is put into play (Derrida 1982: 22), any more than there is any bottom to the infinite oceans of God ("God possesses relationships, faces and realities without limit" [Chittick 1989: 156; Yahia: II.671.5]). The confusion that the infinity of the Real/the Derridean text provides is seen by both Derrida and Ibn 'Arabi to be perfectly desirable,

---

[15] "Falau anā nuh yatī bimithal haza al-aya lafzan ajābu."

[16] "Faghariqu fī bihari al-'alam bi Allah wa huwa al-hayrah."

even if they do lead in radically different directions. For Derrida, the be-wilderingly infinite possibilities of the text lead to one conclusion: that the text is semantically vacuous, a sheet of symbols bereft of depth. Ibn 'Arabi, however, viewing the perplexing variety of people's beliefs, does not come to the conclusion that there is no God but, rather, that there is "Something that cannot be known" that both embodies and is embodied by all of these infinite manifestations.

A second point to be made is that Noah's evangelical failure to save the unbelievers from the flood stems from his refusal to present God as a divine perplexity: "Noah summoned his people *by night*, in that he ap-pealed to their intellects and spirits, which are unseen, and *by day*, in that he appealed to the external senses. But he did not unite the two as in the verse *There is none like Him* (42:11)" (Afifi: 70–71; Austin 1980: 76).[17] Noah literally refuses to con-fuse the idea of God by presenting Him as a simultaneous conjunction of opposites (immanent and transcendent). This monologic attachment to a simplistic understanding of God, essen-tially this distaste for confusion on Noah's part, causes the unbelievers to "recoil" and prevents them from climbing onto the boat. It is an unflat-tering portrayal of Noah for Ibn 'Arabi to present—one that seems to class Noah with the proponents of the Kalam and the other philosophers who fetter (*'iqal*) themselves to a single image of God. Perhaps to recover some shred of orthodoxy, Ibn 'Arabi contrasts this implicit ignorance of Noah with the keener wisdom of the Prophet Muhammad, who (in the Shaykh's opinion) clearly understood something about God that Noah did not:

> In the verse *There is none like Him*, similarity is at once implied and denied. Because of this Muhammad said that he had been granted knowledge [of God] integrating all His aspects. Muhammad [unlike Noah] did not sum-mon his people *by night* and *by day*, but by night during the day [an inner summons implicit in the outer one], and by day during the night [the outer truth being implicit in the inner]. (Afifi: 71; Austin 1980: 76–77)[18]

Unlike Noah, the Prophet is keenly aware of the "actual situation"—he emphasizes neither the *zahir* nor the *batin* (esoteric meaning) at the ex-pense of one another but, rather, blurs the distinction between both. Unlike Noah, the Prophet is not afraid of the con-fusion of God; this natural distance between Noah and Muhammad is not measured in terms

---

[17] "Nuh da'a qawmahu 'laylan' min haythu 'uqluhum wa ruha niyatahum fainnahā ghayb. 'wan-hāran' da'ahum aythan min haythu zahir surāhum wa hissehum wa ma jam'a fi al-da'uwati mithal 'lays kamithliha shay.'"

[18] Austin's notes are in brackets. "Fafi 'lays kamithliha shay' ithbat al-mithal wa nafīhi, wa bihaza qal 'an nefsihi sal Allah alayhi wa selam inahi ūtiya jawa lam'a al-kelim. Fima da'a Muhammad sala allahi alayhi wa selam qawmahu laylan wa nahaza, bil da'ahum laylan fī nahār fi layli."

of respect or divine favor but, rather, in terms of how close each comes to accepting perplexity as a condition of the divine.

One of the more interesting metaphors Ibn 'Arabi uses for such perplexity is that of a deluge, evoking the familiar image of God as a shoreless ocean. It is a metaphor that provides the most scandalous suggestion in Ibn 'Arabi's rereading of the surah; the unbelievers' refusal to join Noah and climb on the boat is no tragic mistake but, rather, a spiritually wiser move, one that saves them from the narrow ontotheology of Noah's ark and allows them to drown ecstatically in the wider seas of "the knowledge of God" (Austin 1980: 79). By refusing to join Noah and heed the call to his transcendent God, they reject an unenlightened clarity in favor of their own perplexing truth—and pay for this choice, as Al Hallaj did, with their lives. Nevertheless, the spiritual stage the unbelievers reach as a result of their refusal is far higher than that of Noah. Once swept away by the flood, if they were ever to find land again (as Noah does), it would constitute no rescue but a spiritual descent: "Were He to deliver them onto the shore of Nature He would be lowering them from an eminent stage" (Afifi: 73; Austin 1980: 80).[19] For true gnostics, evidently, oceans are preferable to arks.

In the *Futuhat* Ibn 'Arabi performs the same controversial gesture, taking familiar condemnations of the foolish and the proud in the Koran and completely inverting their meaning so that they describe those few, distinct from "the common people" (Chittick 1989: 380), who have discovered true perplexity. For example, the wayward described by the Koran in verses 2:17, those "who do not see. Deaf, dumb, and blind, they will never return to the right path," are interpreted differently by the Shaykh in the last volume of the *Futuhat*: "But the *elect* are 'in darkness, they do not see. Deaf, dumb, blind.' (2:17), they do not understand. Sometimes they say 'We are we and He is He,' sometimes they say 'He is we and we are He'" (Chittick 1989: 380, emphasis added). Darkness, incomprehension, and aimlessness are the gifts of the perplexed—"they will never return to the right path." Bewilderment, amongst other things, means loss of direction. Suddenly, "never returning to the right path" seems to be indicative of enlightenment, not ignorance. Ibn 'Arabi infuses the idea of wandering with a positive sense that would be difficult to reconcile with orthodox Islam, given the importance of the path (*al-sirat al-mustaqim*) and its synonymity with the codes and traditions of the Shariah. In his chapter on Noah, Ibn 'Arabi analyzes this difference between the unperplexed—who proceed along a given path toward a goal—and the bewildered, for whom there is no longer any center to journey toward:

---

[19] "Fala akhrajahum ila al-sayf, sayf al-tabiyat lanazil biham an haza al-darjat al-rafi'at."

He who experiences this perplexity is ceaselessly centered on the Pole [God], while he who follows the "long" path [to a distant God] is always turning aside from the [Supreme] Goal to search after that which is [eternally] within him, running after imagination as his goal. He has an [imaginary] starting point and [what he supposes to be] a goal and what lies between them, while for the God-centered man there is no restriction of beginning or end, possessing [as he does] the most comprehensive existence and being the recipient of [divine] truths and realities. (Afifi: 73; Austin 1980: 79)[20]

Ibn 'Arabi's perplexity here is opposed to movement—confusion becomes a paralyzing condition, it robs the believer of a goal, an object, an aim. As soon as one discovers that God is (immanently) in oneself, as well as (transcendentally) Somewhere outside, one no longer needs to make a pilgrimage, for the shrine is already inside the pilgrim. Hence, the paralysis that confusion brings to the "God-centered" (perplexed) man is by no means negative, but simply the rendering unnecessary of an illusory journey to something one already is.

The final point to be made about Ibn 'Arabi's remarks on Noah concerns the social implications of *hayrah* and its subversive potential. The chapter on Noah offers one of the few places in the *Fusus* where the faintly political possibilities of perplexity—discovering the Real within oneself— are alluded to, if not fully explored. Modern critics with political agendas often can be found reinterpreting various medieval mysticisms as revolutionary vocabularies, particularly those that emphasize the divine within the human. The clearest example of this is probably Ernst Bloch's Marxist reading of Meister Eckhart in his *Atheismus im Christentum*. In Ernst Bloch, Eckhart's insistence on the unity of God and the soul becomes a subversive, emancipatory gesture that ultimately sees "the treasure in Heaven [as] the property of man" [die Schätze im Himmel als Eigentum der Mensch] (Bloch: 95). Thus, for Bloch, Eckhart supplies not just an "aspiring subject" but also a "blown-open, descending heavenly kingdom" [gesprengter, niedersteigender Himmel] (287).

All of which does not mean to say a similarly emancipatory reading of Ibn 'Arabi should be attempted—the only chains the Shaykh is keen to break are purely metaphysical. What deserves comment in Ibn 'Arabi's Noah is the way the presence of the perplexed dissolves a certain social

---

[20] Austin's notes are in brackets. "Falhare lahu al-dar wa al-harakat al-duriyat hal al-qutb falla yabrah minhu, wa salhab al-tariq al-mustatil maal ḵharaja 'an al-maqsud talaba ma huwa fihi salahab ḵhayal ilahi ghayat: fallahu min wa illa wa ma bin huma. Wa sahab al-harakat al-duriyat al-abd ulahu fiyalzamhu 'man' wa la ghayat fathakam alayhi 'ila' Falaha al-wujud al-atam wa huwa al-mutā juwa ma'a al-kelam wa al-hukum."

hierarchy—and the way Noah's words (below in italics) present the confusion of the unbelievers as a possible threat to society, one that might
spread if not checked in time:

> If you spare them, that is leave them, they will confuse your servants, mean-
> ing that they will perplex them and cause them to depart from their
> servanthood to [assert] the mysteries of Lordship in themselves, so that
> they will consider themselves as Lords after being servants. They will in-
> deed be servants become as Lords. (Afifi: 74; Austin 1980: 80)[21]

If God is the dissolver of differences ("He has no attributes [sifa]" [Chittick
1989: 73]), then everyone carries within them this capacity to dismantle
hierarchy, regardless of their social position. Noah's fear lies in this perceived
threat of self-discovery; perplexity lifts the servant out of his servanthood,
causes everything to shimmer and change, relocating the Divinity not just
in the hearts of caliphs and kings but even down to the lowest rung of the
social ladder. It is a passage that reminds us of Bloch's observation—in
Ibn 'Arabi, true enlightenment turns servants into lords.

Both Derrida's and Ibn 'Arabi's attitudes toward perplexity—their
repeated mistrust of systems and system builders, their consistent portrayal of clarity as an illusion based on the ignorance of a certain situation, their understanding of a certain dynamic force that pervades all
manifestations/texts without ever revealing itself, along with their belief
that the state of perplexity allows one to glimpse an elusive Other that
remains invisible to those who are trying to think it—all these observations lead us to a number of general points.

Perplexity Is an "Actual Situation"

For both thinkers, confusion is a certain originary state of affairs that
seems to precede God/the text and every attempt to talk about them. For
Ibn 'Arabi, the true gnostic sees through (without dismissing) the theolo-
gizing and philosophizing of his peers; he understands that "the whole af-
fair [of God] is perplexity" (Austin 1980: 254), a divine flux that lies beneath
every image and concept proffered about the Real. The deconstructive critic
replicates this antedating of meaning with confusion by seeing through the
apparent calm of the text and perceiving an "'active, moving discord of
different forces' beneath it" (Derrida 1982: 18),[22] always already about to
subvert and undermine any and every interpretation.

---

[21] "'Inaka tajarhum' ay tad'ahum wa tatarkum 'yadhulu 'abādak' ay yahiruham fi ya kharajuhum
min al-'abudiyat ila ma fihum min asrār al-rabubiyat fiyanzarun anfasahum arbāba."

[22] "Cette discorde 'active,' en mouvement, des forces différentes."

Perplexity Is an Inevitable Situation

The confusion that both *différance* and *al-haqq* perpetrate cannot be overcome; no theological vocabulary can tie the Real to one form, safe and constant, just as no hermeneutics can prevent the "essential drifting of the text" (Derrida 1982: 317). The Real moves through a bewildering variety of manifestations, from *zahir* to *zahir*, just as the text moves through an equally bewildering series of differing interpretations. For both Derrida and Ibn 'Arabi, the perplexing effusion of meanings and manifestations can be neither controlled nor resisted; bewilderment is a semantic fact of God.

Perplexity Is an Honest, Difficult Situation

The word for *khâfir* (infidel, unbeliever) comes from the Arabic root *khafara*, meaning to hide or conceal. Etymologically, a *khâfir* is someone who hides the truth in his or her heart (Austin 1984: 7). For Ibn 'Arabi, this would mean refusing to acknowledge the perplexity of the "actual situation"—that the Real both is and is not the creation, that He is simultaneously immanent and transcendent. The secret of the Akhbarian soul—that it is a part of the Real—is concealed (*khafara*) thanks to the half-truth of transcendence (*tanzih*). "We forbid reflection totally," writes Ibn 'Arabi, "since it makes the possessor heir to deceit and lack of sincerity" (Chittick 1989: 203; Yahia: II.523.2). "Covering" or "concealing" the radical unthinkability of God with our own versions of the deity makes our spiritual lives easier for us; if we desire a true encounter with the Real, we have to be prepared to experience perplexity and not simply seek reassurance in comfortable, familiar images.

Speaking in an interview (within a strictly Christian context) of a "deconstructive theology movement," Derrida has suggested some similar theological applications of deconstruction—more than anything else, of "uncovering" a spiritual authenticity:

> The point would seem to be to *liberate* theology from what has been grafted onto it, to free it from its metaphysico-philosophical super ego, so as to *uncover* an authenticity of the "gospel," of the evangelical message. And thus from the perspective of faith, deconstruction can at least be a very useful technique when Aristotelianism or Thomism are to be criticized or, even from an institutional perspective, when what needs to be criticized is a whole theological institution which supposedly has *covered over*, dissimulated an authentic Christian message. And [the point would also seem to be] a real possibility for faith both at the margins and very close to Scripture, a faith lived in a venturous, dangerous, free way. (Blond: 262, emphasis added)

Despite the difference in contexts, Derrida is saying in effect something remarkably similar to Ibn 'Arabi: The "metaphysico-philosophical" constructions with which various institutions (the Asharites, the Mutazilites) have tried to simplify and regulate the nature of God over the centuries have been based on a "covering over" of the true Divinity. Ibn 'Arabi's *hayrah*, in many ways, provides the Islamic precedent for a "faith lived in a venturous, dangerous, free way." A faith free of metaphysics, free of veils, images and idols.

Perplexity Is a Desirable Situation

For both deconstructive and Sufi alterities, the basic point remains the same: When we are confused, we see things that we miss when we think we know what we are doing. We see the difference of difference.

Heidegger often makes a similar point. When something goes wrong—a broken tool, an unexpected accident, an unfaithful partner—and our projects break down, we truly see for a moment how our world is structured and contextualized around us to give it meaning. In this moment of "breakdown" we glimpse, says Heidegger, the "worldhood of the world" [die Weltlichkeit der Welt]. The perplexing multiplicity of manifestations enables the stunned believer to glimpse the "Godness" of God, just as the continually irrupting images of the Other enables Derrida to glimpse the otherness of the *tout autre*. Thus, a common opposition to rational/metaphysical thought in both Sufism and deconstruction also finds a common response: If metaphysics blinds/veils us from the actual situation—and if confusion is that which disables our rationalizing will to a system—then we will only truly begin to "see" when we learn to desire confusion, not to flee it.

REFERENCES

Afifi, A. E.   *Fusus al-Hikam*. Beirut: Dar al-kutub al-'Arabi.
1946

Austin, Ralph   *The Bezels of Wisdom*. Mahwah, NJ: Paulist Press.
1980

1984   "Meditations upon the Vocabulary of Love and Union
                in Ibn 'Arabi's Thought." *Journal of the Muhyiddin Ibn
                'Arabi Society* 3.

Bloch, Ernst   *Atheismus im Christentum* (found in *Gesamtausgabe*).
1968   Frankfurt am Main: Suhrkamp.

Blond, Philip   *Post-secular Philosophy*. London: Routledge.
1998

Chittick, William G.
1982   "The Imprint of the Bezels of Wisdom." *Journal of the Muhyiddin Ibn'Arabi Society* 1.

1989   *The Sufi Path of Knowledge*. Albany: State University of New York Press.

Coward, Harold,   *Derrida and Negative Theology*. Albany: State Univer-
and T. Foshay   sity of New York Press.
1992

Derrida, Jacques   *L'Écriture et la Différence* [Writing and Difference]. Trans.
1967   by Alan Bass. London: Routledge and Kegan.

1972   *La Dissémination* [Dissemination]. Trans. by Barbara Johnson. London: Athlone Press.

1982   *Margins of Philosophy*. Trans. by Alan Bass. Brighton: Harvester Press.

1987a   *Positions*. Trans. by Alan Bass. London: Athlone Press.

1987b   *Psyché: Inventions de l'autre*. Paris: Editions Galilée.

Guignon, Charles   *A Cambridge Companion to Heidegger*. Cambridge: Cam-
1983   bridge University Press.

Hirtenstein, S.,   *Muhyiddin Ibn 'Arabi: A Commemorative Volume*. Dorset:
and Michael Tiernan   Element.
1993

Kamuf, Peggy   *A Derrida Reader: Between the Blinds*. Exeter: Wheatsheaf.
1991

Kenny, Anthony   *A Wittgenstein Reader*. London: Blackwell.
1994

Midgley, Nick   "Responsibilities of Deconstruction." *University of War-
1997   wick Journal of Philosophy*.

Nasr, S. H.,   *History of Islamic Philosophy*. London: Routledge.
and Oliver Leaman
1996

Netton, Richard   *Allah Transcendent: Studies in the Structure and Semiotics
1989   of Islamic Philosophy, Theology and Cosmology*. London: Routledge.

Nietzsche, F.   *Twilight of the Idols*. Trans. by R. J. Hollingdale. Lon-
1990   don: Penguin.

Pseudo-Dionysius   *The Complete Works.* Trans. by Colm Luibheid. Lon-
1987   don: SPCK.

Turner, D.   *The Darkness of God.* London: Cambridge University
1993   Press.

Yahia, Osman   *Futuhat al-Makkiyya.* Cairo: Al-Hay'at al-Misriyyat
1972   al-'Amma li'l-kitab.

The Liberation of Questioning in Augustine's *Confessions*

Charles T. Mathewes

Concluding his *Confessions*, Augustine chose as the work's final word *aperietur*, "will be" or "shall be opened." The oddity of ending and closing a book on a conjugation of *to open* provokes reflections into the nature of questioning, reflections that open into a larger investigation concerning how Augustine understood the nature of religious belief and faithful life. For him, faithful life is a project of resisting our always premature attempts at conclusion, in order better to see the project of "inquiry into God" as an infinite undertaking, in community with others, organized centrally around reading and inhabiting the thought world of the Scriptures. The *Confessions* turns out to be a story of Augustine learning to ask questions in the right way and to accept the dynamic of questioning as an energy moving him toward God. Appreciating the *Confessions* as a story of "learning to ask questions" illuminates not only the work's content but also its structure, most notably the odd change of tone and topic from books 1–9 to books 10–13.

CONCLUDING HIS *CONFESSIONS*, Augustine left a puzzle that seems to have tripped up at least some of his posthumous copyists. For the work's final word he chose *aperietur*, "will be" or "shall be opened." The oddity

Charles T. Mathewes is an assistant professor of religious studies at the University of Virginia, Charlottesville, VA 22904–4126

This article was initially delivered at a conference entitled "Augustine and the Disciplines" at Villanova University in November 2000, and thanks are due both to Mark Vessey who invited me to give it and to the audience who heard and discussed it. A long time ago Paul J. Griffiths taught a class on "belief" that first instigated my reflections on these matters. Thanks are also due to a number of others, especially Lewis Ayres, Michel René Barnes, Peter Brown, Jennifer L. Geddes, Michael Hanby, Derek Jeffreys, Jennifer McBride, Neil McLynn, Peter Ochs, Karla Pollmann, William Schweiker, Jim Wetzel, and Robert Wilken. The research and writing of this article were aided by a grant from the Louisville Institute, and it was largely composed during a fellowship at the Center for the Study of Religion at Princeton University; I thank James Lewis and Robert Wuthnow for the support of their institutions. For its faults I have only myself to thank.

Journal of the American Academy of Religion September 2002, Vol. 70, No. 3, pp. 539–560.
© 2002 The American Academy of Religion

of ending and thus closing a book on a conjugation of *to open* seems to have been too difficult a *finis* for some scribes to bear. As James O'Donnell notes in his magisterial commentary on the *Confessions*, many manuscripts add on a more fitting "amen," firmly if calmly shutting the semantic door that Augustine seemed to leave open, creaking in the hermeneutical wind. O'Donnell casually works to salvage the reputation of his redactorial ancestors by suggesting that their amen might best be understood as the appropriate and admiring response of the reader to reaching the conclusion of the work. Yet I wonder whether O'Donnell's redaction of the redactors does not itself effectively replicate their error, by subtly foreclosing our potential disquiet at their subtle foreclosing of their own disquiet here, at the end of what is surely Augustine's most fully wrought work.

My mention of disquiet on the part of Augustine's readers goes against the grain of most work on the *Confessions*, which more often imputes disquiet and anxiety to Augustine the writer. Indeed, our unhappy age has exploited Augustine's vulnerability in ways that work fundamentally to foil his own intentions for his openness. For all the modern railing against Augustine's purported "self-hatred," especially as expressed in his concept of sin, we find the notion extremely convenient in helping us avoid our own perplexities—for, after all, perhaps the confusions we meet in our reading are because of Augustine's sins and not our own.[1] We mistake confession for abasement, assuming that the brokenness he details and bewails in the work is reflected in the work's formal structure. We do not see that a confession as profound as Augustine's is not an easy thing and cannot be done by just anyone as shattered and sinful as he represents himself as being. Barth was perhaps overstating it when he said that only Christians sin (then again, perhaps not), but perhaps the recognition of one's own sinfulness is, paradoxically, a real achievement, a mark of real grace. Hence we are always tempted to find an easy answer to our questions about Augustine's text in his self-represented flaws. In this as in so many other ways we fail Augustine (as James O'Donnell [1: xix] has rightly noted), and his text judges us as we presume to judge it.

Even Augustine's ablest exegetes are not always immune to the temptation to impute anxiety to him. O'Donnell himself, the undisputed master of the text of the *Confessions*, provides an example; he provocatively notes that part of the oddity of the book is that it does not seem finally to get anywhere: "*Confessio* and *inquisitio* end with questions still on the table, and the same assurances (Mt. 7:7) that marked the opening of the work.

---

[1] My use of *we* throughout this article is not meant to be presumptuously prescriptive (much less paranoically proscriptive) but, rather, simply invitational, suggesting that many readers may find that they share the prejudgments from which I begin. See Williams: 171n1.

What has changed since then?" (3: 420–421). The common answer to this question, and one he has already provided, is based on the presumption of Augustine's "anxiety":

> Anxiety so pervades the *Confessions* that even the implicit narrative structure is undermined. When on the first page we hear that the heart is restless until there is repose in God, the reasonable expectation is that the text will move from restlessness to rest, from anxiety to tranquillity. In some ways that is true: on baptism care flies away, and the last page looks forward to the tranquillity of endless praise in heaven. But the conversion story leaves the Augustine of this text far more uneasy than we might have expected. The proper culmination for an optimistic *Confessions* would be mystic vision as fruit of conversion. . . . But instead the last half of Bk. 10 and the whole of Bks. 11 to 13—not incidentally the parts of the work that have most baffled modern attempts to reduce the text to a coherent pattern—defy the expected movement from turmoil to serenity and show an Augustine still anxious over matters large and small. It is unclear at what date it became possible, or necessary, for Augustine to endure that continuing tension. At the time of the events narrated in the first nine books he surely expected more repose for his troubles. (O'Donnell, 1: xviii)

Because this passage so compactly and cannily expresses precisely the sort of inquiry-defeating, psychologistic explanation that I have been describing—as well as suggesting a vague dissatisfaction at this "explanation" *as* an explanation (i.e., "in some ways," "than we might have expected")—I use it as the central text to which this article responds. Furthermore, because the anxiety attributed to Augustine here (and also in so many other accounts) is commonly seen to reveal itself in the innumerable questions that riddle the *Confessions*, this article takes as its theme the real meaning and purpose of these questions. For if we do not see the interrogative voice of the *Confessions* as crucial to its purposes, we are in danger of missing something close to the heart of the work as a whole.

I

To explain my focus on "questioning" in the *Confessions* I begin obliquely, by suggesting an analogy with Ludwig Wittgenstein's *Philosophical Investigations* concerning the role of questions in that mysterious text. One commentator on the *Investigations* has noted that Wittgenstein asks 784 questions in it, and of those 784 questions he only answers about 110, and of those 110 answers no less than seventy are *meant* to be wrong (Kenny: 235). At least part of Wittgenstein's point in pressing so many questions is to offer his readers a new way of thinking about philosophical investigations, one that is more tentative, slightly off the grooves of received styles of thinking. I think he was seeking something of a philosophical *conversion* in his readers, although he likened it more to a therapeutic liberation from the stale logical scholasticism and linguistic literalism of his day.

But if there are that many questions in the *Philosophical Investigations*, how many are there in the *Confessions?* Recall, for a moment, the veritable avalanche of questions with which Augustine at times buries the bewildered reader. I think Augustine's intent here is somewhat similar to Wittgenstein's, although he offers undoubtedly a significantly different proposal. For, in a way not dissimilar to the *Philosophical Investigations,* the *Confessions* is, among many other things, concerned with the relation between our ability to inquire and the cause and end of that inquiry—how philosophy is converted into theology, how its origin and end are found in wonder and praise. The explicit asking of questions is only one among many species of seeking (including prayer), of which questioning is perhaps only the most directly intellectual and abstract example.[2] In brief, Augustine suggests that questioning, and "seeking" more generally, is not simply a prolegomenon to faith or praise but, in fact, a vital expression of it.

Hence it is no accident, nor any little thing, that Augustine ends his book with a beginning—both stylistically with *aperietur* and materially through the concluding discussion of the Sabbath day with no evening— or that that inconclusive conclusion comes at the end of a book riddled with questions. For Augustine means to teach us to see ourselves as best becoming the sorts of beings that our questions are trying also to become: creatures who are trying to reach a beginning but have not yet realized it. It is not that Augustine's ultimate aim in the *Confessions* is to make his readers questions to themselves (although book 10 makes it at least plausible that Augustine sees something like that as an inevitable moment, or at least one not to be renounced); rather, the energies we are trying to express in our many modes of questioning are, for Augustine, the energies that we most deeply are or could be. For Augustine, neither we as we find ourselves nor questions as we find ourselves asking them are rightly organized. (For one, they are often overly theoretical and abstract, disconnected from the issues of the heart that serve as their ultimate impetus.) But they are that from which (and by which) we begin the slow *conversio* back to God; and so we should come to understand ourselves as questioning beings in a way far more profound than we usually do.

---

[2] I am grateful to Peter Ochs and Robert Wilken for convincing me of the importance of underscoring the way that speaking of this wholly in the academic language of "questioning" and "inquiry" would fundamentally misrepresent this activity.

My argument, simply put, is this: In books 1–9 of the *Confessions* Augustine narrates, among other things, his struggles to learn to ask questions, and then (in books 10–13) he models that questioning first (in book 10) by showing the failure of such inquiry as an individual, intellectual, interior, and freestanding speculative project and then (in books 11–13) its replacement by the communal and properly speaking ecstatic activity of inquiry as scriptural exegesis. Furthermore, understanding the argument of the *Confessions* in this way helps us not only more adequately to grasp its content but also perhaps to dissolve some of the confusion about its structure. The puzzlement many people feel at the coherence of books 1–9 and 10–13—a puzzlement often precipitously relieved by speaking of the text as incoherent (as O'Donnell seems to suggest in the passage above), structurally "tense," or even by simply ignoring the last three or four books—is significantly lessened by understanding the structure as narrating the diachronic development, and then the (always only infantile) synchronic exercise, of the right sort of inquiring self.

Far from a text seeking "resolution," where that is conceived as an ending, Augustine aims to produce a text showing us what it means to begin: He wants us to picture life as a way of inquiry, conceived not as a narrowly intellectual project but as a whole way of seeking God, exercised not simply in contemplative interiority but in the ecstatic communion with others in the world, framed and formed by the reading of Scripture. In ignoring Augustine's many questions as "mere rhetoric," or by dismissing them (and perhaps him) as signs of a deep "anxiety," we miss something important. We miss the way that Augustine is telling a story about learning to ask questions—learning, beyond the explicit intellectual form of "the question," to inhabit the form of life from which our questions derive. We miss, that is, the openness of Augustinian questioning as pointing beyond itself to a whole mode of life that we are meant to inhabit. We mistake heaven for hell; fearful as we are of questions, we cannot see that the energy they most fundamentally express is a foretaste of the final communion with God—a communion that is anything but static.

It should be clear that although this article is primarily exegetical, concerned with understanding Augustine's enigmatic work, it is not exclusively so. The exegesis of the *Confessions* that follows opens up questions of a broader nature, about the nature of questions and inquiry in general. These questions in turn provoke further reflections about the nature of religious belief as an orientation toward the world, in particular about whether contemporary pictures of religious belief define it in terms too settled and static adequately to represent the dynamism (intellectual as well as affectional) of Augustine's faith.

II

We do not see the openness of Augustinian questioning, in part, because we stubbornly hold onto our presumptions about inquiry in the face of Augustine's narrative. Indeed, readers of the *Confessions* typically bring some version of one of three procrustean conceptual frameworks to the text and attempt to understand Augustine's presentation of the dynamic of questioning in terms of them. In order to exorcise these frameworks from our minds, the better to explore the role of questioning in the *Confessions*, I work through each of them, exposing their various inadequacies; by so clearing the ground I hope to help us begin to recognize something of the radicality of Augustine's vision. (By working through these modes we simultaneously work through three different understandings of questioning itself, for the three frameworks exemplify these three understandings.) I want to talk about questioning, first, as a mode of seeking knowledge in the form of *answers*, about ourselves and about God; second, as a mode of seeking a certain, final, and "unquestionable" faith; and third, as a mode of unknowing, undoing false pseudo-knowledge, either in some form of skepticism or as a mode of apophaticism. Once we have explored all three and seen the insights and limitations of each, I want to explore what it might mean were we to transcend them all and allow for the liberation of questioning from these frameworks, just as Augustine narrates his own questioning's liberation in the *Confessions*.

Most of the time when we think of questions, we think of *answers*, and we imagine the aim of questioning to be the achievement of an answer. This is a very useful model, and it typically serves us well in our everyday lives. But is it helpful to understand the *Confessions* as a quest simply for answers to questions—say, speculative questions about God and the soul? Was Augustine's most basic preconversion flaw the lack of a good metaphysics class in his education? This gets us into the vexed question of Augustine's relation to philosophy and, particularly, Platonism. Much ink, and not a little scholarly blood, has been spilt over this issue. This relation is quite complicated and changes significantly over the length of Augustine's career (I think he was always "later" than we expect); and it is made more muddled by the disputants' anachronistic understanding of "philosophy," presuming it to involve modern philosophy's disassociation of theory and practice. Augustine appreciated philosophy but thought that even it was inadequate; we can be drawn forward by philosophy, but if we allow ourselves to be overcharmed by the song that dialectic sings (as Plato puts it in the *Republic*), we will never realize even the goods that philosophy does offer.[3] Philosophy is the acknowledgment of longings that it itself cannot fulfill.

---

[3] As O'Donnell says, the "Platonic" ascent (recounted in book 7) worked for Augustine—it did what it promised to do; it was just that what it promised to do turned out to be inadequate to the

To imagine that philosophy can fulfill these longings is to fall into the trap of *curiositas*, which threatens to idolize knowledge—an ever present threat because philosophy can be deceived into accepting the self-presentation of our longing for knowledge in such a way as to not realize that that longing does not fully understand itself. But knowledge, in the very attempt to idolize it, is revealed to not be real knowledge at all—or, rather, what is idolized turns out never to have been real knowledge to begin with. *To know* entails willing *to be known*, being willing to be transformed by the activity of coming to know; a life stuffed full of answers is, ironically, empty.[4] The disappointment that invariably accompanies all our clutching at a fact as if it were the *summum bonum* is not really a disappointment at that fact but a self-inflicted wound, caused by the ricochet of our reluctance to let that fact inform us. Following a long line of hermeneutical thinkers such as Heidegger, Gadamer, and Ricoeur, I think that any account of questioning that reduces it to the hunger for essentially *technological* knowledge is dangerous because it obscures the root openness in ourselves to which the phenomenon of questioning attests (see Gelven). By imagining us as starting with questions and finishing with answers, it threatens to depict humans as primordially puzzle solvers, seeking some epistemological completion that, once grasped, will offer some satisfactory resolution to our quandaries. This is, I think, the root understanding of questioning beneath a common picture of science, one captured in the phrase *crescat scientia, vita excolatur* [let knowledge grow from more to more, and so be human life enriched], which is the motto of my alma mater, the University of Chicago, birthplace of nuclear weapons. The danger of understanding questioning as fundamentally a quasi-Faustian seeking after knowledge is that it does not respect the fundamentality of the desire; it seduces us into thinking about ourselves as problem solvers rather than (as philosophy said it wanted to suggest) as beings with a capacity for contemplation and wonder.

By prioritizing the question as puzzlement in this way, this picture of questioning, paradoxically enough, actually downplays questioning's significance. It makes us more primordially knowers than questioners and suggests that our epistemological dealings with the world are a matter more of technicity than encounter: It is the pragmatist's temptation. It misses the expressivist moment of questioning—that aspect of the phenomenology of questioning that seems most important—the vertigo-

---

hunger of the soul (1: xxxiii). In general, my account of Augustine's "Platonism" is in opposition to that long urged by Robert J. O'Connell and now ably systematized in Cary. As a counterweight to this reading, and in support of my own, I would propose Wetzel 1992.

[4] I am indebted to Jim Wetzel and Jennifer McBride for both this thought and its formulation here.

inducing feeling one gets when one asks a *real* question, a question whose answer one does not even know how to begin searching for, yet a question whose urgency is gripping. (I imagine this feeling as the feeling you get when you are on ice skates and you push off from the side wall and glide out onto open ice, with no more banisters or railings to support you.) It does not see that the hunger of longing that the desire expresses cannot simply be fed but must be reoriented.

Augustine realizes this; as James Wetzel rightly says, "The modern fascination with certainty in knowing is *pre*-Augustinian" (2001: 8, emphasis added; see also Burnyeat). Recall here Augustine's account of his achieved understanding of Aristotle's *Categories* (see *Confessions*, 4.16.28–31). Augustine certainly understood the book, but he then idolized the knowledge he had gained and assumed it gave him a final vocabulary, an absolute frame in terms of which all, including God, could be understood. But this knowledge "misled" him, puffing up his pride and hardening (because rendering more apparently unquestionable and thus inescapable) the surface puzzles of metaphysics, which he felt compelled to "see through" (in several senses) in order to reach his goal. Augustine's very intelligence led him ever farther away from God, whereas the "far slower" intelligence of others did not in fact damage them at all. Human knowledge, of the practical-technical or cognitive-propositional sort, is not the heart of the matter (see *Confessions*, 5.4.7–5.5.9). The dynamic energies underlying our desire to know are certainly valid, but those energies must transcend the forms in which we have tried to trap them. In a way, those forms are attempts to subdue the energies, to capture them in patterns that we can predict. It took a story, not an argument, for Augustine to realize that: as he said, after hearing the stories told by the visiting Ponticianus, "The unlearned (*indocti*) rise up and seize heaven, while we here with all our heartless learning (*doctrinis nostris sine corde*)—behold, we remain stuck in flesh and blood!" (8.8.19, my translation). True philosophy occurs where we least expect it.

The above might suggest that "simple piety," unquestioning faith, is adequate to human life, the sufficing aim and appropriate ideal of Augustine's longing. This appeal to faith can be either a powerfully attractive and deeply optimistic apologetic understanding of questioning or an equally powerfully attractive and deeply pessimistic understanding. To threaten caricature, we can call the optimistic position the "neo-Thomist" view and the pessimistic the "Lutheran" view. (These vulgar stereotypes are meant to highlight intellectual temptations [and perhaps something of an ever degenerating genealogical line], not doctrinal or denominational inheritances, and they may be more helpful in the breach than in the observance.) For neo-Thomists, human wondering is always already a wandering and will lead inexorably, if left to itself, to faith; there is a sort of laissez-faire epistemology at work here. For Lutherans, on the other hand, human questioning can be the first step toward faith—but only by being the device God uses for smashing the pretensions of our self-confidence and forcing us to confront not simply the abyssal and abysmal nature of our own interiority but also the continual and inescapable judgment of God on us; questioning does not so much lead us into faith, as perhaps it does for neo-Thomists, as drive us (in)to it. (Kant is perhaps best understood as offering a profoundly Lutheran skeptical answer in an essentially optimistic, neo-Thomist framework.) There is an implicit teleologism in both positions: Questioning is a vehicle we employ to reach a goal, namely, faith; faith beyond question—indeed *un*questioning faith—is the endpoint.

There is something right about these views, about the momentum of questioning's dynamic and about how that momentum is accelerated by our inability to find satisfactory answers. And again, as with philosophy's promise of knowledge of God, faith as establishing right relationship with God is a formulation from which Augustine would not wholly dissent. But, as also with philosophy's claimed telos of knowledge of God, such formulations err (and both differ from Augustine) in taking faith as an endpoint, a conclusion to some story of existential turmoil and struggle, a real cessation of intellectual inquiry. Our age's vision of faith as such an endpoint threatens to obscure what Augustine takes to be a central truth about faith. O'Donnell notes that were the *Confessions* simply a story of Augustine's "getting right" with God, there would be no need for him to write beyond book 8, book 9, or (at most) book 10's famous *sero te amave* section. But he keeps writing. Why? Most basically because, for Augustine, "faith"—or the *conversio* and reordering of the soul to which our term *faith* really refers—is in no way a conclusion; as he comes to realize, it is only the beginning.[5]

The *Confessions* is better understood as a story of Augustine coming to learn how to ask questions, and his quest for the religion and community (if they can be distinguished) that genuinely enabled his questioning desire to be exercised. Think about his rather extended engagement (it was more than a flirtation) with the Manicheans. They seemed to him to offer the best answers to his questions, but he discovered new questions pressing on him, questions that Manichean authorities, in particular Faustus, did not even attempt to answer (*Confessions*, 5.3.3–5.7.13; see Harrison: 23). The same wandering, wondering energy that had brought him to them eventually drove him away as well. After his conversion to Christianity he began to see that it was Manicheanism's mishandling of the nature of faith that underlay their failure. Questions did not lead to some conclusive con-

---

[5] I explore this further in section IV below.

fidence, as Manicheans advertised; they are not most basically the route to faith, they are also and more deeply the route *from* it. Understanding does not seek faith; faith seeks understanding. Questions implicitly entail some unthought assumptions that orient us toward certain issues and puzzlements and away from others; he drew this lesson in his early epistemological treatise *de utilitate credendi*. But he came to see that the implications of this insight into belief extended far beyond epistemological issues, into the nature of creation and time itself. The end is not the same as the beginning, there is no final *apocatastasis* or return, an undoing of history; history ultimately matters.

If questioning is not ultimately about faith or knowledge, is it perhaps really about itself? Perhaps the questions are the point. It is in following this suggestion out that I think we advance toward understanding Augustine's aims. But to advance in the right direction, we must distinguish our route from two nearby paths, those of skepticism and of apophaticism. By *skepticism* I mean a wise pyrrhonic skepticism, a *pia ignorantia* or *docta ignorantia*, a suspicion of philosophical puzzles as simply beyond the ken of humans to solve and requiring instead the suspension of belief.[6] Or perhaps skepticism is the best defense for securing what fragments of truth there are and the best *ascesis* for keeping us open to further truth. And apophaticism seems if not a sibling then at least a kissing cousin of skepticism, often little more than a way to drape skepticism in a theological gown. Such views are today held by many intellectuals: Think of Richard Rorty for the former form of skepticism, Jacques Derrida for the latter form, and Jean-Luc Marion (or, better, John D. Caputo) for apophasis. But for Augustine none of these really worked, and he tried them all. After the failure of the Manicheans to answer his questions, he decided to stay with them until something better came along; then he switched (though only internally and secretly) to the academic skeptics (*Confessions*, 5.10. 18–5.11.21). Even after the "something better" did come along—or, rather, after Augustine came to it, in the form of Ambrose and his preaching of Christianity (*Confessions*, 5.14.25)—he remained in a state of suspension, trapped in skepticism's amber.

Augustine's description of his momentary flirtation with skepticism suggests how it can present itself as a transcendental anesthetic and can ossify into a stale epistemological cynicism, a dogmatic "knowingness" that there is nothing to know.[7] Furthermore, this sort of skepticism, as Augustine notes in *contra academicos*, is delusory; some beliefs are practi-

---

[6] For historical sources on this sort of skepticism, see Toulmin and Miller. A contemporary version of this is found in Phillips 2001.

[7] On "knowingness," see Lear and Phillips 1996.

cally and theoretically indubitable. Nor is it, as some might have it, a clever strategy for "rupturing" authority or the endless deferral of conclusion, a way to resist "closure." Not only is this skepticism not the welcoming openness it represents itself as being; it is really and essentially an act of impatience, a simultaneously paralyzing and deeply impatient stiff-arming of our inquisitive energies, a refusal to commit to something because it does not wholly satisfy one's expectations. Stanley Fish puts it rather well: "Openness to revision as a principle is itself a form of closure, not at all open to ways of thinking or acting that would bring revision to an end" (235).[8] It is essentially an attempt to *avoid responsibility*, an attempt to avoid the hard work, the struggles and the risks, of real knowing.[9]

III

If the aim of questioning cannot be fully or satisfactorily described as knowledge, as faith, or as the wise (or at least knowing) lack of knowledge or faith in pyrrhonic or apophatic skepticism, then just what *can* we say about it? Just what is it that we are doing or trying to do when we live our lives, as Augustine manifestly wants us to do, in unleashing our desire to ask questions? The final books of the *Confessions* offer us often overlooked insights on this issue. I want to focus on two such insights— first, how the proper context of such questioning is revealed to be wonder, prayer, and exegesis, centrally in the community of believers; and second, how a renewed understanding of this experience might inform and alter our experience of living in time, particularly as our living in time has reference to our "end" in what turns out to be a kind of endlessness, a "Sabbath without an evening." Questioning blossoms, for Augustine, into exegesis, which in turn turns out to be a basic mode of being-in-the-world; hence we must finally ask about the character of that mode's consummation and how it might help deepen our understanding of our present existence.

But to get at this we must take a careful look at *Confessions* 9, the work's last "biographical" book; for in the Ostia experience, and in Augustine's attitude to it afterward, we find a crucial clue for understanding the latter books. We must be especially careful about this book because we feel a hermeneutical "gravitational pull" toward reading it as another ending,

---

[8] Although such a skepticism may attempt to "make room for contingency," Fish argues that "contingency is precisely what you can't make room for; contingency is what befalls the best laid plans of mice and men—and that includes plans to take it into account or guard against its eruption" (237).

[9] I have learned much about this from the writings of Stanley Cavell. See especially Cavell 1976, 1979.

one more conclusion in what we imagine to be a book full of conclusions. Our perception of Augustine as a dogmatist seeking closure so totally dominates our capacity to read him that we do not see that every one of his endings is a beginning and can perhaps be more importantly a beginning than an ending. Furthermore, our eagerness to see endings in this autobiographical text may reflect our desire to find endings in our own lives—for we understand endings as inextricably tied to our ability to control our lives. This is why so many accounts (and some translations) of the *Confessions* simply stop with book 9 or feel it necessary to explain why they are carrying on. On the contrary, to borrow from Winston Churchill, book 9 is not the end, or even the beginning of the end; it is, rather, the end of the beginning. Or, rather, and more properly, it is really the *beginning* of the beginning, that place where the book actually starts, the entry into the essentials of Augustine's present condition. All the rest has been prologue (in several senses).

The central event of book 9 is the vision (O'Donnell more aptly entitles it the "audition" [3: 133]) at Ostia. And typically this vision is seen as the culmination of a series of "mystical" visions in books 4 and 7 (and perhaps also the *conversio* scene in book 8)—their culmination in the sense that Augustine finally achieves what he has been seeking all along. After his conversion, catechumenate, and baptism, in an upper room waiting for their return to Africa (and, hence, the end and resolution of his own *Odyssey*), Augustine and Monica talk their way to God—to God's presence, "touching" God with their hearts before falling away again in sighs and further, deeper longing.

Most readers of the *Confessions* see this culmination as a conclusion, a realization of what Augustine sought all along. But it is equally a continuation of the same pattern of temporary intimacies whose fleetingness serves only to increase Augustine's hunger and longing for God. I am not denying that the Ostia experience is significantly different from the earlier ones (although it differs from them no more significantly than they differ from each other).[10] I am saying, rather, that scholars have been too fixated on locating its significance as an *experience*, a dense and discrete "event," rather than as a moment in an entire life—which has the only real "integrity" that human existence allows and a quite limited and leaky integrity at that. (Here we see the degree to which consumerist attitudes saturate our thought patterns.) We typically seek to define the ex-

---

[10] For the ambiguities of all these experiences, and for a challenge to the usefulness of thinking about them as "experiences" at all, see Turner. Not only the chapter explicitly on *Confessions* (50–73) but the book as a whole have been extremely useful for my thinking. And I am also indebted here to O'Donnell (3: 127–133).

perience wholly in terms of the inner character of the experience itself (focused, for example, on the more affective tinge of the Ostia experience) rather than in terms of the place that the episode has in the larger narrative, especially in terms of how Augustine *responds* to it in the moment and how he retrospectively interprets it much later. (This is especially odd given that we typically come to understand our own experience in just this retrospective way; perhaps we are too seduced by the immanence [and imminence] of Augustine's recounting to remember that it is, after all, a *re*-counting.) Now—both immediately afterward in book 9 and most certainly in the "authorial present" of Augustine as he is writing the *Confessions*—the episode, unlike earlier ones, is not impatiently seen as a failed lunge at eternity, a botched attempt at an immediate, immanent experience whose value is in itself (hence, note, essentially nontemporal). Dissatisfaction no longer leads ineluctably to a sense of failure; incompleteness no longer leads to self-recrimination. Now Augustine understands it as a foretaste, glorious in itself but still a foretaste, of a later and greater blessing in heaven. It is not part of a larger project of *apprehensio*, of grasping apprehension, for Augustine has given that up: The project is now only of *attingere*, of touch.[11]

Augustine's new perspective was one of learning to be "eschatologically patient" rather than "apocalyptically impatient."[12] This allowed him a more relaxed attitude than permitted by the habituated demand for a complete comprehension of previous foretastes, a demand that expresses an impatient anticipation of (and implicit demand for) a nearly immediate resolution and end to his questioning. Immediate comprehension— itself a form of resolution—now is no longer Augustine's aim; instead, he has learned to allow an event's significance to emerge over time, to accept that understanding will be—as in the whole *Confessions* itself— essentially retrospective. History is not a series of failed attempts at reaching union with the divine; it is one long lesson in (because one extended act of *ascesis* for) what that union will one day, at the end of days, be revealed to be. (Though even that will not be the sort of conclusion we wish, in our sinfulness, for it to be.) And we, the readers, must learn this lesson as well; we must learn not to read this series of experiences in the way Augustine thought of them at the beginning of the process but, rather, in the way he thought of them at the end, when he was looking back, en-

---

[11] On this, see van Bavel.

[12] By *eschatologically patient* I mean to describe an attitude of fundamental "advental" passivity, a mode of waiting for the messiah; in contrast, *apocalyptic impatience* expresses a basically impatient and controlling attempt to predict "the end," which entails anticipating it, which in turn reveals itself as a desire to avoid judgment. For slightly more on this (entirely stipulative, although I believe heuristically useful) distinction, see Mathewes 2001.

gaged in the process of *recollectio*, a recollection that says (though always, in this life, provisionally) what the events "meant."[13]

In light of this we can see that once Augustine comes to see his life as a whole, as a narratable unity, he sees it as inextricably bound up with, indeed identical to, his quest for God. But this narratable unity is only so narratable *as* a unity (and hence only narratable) within the framework that Scripture provides. Books 1–9 recount his "first" attempt to *understand* Scripture, to come to "read" it, and his life gains its intelligibility by being a typological retelling of the story of the old Adam and the new Adam in Scripture.[14] Indeed, the story of these books can be read as the story of Augustine picking up and setting down a series of different books, from Cicero's *Hortensius* forward, until he picks up a volume of Paul's letters and, with God's grace, can read it in the right way. The biographical story of the *Confessions* is, thus, importantly a *bibliographical* story. And, like all bibliographical stories, it is a story of a quest—the story of Augustine coming to understand and to learn to live with this quest, understood essentially as a quest for the book that is the key to understanding his life, learning to feel the *distensio* of worldly existence and to long properly for the homeland of "rest" to come. Yet this quest is not a freestanding "existential" project, for it gains determinate shape only when read through the lens of Scripture. Exegesis is the primary form of inquiry in the world; ontology, in fact, is a province of exegesis.[15] Only when he understands that this quest—or more precisely the Scripture that gives it its form— itself provides the narrative framework for his life can he undertake it directly. Life is lived in questing, seeking after God, beseeching God for more profound insight, ever deepening (at once affective and intellectual) understanding; but this deepening understanding is always equally a revelation of ever deepening mystery.

It was when Augustine realized the character of his life as such a seeking and beseeching, that it became possible and necessary for him to "endure" the "continuing tension," to use O'Donnell's terms, of living with ever unfolding questions. But it should be clear by now that "enduring" the "continuing tension" of such questioning is in fact not merely something one suffers regretfully; it is, rather, a mark of being alive. To come to see the joyous endlessness of such questioning, and to begin to inhabit it, is to pass from death into life. Perhaps our sense, never completely

---

[13] On this, see Wetzel 1992.

[14] For support for this argument, see Young. O'Donnell speaks of the "union of intellectual and exegetical" (1: xl) in the *Confessions*. More generally, see Stock for further work on Augustine and literality.

[15] See Markus 1996: 27. I thank Michael Hanby for conversations in which I came to see this.

expungeable, that this tension is obviously bad—something we want to escape—simply bespeaks our condition, as sinners, of death in life, our condition as *refusing* to live.

To inhabit this questioning, to undergo this process of conversion from death into life, is finally a project of *ascesis*, one facet of Augustine's larger ascetical project well described recently by Carol Harrison as "training in longing" (97).[16] Where once he expected to find resolution, to find answers—where his attitude was essentially (if implicitly) apocalyptic—now he sees that his life will be lived in deepening awareness and acceptance of the real mysteriousness of God's providence. As Augustine says in *De trinitate*, such knowledge "is sought in order to be found all the more delightfully, and it is found in order to be sought all the more avidly."[17] To us this sounds like an uncomfortable task; but its discomfort is due to our sinful desire to know and control the course of our lives. In surrendering his will to grace, Augustine no less surrendered his intellect; and it was given back to him not with answers to the questions he had asked but with those questions transfigured and transformed. Now he can begin to live, most basically not by seeking knowledge—whether the knowledge of good and evil or the knowledge of God and the soul—but instead by inhabiting an ever deepening sense of wonder and praise.

IV

Understanding book 9 as displaying this fundamental transformation of Augustine's "intellectual project" helps us understand the otherwise quite jarring shift to books 10 and following, the shift from an apparent focus on autobiography to an apparent focus on exegesis. If one's life should be organized around wonder, we have two routes into such wonder, two books— the book of the world and the book of Scripture. Book 10 is readily seen as a transition from the first to the second, as both the vertigo-inducing consummation (because confutation) of the potentially narcissistic fixation on the self in the first nine books and the recognition of the limitations of that route and the need to go beyond it into another route, the route of the community of the Church, as lived out in multiform exegesis of the Scriptures.

---

[16] The idea of "beginning" as a goal to be sought was a central trope in early monastic spirituality; see Burton-Christie: 247–249 (and the book as a whole has been of enormous value for this article).

[17] *De trinitate*, 15.2, translation in Augustine: 396. The role of seeking in *Confessions* seems more explicitly articulated and addressed in *De trinitate*, especially as that text is centrally organized around Ps. 105:4, "seek his face always." It further is elaborated as well in his *Ennarationes in Psalmos*. I am indebted to Robert Wilken for conversations on this matter and, as usual, to Lewis Ayres and Michel René Barnes for all things concerning Augustine's trinitarian theology.

Hence, book 10 signals the turn to God's work in the Church (this is precisely where, interestingly enough, Pelagius gets nervous about Augustine), and it culminates (at *Confessions*, 10.43.70) in what James O'Donnell calls "a passage of such dense eucharistic imagery that it may best be thought of as perhaps the only place in our literature where a Christian receives the eucharist in the literary text itself" (1: xxxvii).[18] Book 11, then, begins as a rebeginning, echoing book 1's beginning, though this time in the plural: "Ut dicamus omnes 'magnus dominus et laudabilis valde'" (*Confessions*, 11.1. 1). Now it is spoken plurally and communally; now we are in the Church.

But what happens, now that we are in the Church? What are we doing (t)here? We wonder, communally, in awed praise of God. As I said above, the medium of our wonder—the device whereby our wondering is structured and oriented—is Scripture. All forms of understanding are forms of exegesis because Scripture is for us the urtext, the hermeneutical key whereby we seek after God. The fact that the *Confessions* seems to have been written in the wake of Augustine's composition of the first three books of *De doctrina Christiana* takes on a new significance in this light: *De doctrina* theoretically elaborates the hermeneutics of *caritas* that is exhibited materially in books 11–13 of *Confessions*. Those books explore the fruitfulness of the hermeneutical diversity enacted in the Church (most explicitly visible in Augustine's discussion of the command to "increase and multiply" [*Confessions*, 13.24.37], which he takes to authorize multiple interpretations of Scripture, so long as they do not violate the rule of charity).[19] Throughout these books, Augustine explores the multiform legitimate modes of inquiry into God, refusing to limit the styles of reading by any criteria save their fruitfulness for increasing charity. (Indeed, he is willing to countenance a range of exegeses so diverse as to seem positively licentious to some.[20])

---

[18] To support O'Donnell, we might note that there is an interesting pattern in books 8–10 of conversion (8), catechesis and baptism (9), and entry into the full mysteries of the Church with the Eucharist (10). This also parallels O'Donnell's account of the three sorts of vision, mapping onto the three kinds of sin (see 1: xxxiv–xxxvi).

[19] See O'Donnell, 3: 399–401. On *caritas* in general, see Pollmann: 121–147, especially 135–143. Pollman's book seems to me to represent a significant advance in understanding Augustine's hermeneutics of charity, and it deserves more attention in English-language literature on Augustine than it has yet received.

[20] Hence I dissent from R. A. Markus's discomfort with Augustine's exegetical strategy and practice, which he labels "extravagant" (1996: 12, 18–21, 35, 37–38). See Bruns, who suggests that the fourfold scheme of medieval hermeneutics for biblical interpretation was "less a method of polysemy than a critique of it," a way to control the "licentious exegetical practice" (he borrows from Gerhard Ebeling here) of endless allegory (140–141). Bruns thinks that Augustine was foundational for this hermeneutical policing; on my view, in contrast, although his authority may have been invoked in support of such policing, Augustine's own approach is far more consonant with an exegetical endlessness than Bruns allows. (Nor do I think there is much difference between "early" and "late" Augustine here.)

The final books of the *Confessions* thus attempt to represent what goes on in this ecclesial community. (Even the mythic solitary reader of the *Confessions* is not solitary, for she or he is in conversation with Augustine and, through him, with others.) This is a radically open, nonelitist account of exegesis, in which the newfound understanding of human life as fundamentally exegetical enables all people, in their daily life and work, to serve as hermeneuts, legitimate participants—as both explorers and exponents—in the community's inquiry, its ongoing ingoing, into God's mysterious providence.[21] But the openness is not simply a "horizontal" one, welcoming the input of all Christian voices, at all levels of erudition. It is vertically bottomless as well, for there is quite literally no *end* to this inquiry—no final, "literal" meaning of the signs apart from their meaning as infinite, gratuitous love, which is a kind of "literality" that works precisely to vex any finality. As O'Donnell says, "The text itself becomes the ascent," and "the failure to make the adjustment has led to serious failures to see the purpose of this and the later books of *Confessions*" (3: 151). Let me explain what I take O'Donnell to mean in somewhat more detail.

The questions we ask of the Bible are questions equally as much about our lives, our destiny, and God. These questions are "answered" in a very literal sense, but the answers do not suffocate the inquiring love we feel; they enflame it. The "rest" and "peace" of which Augustine speaks is a rest occurring on a Sabbath day with no evening, no ending (*Confessions*, 13.35. 50–13.37.52). This makes us rework just what this "rest" is, just what the *otium* will be toward which we are yearning—as well as what the "heaven" is that Augustine now lives his life anticipating. That is, understanding the *Confessions* as a liberation of questioning ultimately entails a radical reshaping of our eschatological expectations and through them an alteration in our understanding of the nature and meaning of time and eternity.[22] But perhaps such is necessarily in store for us if the symbolics of Christian faith express accurately (if obliquely) something of the real nature of God's plan for us. Some of the questions we should ask are the following: What is heaven

---

[21] Augustine's populism is slowing coming to be appreciated; see Markus 1990 and Leyser. See also Markus, who argues that understanding is a form of *communion*, community: "In discovering the meaning of signs we discover a shared world of reference and in so doing we are integrated into our linguistic community" (1996: 30). I would only add that such "integration" is never total; language is just as riddled with fissures as is any community. For the general point that theology is best understood in this populist, "pastoral" sense, see Charry.

[22] I am alert to discussions of how "eternity" must be distinguished from perennial time. But I think that we have allowed our understanding of Augustinian "eternity" to remain too negatively related to our phenomenal experience of time. I think there is some use in thinking about eternity as related positively to our experience of "beginning"—an experience that, I note, we seem to "experience" in this present life only retrospectively. I have been much informed by Hannah Arendt's thinking about "natality" on these matters and Abraham Joshua Heschel on "Sabbath."

like? What will it mean to live endlessly, in eternity? Such questions may sound profoundly naive; but perhaps, as the Polish poet Wislawa Szymborska suggests, "the only pressing questions / are naive ones." The "naive" questions get at something profoundly important, namely, the nature and implications of the radical open-endedness of God's creation, the way that Creation has no real *finis,* no cessation or closure.[23]

Augustine was not unique in asking such questions about our "end"— witness Gregory of Nyssa's near-parallel attempt through his idea of *epekstasis* in the *Life of Moses.* But it was not the obvious route to follow in his time. Origen, for example, assumed that the order of the whole of creation imitated the cyclical order of patterns *within* creation.[24] But the deep logic of Christian thought implied a fundamentally different understanding of the nature of creation's ultimate end, and Augustine's work may be usefully seen as seeking more fully to articulate that logic. Whether that is in the end ultimately different from saying that Augustine's work determined the course of Christian thought is a topic that I will not address here. But it is certainly clear that Augustine's vision was quite radically distinct from many offered at the same time; and if others such as Gregory were traveling the same route, it was a route that needed all the traveling it could get, if it was finally to make clear the profundity of its path.

Augustine's task in the *Confessions* is not exclusively, or even most directly, to narrate any conclusive resolution. It is not the story of the achievement of a goal essentially "external" to him, some sort of firm acquisition of what is beyond him. That is because God is *interior intimo meo*—"closer to me than I myself am" (see Mathewes 1999). His task is, rather, to narrate one's becoming the sort of creature who can begin properly to pursue, dynamically and with others, such an "external" aim as the

---

[23] See Wislawa Szymborska's "The Century's Decline." For two examples of the surprising fruitfulness of asking "naive" questions such as these, see Russell and Zaleski.

[24] Peter Brown suggested to me that, because Augustine knew that Paulinus of Nola was translating Origen's *On First Principles* into Latin at this time, perhaps he had as one intention (among many) to offer a different vision of time and history than that offered in Origen's work. The problem with Origen's proposal is that his account pictured time as cyclical, essentially a closed system; it assumed that creation is basically symmetrical, a zero-sum game, arising from nothing and descending back into it again in nihilation. On this account, time is understood to be only a measure of change in matter and has no ultimate purpose outside of itself; history "signifies" nothing. Yet not only does this account do damage to history, it has no place for God's grace either—for "grace" as Christians conceive it is precisely God's insistence that what God has created God will not *de*create, that creation itself is not trapped in a zero-sum logic, and that being is not "borrowed" from nothingness (which then would always have a final claim on it) but, rather, is blessed as God's will for all eternity. Furthermore, by rejecting the concept of grace, this Origenist picture refuses the kind of relation that Christianity has come to understand God as having with creation: Because the world is a finite, closed system, once God creates it, God neither affects nor is affected by its reality. For a variety of deep reasons, then, one might read Augustine's account of the Sabbath without an evening, and all of its implications for him, as quite radically opposed to Origen's cosmology.

inmost heart of all creation. He aims to articulate a form of ecstatic *ascesis*, a form of self-formation, and self-discipline, that has at its center precisely *not* concern with the self. It is the root of the hermeneutics of charity and also, though in a different way, *amor Dei*.

CONCLUSION

I conclude with some caveats. First, by portraying Augustine as more centrally dialogical than metaphysically dogmatic, I am not trying to exonerate Augustine from accusations of "Platonism." But that is because I think our vision of what "Platonism" is needs profoundly to be rethought—at least as regards Plato and possibly (although I am not as sure) as regards Middle Platonism and Neo-Platonism. Admitting the presence of a fundamentally dialogical imagination within Plato's texts ought not to be difficult because Plato's metaphysics is better seen as an orienting device for further inquiry than as an absolute, well worked-out "final vocabulary" to which Socrates eventually leads all his dimwitted interlocutors.[25]

Second, I am not trying to be postmodern. Nor am I trying to be premodern. (After all, it was a premodern scribe who obscured the puzzle with which this article begins by planting that last, conclusive *amen* after Augustine's *aperietur*). Really, I want to avoid all such Cecil B. DeMille-esque categories. I am simply trying to suggest that Augustine's discipline of the self may cut across our conceptual categories—and I leave who is included in this "we" open, although I invite you to acknowledge your presence in it—in ways that make it very hard for us to get his project into focus. Nor am I claiming that the *Confessions* is in all respects an accurate report of Augustine's life; whatever else it is, it is an elaborately wrought *theological* text. But my argument need not be merely interesting to theologians like myself. I think that understanding the text as a process of "learning to begin" throws into question a number of the understandings of Augustine's purported Platonism and show us (once again) that etiological labeling, as intricate and interesting a task as some may find that to be, is a far cry from understanding. It also may help us to rethink our typical fixation on religious belief as a final end, a conclusion in some quite definite, determinate way. I think this is a fundamentally flawed understanding of what religious belief is and what it does, and we would be wise to resist its encroachment on our understanding as much as possible.[26]

---

[25] For more on this, see Reeve: 117. On the difference between Plato's metaphysics for "agents" and our metaphysics for "spectators," see Lear: 148–166, 219–246.

[26] I leave to others the question of whether, and if so how, this account might speak more broadly to questions of "belief" for other religious traditions.

But beyond this, my main aim is to convince readers to share my wonder at just what Augustine thought he was doing in ending with an opening. And perhaps such wonder, or some more sophisticated, gussied-up version of it, was just what Augustine most directly intended to excite in his readers. As Paul Ricoeur has said, "The beginning is not what one finds first; the point of departure must be reached, it must be won" (348). In our end is our beginning. Only after we have seen through our doubts', our suspicions', and our questions' self-presentation—only once we have seen them as wanting to be wonder—can the Christian life truly begin.

REFERENCES

Augustine 1991	*The Trinity.* Trans. by Edmund Hill. Hyde Park, NY: New City Press.
Bruns, Gerald L. 1992	*Hermeneutics Ancient and Modern.* New Haven: Yale University Press.
Burnyeat, Myles 1999	"Wittgenstein and Augustine *De magistro*." In *The Augustinian Tradition*, 236–303. Berkeley: University of California Press.
Burton-Christie, Douglas 1993	*The Word in the Desert: Scripture and the Quest for Holiness in Early Christian Monasticism.* New Haven: Yale University Press.
Cary, Phillip 2000	*Augustine's Invention of the Inner Self: The Legacy of a Christian Platonist.* New York: Oxford University Press.
Cavell, Stanley 1976	*Must We Mean What We Say?* Cambridge: Cambridge University Press.
1979	*The Claim of Reason: Wittgenstein, Skepticism, Morality, and Tragedy.* New York: Oxford University Press.
Charry, Ellen 1997	*By the Renewing of Your Minds: The Pastoral Function of Christian Doctrine.* New York: Oxford University Press.
Fish, Stanley 1999	*The Trouble with Principle.* Cambridge: Harvard University Press.
Gelven, Michael 2000	*The Asking Mystery.* College Park: Pennsylvania State University Press.
Harrison, Carol 2000	*Augustine: Christian Truth and Fractured Humanity.* Oxford: Oxford University Press.

Heschel, Abraham Joshua 1977	*The Sabbath: Its Meaning for Modern Man.* New York: Farrar, Straus and Giroux.
Kenny, Anthony 1959	"Aquinas and Wittgenstein." *Downside Review* 77: 217–235.
Lear, Jonathan 1998	*Open-Minded: Working out the Logic of the Soul.* Cambridge: Harvard University Press.
Leyser, Conrad 2000	*Authority and Asceticism from Augustine to Gregory the Great.* Oxford: Clarendon Press.
Markus, R. A. 1990	*The End of Ancient Christianity.* New York: Cambridge University Press.
1996	*Signs and Meanings: World and Text in Ancient Christianity.* Liverpool: Liverpool University Press.
Mathewes, Charles 1999	"Augustinian Anthropology: *Interior intimo meo.*" *Journal of Religious Ethics* 27/2: 195–221.
2001	"Faith, Hope, and Agony: Christian Political Participation beyond Liberalism." *Annual of the Society of Christian Ethics* 21: 1–27.
Miller, Peter N. 2000	*Peiresc's Europe: Learning and Virtue in the Seventeenth Century.* New Haven: Yale University Press.
O'Donnell, James J. 1992	*Augustine Confessions.* 3 vols. Oxford: Clarendon Press.
Phillips, Adam 1996	*Terrors and Experts.* Cambridge: Harvard University Press.
2001	"An Answer to Questions." In *Promises, Promises: Essays on Psychoanalysis and Literature,* 174–180. New York: Basic Books.
Pollmann, Karla 1996	*Doctrina Christiana: Untersuchungen zu den Anfängen der christlichen Hermeneutik unter besonderer Berücksichtigung von Augustinus, De doctrina christiana.* Freiburg, Switzerland: Universitätsverlag.
Reeve, C. D. C. 1988	*Philosopher-Kings: The Argument of Plato's Republic.* Princeton: Princeton University Press.
Ricoeur, Paul 1997	*The Symbolism of Evil.* Trans. by Emerson Buchanan. Boston: Beacon Press.
Russell, Jeffrey Burton 1997	*A History of Heaven: The Singing Silence.* Princeton: Princeton University Press.

Stock, Brian   *Augustine the Reader: Meditation, Self-Knowledge, and*
1996   *the Ethics of Interpretation.* Cambridge: Harvard University Press, Belknap Press.

Szymborska, Wislawa   "The Century's Decline." In *View with a Grain of Sand:*
1995   *Selected Poems.* Trans. by Stanislaw Baranczak and Clare Cavanagh. New York: Harcourt Brace.

Toulmin, Stephen   *Cosmopolis: The Hidden Agenda of Modernity.* Chicago:
1990   University of Chicago Press.

Turner, Denys   *The Darkness of God: Negativity and Christian Mysticism.*
1995   Cambridge: Cambridge University Press.

van Bavel, T. J.   "God in between Affirmation and Negation according
1993   to Augustine." In *Augustine: Presbyter Factus Sum,* 73–98. Ed. by Joseph T. Lienhard, Earl C. Muller, and Roland J. Teske. New York: Peter Lang.

Wetzel, James   *Augustine and the Limits of Virtue.* New York: Cam-
1992   bridge University Press.

2001   "The Theatre of Memory: A View to Augustine's Postmodern Certainties." Unpublished MS.

Williams, Bernard   *Shame and Necessity.* Berkeley: University of California
1993   Press.

Young, Frances   "The *Confessions* of Saint Augustine: What Is the Genre
1999   of This Work?" *Augustinian Studies* 30/1: 1–16.

Zaleski, Carol   *The Life of the World to Come: Near-Death Experience*
1996   *and Christian Hope.* New York: Oxford University Press.

More Lurid Than Lucid: The Spiritualist Invention of the Word *Sexism*

John B. Buescher

Nineteenth-century American spiritualists coined the word *sexism* long before its modern incarnation in order to refer to a complex of ideas about human sexuality and reproduction that were consonant with the general advancement of women's rights. Among these ideas was the belief that spirit and mind were ascendant over matter and could act directly on it. In their view, a woman's sensitive spiritual nature gave her the power to join spirit and matter. She could provide a way for exalted spirits to enter the world through her, in the mental character and even the physical form of her offspring, by focusing her own and others' spirits into the embryo growing within her, as if she were making a photograph. The goal of enhancing this ability would justify changing law and custom to ensure women's autonomy and freedom, especially to protect their decisions about sexual relations in order to regulate favorable and unfavorable impressions on the embryo. Emphasizing the embryo's sensitivity to spiritual impressions, however, also led some progressives to the conclusion that women's autonomy should be restricted. Women had to be kept away from even immaterial influences that would adversely affect them during pregnancy.

THE LOOSELY ORGANIZED movement that called itself "spiritualism" or "modern spiritualism" began in America shortly before 1850 and blossomed in the second half of the nineteenth century. It was based on the belief that the spirits of the deceased had begun to communicate directly with the living, delivering to them, mostly through entranced spiritual "mediums," messages of hope, comfort, and uplift.

John B. Buescher is an independent scholar in Annandale, VA 22003.

Journal of the American Academy of Religion September 2002, Vol. 70, No. 3, pp. 561–592.

Many aspects of spiritualists' beliefs and speculations tied spiritualism to the social reform movements of the time. Ann Braude, in her ground-breaking work *Radical Spirits*, has shown how spiritualism, by recognizing that the divine could manifest or speak through anyone, entwined itself with the women's rights movement. The relationship was based on a vision of equality and universality and an appreciation of the freedoms, rights, and powers of all, male and female (Braude: 56–57). Braude has also shown how spiritualism supported the advancement of women's status by focusing on women's differences from men. It helped feminize religion, for example, by elevating the religious status of the sensitivities regarded as typically feminine that were needed to be an effective trance medium (Braude: 82–84).

This article examines other links between spiritualism and the women's rights movement of the time, not only links based on the idea of the equality of the sexes but also links based on the idea of their differences—particularly the notion that women were the superior mediators of the divine on earth, translating spirit into matter through the biological process of human reproduction. Spiritualists commonly held this view, but some saw it as a literal description of human reproduction and some saw it as a less literal but still useful and beautiful vision that would impel a radically reformed world.

Sexism, as defined by *The Oxford English Dictionary* (*OED*), is "the assumption that one sex is superior to the other and the resultant discrimination practised against members of the supposed inferior sex, esp. by men against women; also conformity with the traditional stereotyping of social roles on the basis of sex." Both the *OED* and *Merriam-Webster's Collegiate Dictionary* give the first citation of *sexism* as 1968. But the word had a previous incarnation, with a different meaning, 100 years earlier, when spiritualists coined it during a controversy about sexuality and women's rights. Uncovering that controversy reveals the links between spiritualism and the women's rights movement that are the focus of this article.

Spiritualists' ideas were spread through independent spiritualist news-papers and through itinerant trance lecturers and spirit mediums who answered to no one else for their volatile inspirations. Their speculations were not entirely consistent or internally coherent. Their collection of ideas on the subject of human sexuality and reproduction resembled a loosely shared dream more than a systematic theory. It touched very lightly on everyday observation and science but then extended into improvised flights of extravagant fantasy, guided by visions of a spirit-led revolution.

Spiritualist ranks were filled with prophets, oracles, and seers who spoke in a trance state with a supernal authority about things otherwise unseen. They did not hesitate to overstep the bounds of the language in order to express things that were not entirely of this world. They created and used many neologisms (Brittan 1855d).

At the quarterly meeting of the new Massachusetts Spiritualists Association in October 1866, the president of the association, Amasa C. Robinson, formed a committee to revise the organization's constitution and declaration of principles, which Henry Clarke Wright had drafted earlier that year. Wright was a spiritualist, an ex-Congregationalist minister, an old-line Garrisonian abolitionist, a writer on social reform, and a lecturer on women's rights (Colby 1866a, 1866b, 1866c, 1866d).

Robinson, a spiritualist medium, lecturer, and shoe manufacturer from Salem, placed himself on the Revision Committee. Edward Smith Wheeler, a well-known trance "improvisator" and lecturer from Boston, was the second member of the committee. The chairman was John Henry Watson Toohey from Boston, an Irish immigrant who had started life as a Catholic but had turned Baptist, then had become a Universalist preacher, and finally had become a spiritualist lecturer and homeopathic physician. In his remarks to the meeting, Toohey talked of spiritualism as far more than contacting the spirits of the dead. "Spiritualism, as I understand it, is the science of life," he said, "the actual utterance and echo of life itself. It formulates the many phased manifestations of Nature and makes Spirit pivotal to all things that live, move, and have a being." He believed that spiritual realities were more fundamental than material realities, as he made clear when he spoke about the capacities of spiritual mediums. He distinguished the physical ("organic") differences between the sexes from their deeper mental or spiritual ("constitutional") differences: "The medium may be man or woman—woman or man—but in either case the characteristics will be *feminine*—negative and positive. The qualifications are constitutional, if not organic, and for the time, become fundamental—*mere* sexism being of secondary significance. Thus nature complements herself—and out of seeming disorder, brings divinist order; out of physical weakness and mental darkness, immortal light!" (Colby 1866d: 2).

Toohey used his word *sexism* to mean, in part, the physical and outward sexual characteristics that placed one in the category of male or female. The *ism* suggested that these categories were somewhat superficial and could be at odds with deeper components of a person's nature. He soon used the word again, with a different and more complex meaning.

At the association's next Annual State Convention—its second, in Boston in January 1867—the Committee on Revision made its report to the membership. Most of the constitution and the principles in the declaration created little controversy, although the membership debated whether the preamble should contain language that set spiritualism apart from Christianity—or at least apart from the established churches. Some who spoke were also uneasy with the idea of defining a creed for spiritualism—many of the independent, unconventional minds that found their place in spiritualism chafed at anything that would bind the movement to dogmatic pronouncements. Instead, they suggested, the only point on which spiritualists agreed was the bare fact of spirit–human intercourse. But committee member Wheeler "asserted that Spiritualism was not a mere chaos of phenomena, and had grander uses than the development of merely sympathetic spirit-intercourse" (Colby 1867a).

One of the articles of the declaration, however, created an intense controversy. It stated the principle of "the equality of the sexes, and the moral integrality of sexism" (Colby 1867b; Dixon 1867). Those present debated it at length before they finally passed it. After the convention, Frank L. Wadsworth, the editor of the Chicago-based spiritualist newspaper *The Spiritual Republic,* received a copy of the proceedings. He wrote that he was confused but—on the alert because of what he saw as the preamble's objectionable anti-Christian tone—suspicious of what *sexism* might mean:

> "The equality of the sexes," is understandable, and we find nothing but what accords with Christ in that, but the "moral integrality of sexism," is a puzzle to us.
>
> Ladies and gentlemen of the Association, what do you mean by it? "Sexism" is a term we can't find in *Webster,* and you haven't defined it. What sort of an *ism* is it? Is it an ism of theory, or practice? How does it differ from other isms concerning sex?
>
> Do you mean by this new term, the use of the sexual functions? If so, do you mean the monogamic marriage of the N[ew] T[estament], or the composite one of the Bible Communists [John Humphrey Noyes and the Oneida Community], or that rather indefinite looseness termed free love? If the authors or author of this luminous phrase, has some recondite meaning concealed in the words, "moral integrality of sexism," we opine it is one which means nothing at all new, or else it conceals what those who adopted it neither understood nor approved. Gentlemen, please use plain words, which express just what you mean, and what the people can understand. We very much expect to find a cat under this mealy covering, if indeed there be not a toad squat at the ear of Eve, which only needs the point of Ithuriel's spear to develop the skulking fiend in all his ugliness. We are the more inclined to this opinion by finding so much which is susceptible of a double sense. (1867b)[1]

---

[1] The cat in mealy covering refers to Aesop's story of the cat who disguised herself to catch a mouse by rolling in flour; the "toad squat at Eve's ear" refers to Satan in disguise, in *Paradise Lost.*

Lita Barney Sayles was a spiritualist and women's suffrage activist from Connecticut, but she, like many other spiritualists, was no radical, and she now wrote Wadsworth. She had attended the Massachusetts Spiritualists Association Convention, and she confirmed his suspicions. She wrote that even though she had been present when the convention received and discussed the committee's report, she was still confused about what the committee had intended by the word *sexism*. She suspected, however, that they had deliberately coined the word in order to hide their intention to encourage promiscuity. They had turned "sex" into "sexism," suggesting that it was acceptable to have sex with whomever one wished, whenever one wished, and they had tried to dignify it as a philosophy, an "ism." She explained her reasons for suspecting this:

> A gentleman who was "in the ring," upon being pressed hard to know if this article did not intend to declare that every man and woman had a right to do as they pleased in regard to their sexual relations, shrugged his shoulders, and smiled, knowingly, and answered, "You don't want me to say, do you?" and *would not deny it*. Another reason is that when the explanation of the term was urgently called for, and the Chairman of the Committee, rose to respond, there was nothing expressed by what was replied, except to reiterate the "integrality of sexism," which was more lurid than lucid. Some pure souls there knew well enough to what the expression pointed, and spoke against it, but the majority had so much confidence in their Committee that it was almost sacrilege to question their immaculateness. (196)

In fact, medium and psychic healer Levi K. Coonley had fiercely objected at the convention to the article about "the integrality of sexism." He had said, "The phraseology is obscure, but it cloaks the assertion of the moral right of social disorder; of the rectitude of promiscuity and miscellaneous sexual relations, regulated solely by the wayward fancy of those who chose to indulge in such a mode of life." He had implied that Toohey was a libertine, for he "was the same in public as in private, and was always ready to act in accordance with his public avowals" (Colby 1866b).

The opposition defined the word in one way, but the committee members who created it defined it in another, apparently trying to capture a complex of ideas. These had begun to coalesce during the spread of the free love doctrine among radical reformers, as *The Spiritual Republic* editor hinted.

Henry Wright, the author of the original Declaration of Principles, was a free lover. Yet what he promoted was not at all crass but, rather, high minded:

> The soul of each man or woman is the only manger in which the true savior can be born. . . . The pre-natal life and education of man is being

discussed all over the land. The right of woman to decide for herself, when, how often and under what circumstances she shall assume the responsibilities and be subjected to the sufferings of maternity is to be a settled principle of the coming republic. That it is a crime of blackest hue for husbands to impose maternity on their wives when they know their nature does not call for it. That the husband will see and worship the God in his wife, and not the mere animal. No more "unwelcome children." That children have a right to demand of their parents healthy bodies and healthy souls, a love origin, and a welcome into life. (1867: 139)

"Sexism," therefore, involved a new recognition and affirmation of the particular powers of each sex in biological reproduction, especially of the female, whose contribution had sometimes been regarded as merely passive, as providing the bed in which the male's seed could grow. Now the female was to be seen as the primary agent in reproduction and the male as secondary. The male only "had power over the germ, before the mother [took] charge of it, and by influencing it, through her thoughts and feelings after conception." The female's power over the child "must of necessity be all but absolute; inasmuch as under the action of the forces of her organism, the entire process of organization is performed" (Wright 1863: 80–81).

In itself, this elevation of the mother's role in heredity was not new. Swiss naturalist Charles Bonnet had long before theorized that the female held within her, but only in a general form, the germinal structure of all future generations, that her egg was acted on only in a general way by the male's semen, and that the individual characteristics of her child were developed as it grew in her womb.

Wright went further and described mental or spiritual influences on the formation of the embryo. He frequently praised the reproductive theory of William Byrd Powell, a phrenologist and irregular physician, "a peripatetic head-reader," as one of his critics put it, who "declared his ability to discover a man's religious tenets by the [physical] developments of his head" (Powell: 12). According to Powell, and to many others afterward, the particular temperaments of the man and woman, during the moments of sexual intercourse, determined the well-being of the child they conceived, in a way reminiscent of astrological influences (Keckeler: 72–81; Pancoast: 191–192; Powell: 179). The mental state of the father and mother were imprinted on the mother's womb as if it were a sensitive photographic plate.

Two years before the Massachusetts Spiritualists Association Convention, spiritualist editor Samuel Byron Brittan had published his own work on "the influence of the mind on the body." In line with Powell's idea, Brittan believed that "the singular effects produced on the unborn child, by the sudden mental emotions of the mother, are remarkable examples of a kind of *electrotyping* on the sensitive surfaces of living forms. It is doubt-less true that the mind's action, in such cases, may increase or diminish the molecular deposits in the several portions of the system" (Brittan 1873). As early as 1857, he had written:

> The parents fully and completely daguerreotype all their constitutional characteristics and their conditions and affections upon the spiritual and natural form and nature of the offspring. The child is the combined min-iature type or focal representation of all the faculties, proclivities, habits, states, ruling affections and conditions of the parents at the time it was begotten and conceived, and afterward, in its growth and development, it discloses all these traits and conditions, and retains them through life. (1857b)

Elizabeth Lyle Saxon, suffragist, temperance activist, and social re-former, wrote to Brittan that

> women are the builders and creators, under Providence, of the human frame; and until men and women alike learn the laws of Nature and Life— boldly and freely learn, with reverent hearts and a desire for all good, they will continue to send forth monstrosities of mind and body and fill pris-ons and asylums. Every deep abiding grief; every angry emotion, is in a degree daguerreotyped on the minds of our unborn children. (531–532)

More profoundly, however, many also thought it was daguerreotyped on their bodies, in a way, one might say, that developed in the midst of wide-spread interest in homeopathy and that relied on the Doctrine of Signa-tures. Saxon wrote that after a man of her acquaintance had taken up drink, all his children were born with physical deformities. Minister, mesmer-ist, and (later) spiritualist John Bovee Dods wrote that

> if a woman were to conceive while wrapped in total darkness, and never see the man by whom she conceived, nor get the most distant impres-sion of his image, and could she, at the moment of conception, be con-signed to a sleep of profound insensibility till the time her delivery came, she would unquestionably bring forth an offspring exactly in her own image. It would be as perfect a fac-simile of her own organism, form, and features as the second bank-plate was of the first from which by galvanic action it was produced. (239–240)

Tying spirit to matter and, finally, Heaven to Earth occurred through a materialization of the spirit, by means of a technology of visual reproduc-tion, through seeing. Women precipitated spirits into the world as pho-tographers precipitated immaterial images onto a silver plate.

The notion that thought and feeling materialized in the embryo, par-alleled that of spirit photography, of "spirits imprinting their forms" on a sensitized material substrate—the metal or coated glass plate (Moses).

Back to the very beginnings of photography, some speculated that the objective universe might really be just images and signs that took on form—"for aught we know to the contrary, other worlds of the system may be peopled and conducted with the images of persons and transactions thrown off from this and from each other; the whole universal nature being nothing more than phonetic and photogenic structures" (Blavatsky 1877: 321–322; Willis: 70). Conversely, the womb was "peopled" by means of images and thoughts, or, as the spirits taught Boston trance medium John Murray Spear, "it may be declared that mind impregnates matter and hence then comes what is called birth" (1858b).

Boston engraver William Howard Mumler made the first well-known "spirit photographs" in 1862, but for almost a decade photographers had been trying to capture an image of a spirit (Briggs; Brittan 1854, 1855a, 1855b, 1855c; Buescher). In other new ways, too, the immaterial had been inscribing itself upon the material. Massachusetts mediums received spirit messages as writing or pictures spontaneously appearing in complex red lines or welts upon their bodies (Bartlett: 17, 22–23; Hardinge 1870: 107–108). One medium who had later imitators, Elizabeth J. French, produced nearly instantaneous spirit drawings of flowers on blank paper placed inside light-proof boxes: "The friends of the medium say, that by some unknown process of chemistry, the substance of the lead pencils is suddenly precipitated upon sketches already limned by spirit artists, in such a way as to *bring out* the pictures by some act similar to that of our ordinary photography" (Hardinge 1871: 55; Howitt: 177).

The parents' emotional and mental states during coition would determine the embryo's own subsequent mental patterning but also whether it would be free of biological defects and disease. Sexual excitement was an electromagnetic charge that built up in the body and coursed into one's sexual partner. This charge would effect the impression onto the mother of the biological pattern of the child. For "every person is continually giving off subtle emanations which partake of his physical, mental, and spiritual characteristics, and which tend to impart the same to all persons and things about him" (Newton 1863). Spiritualists even declared that objects, too, continually radiated all the "scenes" of their history and "daguerreotyped" them on everything surrounding them, reducing the material universe, in a sense, to a collection of images, all of which were mentally retrievable by sensitive mediums (Denton: 276–279).

A pregnant woman's mere viewing of a photographic or lithographic reproduction could directly affect the child growing within her. An unlovely mother might produce a beautiful child, for example, as Britten reported of a particular case: "The boy is doubtless indebted for his fine form to the presence of a beautiful French Lithograph in his mother's sleeping apartment, and which presented for her contemplation the fault-less form of a naked child" (1873).

The profound biological impact the mother's emotional and mental well-being had on the embryonic child was a significant part of the reason why "the unwanted child" (Wright's phrase from his popular 1858 book of the same title) had to be so carefully avoided. If the mother was forced to have sex with someone with whom she was not temperamentally attuned—even if just for that moment—if she did not feel deep and pure love and affection for her partner, then she could anticipate dire biological consequences for the resulting child. When a man forced a woman to have sex, it was certain to affect the biological issue—not just because of the terrible emotional and mental state of the woman but also because of the monstrous inner condition of the man.

Whether the woman happened to be married to the man who had forced himself on her made no difference. A marriage license, after all, could not regulate a woman's affection. Only she could know, in the privacy of her heart, the rightness of any sexual act (Braude: 125–136; Carroll: 40–41). "It is for her nature to decide," wrote physician and spiritualist Thomas Low Nichols, "both whom she will admit to her embraces, and when; and there is no despotism upon this earth so infernal as that which compels a woman to submit to the embraces of a man she does not love; or to receive even these, where her nature does not require them, and when she can not partake in the sexual embrace without injury to herself, and danger to her offspring" (150).[2] The result was the mental and physical degradation of the human race. Dr. Edward Bliss Foote wrote:

> The human family is sick; our planet is a huge revolving hospital. . . . What's the reason? The only answer is, startling as it may appear when given, the children of this world are but the creatures of accident. Comparatively few of them are wanted at the time of their birth. They are the unwelcome product of an amative spasm. Through nine weary months they are borne about in the wombs of wretched-minded mothers, no small number of whom, surrounded by unfortunate circumstances, loathe the act which rendered them pregnant. (4)

Various doctrines and practices that were labeled as "free love" were often espoused by spiritualists. Whatever else "free love" may have en-

---

[2] About the physical impression on the embryo made by the parents' thoughts, Nichols seems to have been ambivalent. On the one hand, he wrote that "particular talents, tendencies, tastes, idiosyncrasies, and affections of every kind" are impressed on the child's "body as well as the mind" while it is in the womb (194); on the other hand, he also wrote that "all which makes the basis of the character, mental and physical, must reside in the germ and the spermatazoon" (169).

tailed, its core was the conviction that the touchstone of sexual behavior must be each individual's decision, not the conventional contract regulated by church and state in the institution of marriage (Sears: 8–9, 20–21). Mutual affection and love, freely given and received in pairings of suitably balanced male and female energies implicitly referred to by the term *sexism*, was the true basis of "marriage."

Was this a call to deepen and "spiritualize" the marriage institution, adding to it love and mutual respect? Or was it a call to cast aside the marriage institution altogether, as an oppressive relic of the past, and for each person to follow, "as the voice of God," her or his sexual yearnings wherever they might lead, to be as angels, as, it was said, angels "neither marry nor are given in marriage"? This issue was argued by more conservative spiritualists (such as Sayles) who appear to have constituted the majority of spiritualists and more radical "free love spiritualists."

Free lovers argued that the institution of marriage defined the oppression of women and disregarded the natural exchange of love between men and women. It was to blame for the degradation (even the biological degradation) of the human race. As it came to be expressed in stark, radical terms by Victoria Woodhull in 1872, their claim was that marriage itself is slavery and prostitution, that "the barter and sale of wives stands on the same moral footing as the barter and sale of slaves," and that "the god-implanted human affections cannot, and will not, be any longer subordinated to these external, legal restrictions and conventional engagements" (11).

Most spiritualists opposed any move to sever the connection between sexual relations and the marriage contract. No matter whether one was (relatively) a conservative or a radical, however, spiritualists commonly believed that women had to be given personal power over their "generative function" commensurate with their biological power. Toohey called the reform principle that held that as its goal *sexism*.

Spiritualists looked to a "natural" law of sex, whereby spiritual feelings of attraction, regarded as manifestations of a subtle form of magnetism or electricity, would determine sexual relations (Guarneri: 360–361). The committee that coined the word *sexism* meant sexual naturalism and the unhindered flows of mutual attractions, in line with the calculus of "amatory affinities" that French social philosopher Fourier had envisioned (1.161–199). It was a reform philosophy by which women were to be liberated from oppression and arbitrary constraints (Spurlock: 87–98).

Toohey, when asked at the convention to explain "the integrality of sexism," called it a radical article that was a flat denial of the saying of [Alexander] Pope, that "every woman was at heart a rake"; or "man was always a damned rascal," whenever there was "a lady in the case," as ran the thought of those who had formed their ideas upon the precepts of the church, which taught the total depravity of humanity; whose Christian fathers had sullied the character of woman by vile aspersions; whose maxims taught the essential immorality of marriage—asserting that it was incompatible with a saintly life. We must rescue woman from this degradation and assert the natural, normal life of manhood and womanhood: the integrality of sexism. (Colby 1867b)

Sex was both natural and good, not inherently evil. "Often, years ago," Toohey said, "men were arrested for teaching physiology. The demand now is for the truth, the whole truth, and, if possible, nothing but the truth. To make that truth manifest is our labor." The very fact that people assumed that "the integrality of sexism" was an invitation to immoral behavior, Toohey said, demonstrated how badly the idea needed to be promoted. *Sexism* meant the natural goodness of the sexual processes, including the sex act. He denied that the article "favored the idea of immorality or disorder." It "had nothing to do with promiscuity." It was "universal, and simply meant that love was not a thing to blush for, as was quite commonly thought" (Colby 1867b).

Committee member Edward Wheeler also endorsed the article and said it was not meant to elevate "the looseness of an immoral life" or to disparage "a permanent monogamic marriage." He said that he "recognized the truth of marriage, and knew that in its nature it was *sacramental.*" But, he added, "the mere assertion of marriage was not entitled to respect, unless the relation was *vital* and *true.*" Attorney Isaiah Coffin Ray, from Nantucket, in support of the article at the convention, replied to an objection that the article "struck at marriage." "What was marriage?" he asked and then answered his own question: "That which passes for the thing in law and society is not altogether lovely; *it makes man and woman one, and man is the one.* I care not how much of that sort of thing comes to an end. Make marriage slavery, and I care not who destroys it."

The influence of the Protestant dissenting tradition is evident here, in the willingness to "come out" of the worldly institution of marriage, once it had been perceived as a power contrary to God's "true" law of marriage. But the emphasis here on the natural law of sexuality—as distinct from the mundane laws governing it—was also influenced by the earlier writings of Charles Fourier and those of Swedish visionary Emmanuel Swedenborg. Fourier sharply distinguished between what he saw as the natural law of "passional attraction," which brought disparate things and isolated people into harmonic combinations, and what he described as the arbitrary and whimsical duties and conventions that human society set up to regulate behavior.

Swedenborg believed that all things, inanimate and animate, had correspondences in the spiritual world and that they all evolved, from the lowest elements to the highest beings, through sexual relationships in one form or another. Boston physician Harriot Kezia Hunt, although not a spiritualist, was a Swedenborgian, and expressed the belief in this way: "My profession assumed a magical power over me, just as in proportion as I recognized the material body as a *type* only of the spiritual" (Hunt: 197). Indeed, it was not just a "type" but, in the words of John Dods, a "visible daguerreotype" of God's spirit (223).

The spirit guides that spoke through Boston spiritualist medium John Spear had discoursed on such an idea in 1858 (the year before the publication of Darwin's *On the Origin of Species*), calling it not "sexism" but "sexualism": "Sexualism is universal. Planets are male and female. They copulate, cohabit, conceive, pass through gestational conditions, give birth to offspring with as much regularity and precision as the lower and grosser orders of animate life" (1858a). The Massachusetts Committee, when it coined *sexism,* would have invoked this idea of evolutionary progress. It was a philosophy that looked to the natural laws of physics and biology as a future basis of society and rejected the manmade laws that currently defined sexual relations. Spear's spirit guides asked rhetorically, "Think you that thru any legislative bull capacitated to frame personal laws or civil codes, that will repress or govern the sexual relations of the planetary world; in other words, can man institute laws that should jostle the mechanism of the infinite?" The spirits had good reason to ask this through Spear: He had decided that his true spiritual affinity was not his wife of thirty years, but Caroline Hinckley, who was visibly pregnant at the time this discourse was given to him in trance. Hinckley acted as his amanuensis, writing down the words uttered through him.

In the year of the Massachusetts spiritualist convention in Boston, Elizabeth Osgood Goodrich Willard, a physician from Chicago, gave the name "sexology" to her attempt to describe a society that ensured individual freedom and equality of the sexes from a scientific study of the natural laws governing sex. Her laws of genetic inheritance, however, included the notion of "transmission by impression," essentially the idea that spirit informed the flesh, that mind controlled matter (184–185). This mechanism could be described, in the end, only through the assertion of sympathetic magic, but Spear's Boston associate Alonzo Eliot Newton had dignified it the year before as the workings of the Holy Spirit. "These magnetic emanations moving from one sexual partner to the other," Newton wrote, "possess all the distinctive personal *qualities* of the persons from whom they proceed—in fact, are in some sense *the persons themselves*, projected into contact with others" (1866).

If sex could liberate people from artificial constraints, so might its unabashed outing, with a kind of scientific equanimity, beyond embarrassment about body parts or functions, making it possible to investigate the laws of nature regarding "sexual hygiene" without squeamishness. Humans could use their improved understanding to reorder human society and to create better human beings. "Sexism," therefore, involved a commitment to science (at least in theory) and to human control of the biological future of the race.

This was a point of contention between those who looked to a future in which humans would breed according to natural laws in order to produce the best offspring and those who saw the idea of evolution—especially human-directed evolution—as an affront to the Creator. Some among the conservative wing of spiritualists rejected this application of science to human sexual relations, saying that Henry Wright was "wrong for declaring that God does not make man, that man makes man" (Wright 1863: 24–28). Despite that, most spiritualists, even if not ultraradical, believed that a rational reform of sexual relations would improve society.

Sexism, therefore, also carried the meaning of a scheme of social engineering, a supposedly scientific system of human reproduction. In 1869 John Humphrey Noyes introduced a system of breeding he named "stirpi-culture" into the Oneida community (Andrews 1870b).[3] He believed his system had heavenly warrant. He distanced himself from the spiritualists of the time, but they, too, believed that heaven, through the spirits, was communicating to many the broad principles on which ennobling sexual combinations could be made. The spirit of Isaac Newton announced to medium and radical free lover John Spear that there was a precise calculus to these combinations. Through it, humans could be manufactured, automatically, with the same precision as one might manufacture "a hoe or a spade" (Spear 1873: 10). At least one spiritualist experimenter in sexual science and utopian social reconstruction tried to go farther down this road toward decoding biological inheritance. Orson Squire Fowler, perhaps best known as a phrenologist, regarded the intentional improvement of the human stock as the golden key for all the various societal reforms of the Age (275–277). His nephew, Samuel Theron Fowler, believed that angels had dictated to him the specific code by which elementary spiritual qualities combined and recombined in matrices that expressed themselves in the material form of the human being (81–146).

---

[3] Around this time Noyes read Francis Galton's 1869 *Hereditary Genius: An Inquiry into Its Laws and Consequences*, but Galton invented the word *eugenics* only in 1883.

The conceptual link between a revolution in sexual relations and spiritualism consisted in the belief that the development of people's powers as spiritualist mediums made them more sensitive to higher, divine influences. When their minds were thus uplifted and opened to spiritual influxes (in the manner of Swedenborg), the children they would give birth to would be similarly uplifted in mind and body. Spiritualism, under this belief, was a spirit-directed program of human evolution. In religious terms, it would eliminate the need for a separate "regeneration" by involving and expressing the Spirit directly in "generation," bypassing original sin, one might say, and, in its most radical formulation, achieving the millennium. The spirits were coming, and they would carry out a sexual revolution with flaming swords, as Victoria Claflin Woodhull told the 1873 convention of the American Association of Spiritualists, of which she was the president:

> They will laugh at your professed ownership in sex, and tell you to enforce it if you can. They will snap their fingers at your officers and spit upon laws as I have been taught by them, to do. Nor will they wait for divorces either. They will love whom they will; and in their loving, lift us of earth, to their level. I know there are thousands who have been sexually inspired of spirits; and many more whom spirits control and through whom they receive the benedictions of love. Once and for all I tell you, Oh, children of earth, that you had better put your houses in order and await the coming of the bridegroom or the bride. Accept sexual freedom while yet it can be attained, by degrees, and not wait until it shall tear your souls at its sudden coming. (1873: 12)[4]

The excitement within the spiritualist community was enhanced by the conviction that a concentrated and purified revolutionary mind or spirit could imprint itself as a pattern on the physical organism. At the "pivotal moment" of the sexual climax, Heaven's Gate would open on Earth, and the highest spirit would find a way to inscribe itself on matter. The best that the man could do at that moment, in the photographic metaphor, was to be "pure," to avoid acting as a distorting lens or filter, so that the clear spiritual light could flow into his partner.

Some believed that the noble spirits of the past were preparing to condense their energies and reenter the world by impregnating sensitive and cooperative women, who would produce a new, elevated human–spirit hybrid race. The Communion of Saints would then occur on Earth. Spear's associate Newton explained in 1856 that the spirits "contemplate the introduction of a higher order of existences, through a divine marriage and

---

[4] Correspondents to *The Religio-Philosophical Journal*, an important anti-Woodhull and anti–free love spiritualist newspaper, believed that Stephen Pearl Andrews had actually written this speech.

holy association of persons; who shall bring forth offspring correspond-
ing to their improved, elevated, and spiritualized conditions" (Spear 1857:
iv). Thaddeus Spencer Sheldon, another associate of Spear, gave a speech
at a spiritualist convention that he attended with Newton and Wright in
which he "discharged a whole broadside of ideas novel and startling to
conservative minds." He explained that "it is possible for advanced minds
in finer conditions (spirits) to associate, concentrate their psychological
powers, and by acting upon receptive mothers, without miracle, to reproduce their present combined characteristics in a human child," eventually
making it "possible to introduce into the world astronomers, mathe-
maticians, poets, artists, metaphysicians, moralists, organizers and better
types of humanity generally, as they may be desired, as it now is to improve the stock of animals on the farm" (Newton 1858).

During the 1860s and 1870s, when the spiritualist community widely
embraced the notion that mind informed, if not actually conjured, matter, in the sense that thoughts during sex imprinted themselves on the
child, spiritualists came to regard the "full body materializations" of spirits
as the highest achievement of the spirit medium. These demonstrated that
spirit would organize itself, embody itself, in a palpable substance. Spirit
would give birth to a human form. The "cabinet materialization" of the
spiritualist séance that developed at that time would seem to have been
an unselfconscious and unconscious performance in which the closeted
female medium materialized (or, one might say, gave birth to) spiritual
beings who emerged from the cabinet and embodied themselves in glorified forms. The medium herself as well, one might say, was both liberated and reborn in a glorified form from the cabinet, the darkroom where
her new self had been developed and where her old self was yet enclosed
(Hawken: 37).

By the early 1870s some spiritualists even used the spiritualizing of sex
to anticipate the elimination of purely *human* sex altogether. The believers called themselves "Alphites" (or "Alphaists")—and published their
ideas in *The Alpha*, a journal that more generally advocated sexual absti-
nence and was edited by physician Caroline Brown Winslow. Women in
an ennobled or spiritualized condition, they suggested, would ultimately
be able to reproduce merely through the visitation of the Spirit(s)—repeat-
ing Mary's immaculate conception and "divine" (because uncorrupted)
maternity. Spiritualist trance lecturer Addie Lucia Ballou developed this
vision (she wrote that it came to her in a trance state) in a series of articles
in 1872–73 on what she called "spiritathesis" in the nationally distributed
spiritualist newspaper *The Religio-Philosophical Journal*. How many of
even the most radical regarded this as a literal possibility, as opposed to a
beautiful dream, is impossible to say.

This gave a particular meaning to the widespread, potent, but only vaguely articulated notion of "generation separate from sexual conditions," an idea perhaps first explained as the basis of social reform by Charles Fourier, who divided the "passion of love" into material and spiritual functions (1.184, 2.69–83). The idea found its way, in contradictory forms, into such diverse theories as John Humphrey Noyes's "male continence" system at Oneida, which separated the "amative" function from the "propagative" function of sex, and Mary Baker Eddy's tentative speculations on the possibility of asexual reproduction in humans.

The radical spiritualist interpretation was that spirit, mind, or feeling (even sexual arousal or orgasm) could become so much the master instead of the slave of matter, that it could *cause* conception, whether or not the physical act of sex occurred. This meant that women might imagine a time when sex with men would be obviated, even in order to have children (Waisbrooker: 1–3). As Newton put it, whoever a child's earthly father is, the real paternity for every conception is accomplished through an "overshadowing of the Most High" (1879: 6). Women—and the spirits—might therefore become ascendant or even all sufficient, an idea that, after changing the literal reference to "spirits" to the more general "spirit," found an echo within the early New Thought movement (Satter: 12, 148–149).

At a minimum, even if men were not to be cast out of the temple of sex altogether, men and women's sexual energies and "magnetisms" had to be equalized during the sexual "exchange"; otherwise, the imbalance would distort the divine imprint on the embryo.[5] For this reason, both Woodhull and another Spear associate, Paschal Beverly Randolph, repeatedly stressed that men, through what they called "equilibration," had to take care to bring their women partners to sexual climax and not simply stop after their own climaxes, leaving their partners unfulfilled. In every sense, women had to be given the freedom to find their own fulfillment.

At the time of the Massachusetts Spiritualist Convention in 1867, Randolph was in Boston running a clinic where he taught "sexual hygiene." He explained that a woman was entranced during orgasm and that, during those moments, she was completely open to impression from her partner's mind, who acted, in turn, as a channel for high (or low) spirits to enter her (45). The mother, as the true agent of reproduction, was a

---

[5] Here was a point on which "sexual hygienists" differed widely among themselves—some taught that male and female had opposite magnetic "charges," positive and negative, and therefore could "attract" each other as "affinities." Others, however, regarded the force of attraction as something like gravity or regarded specific attractions between two individuals as lock-and-key relationships. Others regarded male and female "affinities" almost in a taxonomic sense, as two individuals who had a large number of essential similarities.

kind of aperture for Heaven to appear on Earth, a gate through which the spirits of the race would pass into the future generation. For the spiritualists' reproductive theory, the mother's body was, in fact, the place where Heaven and Earth were joined, where spirit and matter were reconciled, where the contradictions between religious and scientific discourse were resolved (Taves: 166–167).

A woman, sensitive to the spirits, could deliver a heavenly being into the world, a material being formed entirely by mind or spirit and undiluted by the physical constraints and laws of the mere present:

> The thoughts, or rather, the elements of the being . . . have been influenced & absorbed to her being from various sources, from various persons, and let her cohabit with whom she will, that offspring is legitimately and naturally hers & no one human being is the author or sustains the relation of father to it in any true sense. . . . It may be declared that mind impregnates matter and hence then comes what is called birth. If two persons could be brought into the copulative condition destitute of mind, there could be no birth. It is mind which passes to the sexual organs, which originates birth. (Spear 1858b)

It seemed possible, then, in a utopian world, to render men entirely beside the point, either to the question of heredity or even to the bare fact of reproduction. Women and spirit (or spirits) would do the whole work. It would be an era of women's dominion, not men's.

Spiritualist and women's rights activist Eliza Woodson Burhans Farnham captured the idea. She wrote that, through women, "the race is destined to rise to a more exalted position than ever before it has held, and for the first time to form its dominant ties of relationship to that world of purer action and diviner motion, which lies above the material one of intellectual struggle and selfish purpose wherein man has held and exercised his long sovereignty" (311).

The spiritualists' sexual revolution led in contradictory directions simultaneously—toward unhampered individual freedom in sexual choice but also toward reforming and regulating individual sexual activity under a plan of social engineering. It also led simultaneously to license as well as asceticism.

The revolution led some toward an appreciation of the immanence of the divine in earthly ecstasy and toward uninhibited sexuality and the acceptance of pleasure, regarded as angelic or as the working of the spirit. Frank Wadsworth, the editor of *The Spiritual Republic*, like many others in and out of the spiritualist community, parodied this "free love" as "free lust" (1867a).

The revolution also led some toward transcendence and toward an ascetic ideal of thoroughly eliminating "animal passion" in the human organism. Women would no longer need protection from men's sexual predation, even if they were to walk around in the nude, like Eve in Paradise. Actual sexual intercourse would be hedged about with so many preconditions for bringing the minds and bodies of the man and woman into the very highest sacramental purity that it might occur, like some grand conjunction of planets, only on the rarest of occasions and then only for the purpose of conceiving a child.

The language of the one group of sexual reformers was sometimes indistinguishable from that of the other. Groups and individuals sometimes vacillated, passing from license to asceticism and back again. Theorists at the time who intended to reform sexual relations saw indulgence and denial as variations on a single theme of continence (Gordon: 159–185). The common goal was to live "as angels," to recapture the innocence of Eden. This was why Wheeler's explanation that "the integrality of sexism" meant "the morality of sacramental marriage" did not satisfy those who suspected that its real meaning was the morality of extramarital sex (Wadsworth 1867c). For free lovers commonly distinguished between false marriage— that which was merely sanctioned by church or state—and true marriage— a natural and profound spiritual bond of love (Brown 1861: 7–9).

Both the libertines and the ascetics sounded much the same on this subject. For both, a woman "in the highest condition" was clothed "only in her aura" (Spear 1857: 307). Farnham, on the platform at a spiritualist conference in May 1857, quoted Spear's spirit messages on this: "Spiritualism comes, then, to call out a few persons who shall be divinities, or goddesses in human form; who shall know no shame; who shall seek no fig-leaf coverings; who shall be so pure that garments shall not be used for purposes of concealment, but only for comfort and convenience" (Spear 1857: 621). Then she added her own comment: "It is expected that the low, lascivious, will treat efforts of this sort with contempt. It is expected that persons undertaking to reach this high position will be misinterpreted; but the end to be reached is of higher moment than all the sacrifices which may be required" (Brittan 1857a).

The attempts to "reach this high position" included experiments "to elevate, to holyize, to divinize and spiritualize woman," to "bring her into a condition where low thoughts cannot be generated in her mind," and "to so live, be so pure, so holy, that evil can find no place in her bosom, and by a law of necessity she cannot attract evil." Part of what that meant was revealed in the autumn of 1857 when newspapers reported that "spirits" had directed the residents of Spear's utopian community at Kiantone, New York, to do without clothing.

Spear's radical free love associates apparently practiced a group training to desensitize the participants to frank sexual language and perhaps other sexual behavior and then to resensitize them to it as sacramental. In this training each woman was to "be brought into that condition where conversations can be free on subjects of this character, so that blush shall not matte her cheek." The point was that

> persons must be so educated, purified, and spiritualized, that they will cease to think of the sexual organs with other than high and holy feelings; the false modesty which is startled at conversation on vital subjects must be eradicated from the mind. Man must come to that state wherein he will feel that the human form is divine, that every organ is holy, that all the functions are pure. (Spear 1857: 257)

Woodhull's 1873 speech to the American Association of Spiritualists also recommended the therapeutic use of blunt sexual language, to draw what had been hidden into the light of public discourse, and configuring "free love" as "free speech."

"Sexism," as the "scientific" practice of sex, also included a philosophy of ecstatic experience. Some considered that this was to be achieved through *coitus reservatus*—what today would be called Tantric sex—a practice that appears to have been fairly well known within the utopian spiritualist and radical communities of the time. It was not undertaken simply as a method of birth control but as a way to exercise and increase one's magnetic and electrical attractive power.[6] Newton wrote that the man's retention of his semen had the effect, through an inner alchemy, of transmuting it, "the concentrated essence of all the life-forces of your being," as he told his readers, "distilled and compounded with marvelous chemistry in the most wonderful of laboratories," into ecstasy and enlightenment:

> This element when retained in the system—the mental powers being properly directed—is in some way absorbed and diffused throughout the whole organism, replacing waste, and imparting a peculiar vigor in every part. It is taken up by the brain, and may be coined into new thoughts— perhaps new inventions—grand conceptions of the true, the beautiful, the useful—or into fresh emotions of joy, and impulses of kindness and blessing to all around. (1875: 30)

A name for the philosopher's stone of transmuted sexual energy of either sex was "the elixir of life," as in the title of Woodhull's keynote

---

[6] Noyes's followers at Oneida called the technique "male continence," but spiritualist physician Alice Bunker Stockham later called it "karezza," and it was also known as "magnetation" (Sears: 209–213). Not all the sexual theorists in the spiritualist movement recommended *coitus reservatus*; P. B. Randolph, for example, did not, although he, like other spiritualist healers, purveyed equipment meant to help men guard against "spermatorrhea" or loss of semen outside of sexual intercourse.

address to the spiritualists' convention.[7] This energy was supposed to maintain the body's youth and to make it possible, after death, to materialize at will back on Earth (Waisbrooker: 3–4). As Woodhull declared to the convention, "The law of life! The law of love! These are what we need to discover, advocate and practice; and when we shall have done all this, and not until then, farewell all human misery. Not till then can the millennium be ushered in—death banished the earth, and the resurrection accomplished" (American Association of Spiritualists: 45). This would be accomplished either by the spirit's taking on a glorified form—suggestive to some of Jesus' appearances after his resurrection—or, during the especially "sensitive" period of pregnancy, by the spirit inhabiting a growing human embryo.

Some spiritualists who might have been expected to acknowledge themselves as unabashed free lovers (at least in theory) also wrote against promiscuity—and not just as found in the "degraded prostitution of loveless marriages." One reason for this was perhaps the desire to deflect conservative criticism (or even, perhaps, legal prosecution), but another may have been the wish not to cast pearls before swine, not to teach free love to those who were impure and who would therefore misunderstand and abuse it. Those within the spiritualist community who wished to identify the libertines among them found the true positions of the various writers and proponents of sexual reform difficult to divine and equally difficult to describe frankly and publicly.

The spiritualist newspapers, for example, merely criticized the free love members of John Spear's "Sacred Order of Unionists" for quoting Paul's letter to Titus—"To the pure, all things were pure" (Hardinge 1870: 237–238)—without saying unequivocally that they were using it to justify their sexual practices. Spear associate Newton recommended that "in God's name, then, give [woman] her freedom to move in such orbit as she will—gathering honey from any and every opening flower, and lovingly bringing the same to the domestic hive" (Spear 1857: 611–612).[8] Newton also compared the healthy benefits of secrecy (as in the group's esoteric practices) to those that a man received from maintaining his "reserve" of se-

---

[7] The term *elixir of life* had a more general usage too: As a young woman married to Canning Woodhull, for example, Victoria was a part of his traveling mesmerist and patent medicine show. The medicine they sold was called "The Elixir of Life."

[8] Around the same time Newton used his metaphor of the bee, Samuel Brittan, then editing *The Spiritual Age*, published an article by zoologist Rufus Browne about the new findings of Carl Theodor Ernst von Siebold on parthenogenesis in bees. This consisted in "the deposition of fertile ova by true virgin females, that is, by individuals whose complete development renders them fully competent to perform the sexual act in the ordinary way, but which are kept from doing so by exclusion from the males" (Browne). One presumes the Alphites would have welcomed human cloning.

men (Newton 1862: 2; 1875: 41). "*Reserve*," he wrote, "is the grand secret of power everywhere." On the other hand, in the early 1870s when Woodhull, as both spiritualist and free lover, became a lightning rod for public criticism against her free love views, Newton also discoursed at length in the Boston spiritualist newspaper, *The Banner of Light*, against what seemed to him to be her philosophy of unreserved licentiousness (Jones 1873a, 1873b; Newton 1872).

Spiritualist lecturers James Martin Peebles and Joseph Osgood Barrett, who both (at least at first) supported Woodhull as a pure soul, also wrote a condemnation of free love: "Virile qualities were never more degraded than in those . . . masterful licentiates who mistake a slop of animal sentiment for a well of water springing up into everlasting life, and sink in the bottomless bog of demoralized passion with cries of glory unto the rock on which their feet are planted" (Barrett: 100). Woodhull herself would later declare that she had never meant what she had been thought to mean.

The same confusions had been present in the Massachusetts Spiritualists Association's debate over the word *sexism*. Revision Committee member Edward Wheeler, for example, criticized Levi Coonley, who had accused Toohey of encouraging promiscuous behavior, for a statement Coonley had made that "if we elevated hell itself high enough it would become the golden floor of heaven" (Colby 1867b: 3).

Sexism meant, in part, recognizing the biological distinction between the sexes. Recognizing the distinction was meant to free women and to protect their particular rights *as* women, particularly their reproductive rights. Women, according to Henry Wright, exercised a special dominion of power. They had an "empire over the character and development" of their children and, so, over the entire race. Recognizing and protecting that dominion was supposed to be the key to the liberation of women (Hardinge 1867; Stanton: 861). It was meant to change maternity from being a burden and a bond, an instrument of women's oppression, to an instrument of women's liberation, for it would require social changes that would give each woman the power to produce the best offspring possible.

Emphasizing a mother's power over the child's embryonic development, however, could not, in itself, justify her liberation. The science of human sexuality had, at first, seemed to be a partner with (and provide a plan for) schemes of rapid reform and social engineering (Laqueur: 16–24), in which the woman came into her own as the true artist in control of creating her offspring. This "science" of human sexuality developed in the nineteenth century in various ways, often through mere speculation, that were not conducive to women's rights (Tuana: 35–38). Some conceptual models of human reproduction, having considerable weight in the spiritualist community, imagined the biological processes in a way that the woman became the passive victim of external influences, not the active agent in an "artistic maternity." They provided a rationale to restrict her freedom and movement and associations, to closet her, in order to ensure that unhealthy psychic influences would not be transmitted through her to her offspring. Emphasizing that a woman had a special power and sensitivity ironically made her the slave of what she was exposed to, in her metaphorical role of camera, as if her shutter were stuck open and had to be manually covered over.

This made her helplessly vulnerable to sexual impressions and influences (Braude: 177, 190; Moore: 119–121). To continue the photographic metaphor, she needed to be kept in the dark so that she would not automatically reproduce the image that impinged on her. Portraying women as especially powerful "sensitives" or mediums—as if they were photographic plates—ultimately made them dependent on men to protect and guard them (Wright 1863: 76–79). Where this led was evident in Levi Coonley's declaration that mediums were not responsible for their immoral (that is, sexual) behavior because, at least in trance, they were helpless to resist impressions:

> He believed that there was no class of society who were more upright and pure than they; but the very fact of their being mediums signified that they were the subjects of influences which were of the earth as well as of the heavens; it was true that mediums reflected the conditions around them, externalizing the spiritual state of the social life of the age, as well as the life in the [heavenly] spheres, and, as they were not considered as they should be, they suffered in consequence, not so much, perhaps, because of any special fault of their own, as of the elements which were thrown upon them, and of which they became the victims. (Colby 1867b)

The consequences for women's freedom and autonomy were retrograde. Under this regime individual rights became less important as a goal in human sexual relationships, and the social and biological engineering of the race became more important. Under this model of sexuality a young woman might not even be allowed to read a novel that stirred the passions or allowed into a theater to see an exciting play. California spiritualist newspaper editor Julia Schlesinger left a San Francisco theater one night appalled at the graphic representation of murder and mayhem she had witnessed. She wrote that she was ready to try to prevent other impressionable women from seeing it:

> The result was depressing in the extreme; and the thought came what must be the effects of witnessing such plays upon a delicate, sensitive, pregnant woman? Surely the mental picture engraved upon the impressible

mother's mind must result disastrously upon the embryo child. It is well known that a momentary fright or sight of some repulsive object will leave an indelible impression upon the unborn babe, thus disfigured for life. Is it not probable that the impress of some horrible crime thus stamped upon the unborn, may, in years to come, yield the fruit of murder? (256)

It was a line of thought that spiritualists had long pursued. In 1875, for example, Addie Ballou had led a petition drive asking Massachusetts Governor William Gaston to commute the death sentence of young serial murderer Jesse Pomeroy to life imprisonment. She argued that Pomeroy was less than fully culpable because he had been made prone to butchery and murder when his mother, while he was still in her womb, repeatedly visited the slaughterhouse where his father was employed and watched his work (Schlesinger: 146–147).

The fear about uncontrolled and wanton influence on "the race," however, was wider still. The anxiety among whites after the Civil War about the large numbers of free blacks and non-Anglo immigrants in the country had its particular effect on the complex of ideas about sexual inheritance and the elevation of the race. This was reflected in spiritualists' notions about "the real reason why spirits have come to Earth," as one spiritualist put it (Henry Brown). That reason, it seemed, was to counteract "downward" pressures on the race, and the spirits would accomplish that through mixing their ethereal essences into the reproductive pool (Chase: 81–84). For some spiritualists, the "race" that the spirits were going to protect was the human race as a whole, but for some other spiritualists, it was plainly the white race (Andrews 1870a). The other races might progress to become white or might simply fade away, as it were. Some spiritualists who had been ardent antislavery activists, such as Warren Chase and Stephen Pearl Andrews, who might have been expected to resist theories of racial superiority, were instead their eager proponents.

During and after the Civil War, spiritualists, working from flawed notions of biological inheritance, advocated "progressive" public policies that would protect and promote "blood purity." They opposed the practice of vaccination (because it involved injecting the blood products, i.e., cowpox antibodies, from another, lower species into humans, thereby "contaminating" their blood). They supported antimiscegenation laws.

Many of them opposed Darwinian evolution, even as they embraced a "spirit-inspired" form of Social Darwinism. Although most spiritualists were progressives and held that the Earth and its creatures evolved and developed, they—like evolutionists influenced by Jean Baptist Lamarck—also believed that this process was purposeful. Spiritualists believed it was ultimately guided by an immaterial, spiritual intelligence. In this they were encouraged by Alfred Russel Wallace, codiscoverer with Darwin of the modern theory of evolution, who was finally at odds with Darwin on the question of whether it was a teleological process. Wallace had become a spiritualist.

One challenge of the materialism that appeared to be implicit in Darwinian theory arose from the question of whether the human "spirit" might simply be a product of biological evolution, an epiphenomenon of the physical organism. Spiritualism could not accept that, for it had described a universe full of intelligent, active spirits that had detached themselves from their bodies. Not surprisingly, some spiritualists proposed explanations for how the human spirit or soul had been implanted into physically evolved apes: Spiritual beings from other planets—or angels— had originally seeded the intelligent spirits of the human race onto the Earth and had recently begun doing so again in order to rejuvenate the race, essentially to insure that the human species would not "bolt" and revert to the degraded animal state it occupied before it had become an animal–spirit hybrid (Blavatsky 1888: 81–86; Newton 1857).

Shortly after the turn of the century, the modern understanding of the mechanisms of genetic inheritance had overcome ideas about female biology that had restricted women's social roles. It demonstrated that hereditary characteristics had a comprehensive material basis and that they were derived equally from both parents. It also undercut the idea that spiritual states and immaterial characteristics were translated into the womb and inherited by the child. Such of these as might influence the child were shifted to the category of "nurture" rather than "nature" and located in the period after birth.

The earlier reproductive notions nevertheless lingered on past the turn of the century. In her 1920 book *Woman and the New Race*, Margaret Sanger hinted that "weighty medical authorities" still accepted that "through the female alone comes those modifications of form, capacity and ability which constitute evolutionary progress" (228).

The spirits had instructed John Spear in 1858 that a sensitive woman could channel (as we would say today) the actual spirit of Reubens, Archimedes, or Galileo into the unborn child growing within her by constantly looking at Reubens's paintings or by studying astronomy or mathematics (Spear 1858b).[9] Similar language appeared in the closing words of Sanger's book. By that time, however, it would seem to have lost the force

---

[9] Spear's associate P. B. Randolph wrote of "living pictures" (116) and referred the origin of the practice to Hermes Trismegistus, but the provenance of this "translated" text of Randolph is unclear (Deveney: 364). The spirits consecrated Spear's and Hinckley's son as "The Mathematician," perhaps because Hinckley had to devote considerable energy during her pregnancy to keeping track of the finances of Spear's little utopian settlement.

of a literal description of the biological mechanics by which spirit animates matter and by which the actual spirits of the exalted dead might reinhabit the world. Despite her rearguard defense of the earlier reproductive model placing the responsibility for heredity only with the mother, Sanger's language here would seem to have been more rhetorical:

> When the womb becomes fruitful through the desire of an aspiring love, another Newton will come forth to unlock further the secrets of the earth and the stars. There will come a Plato who will be understood, a Socrates who will drink no hemlock, and a Jesus who will not die upon the cross. These and the race that is to be in America await upon a motherhood that is to be sacred because it is free. (234)

The newer science of genetics, however, as it took shape toward the beginning of the twentieth century, with the insights of August Weismann and Gregor Mendel, rejected the inheritance of "acquired characteristics," including momentary, mental, or spiritual ones. Its consequence was to allow women a basis on which to regard themselves as independent agents of heredity, equal with men, with the right to control their own reproductive activity.

By the time the word *sexism* came along again in 1968, its new usage referred to an inappropriate discrimination between the sexes, not to an appropriate discrimination between them. If the word *sexism* in its first meaning was meant to help elevate women, then, in the meaning it would have one hundred years later, in its second incarnation, it was meant to uncover, and help to remove, false limits on their rights.

REFERENCES

American Association of Spiritualists 1873
Proceedings of the Tenth Annual Convention of the American Association of Spiritualists, Held at Grow's Opera Hall, Chicago, on Tuesday, Sept. 16. Chicago: American Association of Spiritualists.

Andrews, Stephen Pearl 1870a
"How to Kill Mosquitoes, Flies, Wood-Lice, Bed-Bugs, Cockroaches, Centipedes, Prairie Dogs, Wolves, and Other 'Varmints.' The Pantarch's Recipe." *New York Woodhull and Claflin's Weekly*, 22 October.

1870b
"Stirpiculture; Scientific Propagation; the Founding of a New Race of Human Beings. The Men and the Women of the Future—How They Are to Be Generated. The Reconstruction of the Physiology of Man." *New York Woodhull and Claflin's Weekly*, 10 September.

Ballou, Addie Lucia   "Spirithathesis, or The Birth and Development of Spirit"
1872   *Chicago Religio-Philosophical Journal,* 22 June 1872–
5 July 1873, nos. 1–7.

Barrett, Joseph   *The Gadarene: or, Spirits in Prison.* Boston: Colby and
Osgood, and James   Rich.
Martin Peebles
1874

Bartlett, George C.   *The Salem Seer: Reminiscences of Charles H. Foster.* New
1891   York: United States Book Co.

Blavatsky, Helena   *Isis Unveiled: A Master-Key to the Mysteries of Ancient
Petrovna   and Modern Science and Theology.* Vol. 1. 6th ed. New
1877   York: J. W. Bouton.

1888   *The Secret Doctrine: The Synthesis of Science, Religion
and Philosophy.* Vol. 2. London: Theosophical Publishing Co.

Braude, Ann   *Radical Spirits: Spiritualism and Women's Rights in
1989   Nineteenth-Century America.* Boston: Beacon Press.

Briggs, Robert R.   "Sitting for the Picture of a Spirit." *New York Spiritual
1855   Telegraph,* 5 May: 7.

Brittan, Samuel Byron   "A Wonderful Spirit-Photo." *New York Spiritual Tele-
1854   graph,* 9 December: 127.

1855a   "Spirits and Photography." *New York Spiritual Telegraph,*
3 March: 174.

1855b   "Spiritual Forms Daguerreotyped." *New York Spiritual
Telegraph,* 24 February: 171.

1855c   "Spiritual Light Daguerreotyped." *New York Spiritual
Telegraph,* 31 March: 190.

1855d   "Spiritualist Terminology." *New York Spiritual Telegraph,* 15 September: 71.

1857a   "New York Conference." *New York Spiritual Age,* 13
June: 31.

1857b   "Progenitive Law." *New York Spiritual Age,* 19 September: 79.

1864   *Man and His Relations: Illustrating the Influence of the
Mind on the Body, the Relations of the Faculties to the
Organs and to the Elements, Objects and Phenomena of the
External World.* New York: S. B. Brittan and Son.

1873   "Relations of Mind to Offspring." *New York Brittan's
Journal of Spiritual Science, Literature, Art, and Inspiration,* April: 327.

Brown, Hannah F. M.   *The False and True Marriage: The Reason and Results.*
1861   2d ed. Cleveland: Viets and Savage.

Brown, Henry   "Angels Our Saviors, or Spiritualism versus Race De-
Harrison   terioration." *Chicago Religio-Philosophical Journal,* 4
1880   September.

Browne, Rufus King   "Parthenogenesis." *New York Spiritual Age,* 26 Septem-
1857   ber: 85.

Buescher, John   "Photographing Heaven." Available at www.spirithistory.
2001   com.

Carroll, Bret E.   *Spiritualism in Antebellum America.* Bloomington: In-
1997   diana University Press.

Chase, Warren   *The Gist of Spiritualism: Viewed Scientifically, Philo-
1865   sophically, Religiously, Politically, and Socially; in a Course
of Five Lectures, Delivered in Washington, D.C., January,
1865.* Boston: Colby and Rich.

Colby, Luther, ed.   "Massachusetts State Convention, Third Quarterly Meet-
1866a   ing, at Lawrence, Mass., Oct. 10, 11 and 12, 1866." *Boston Banner of Light,* 20 October: 5.

1866b   "Massachusetts State Convention, Third Quarterly Meeting." *Boston Banner of Light,* 27 October: 3.

1866c   "Massachusetts State Convention, Third Quarterly Meeting." *Boston Banner of Light,* 3 November: 3.

1866d   "Massachusetts State Convention, Third Quarterly Meeting." *Boston Banner of Light,* 10 November: 2.

1867a   "Second Annual Convention of the Massachusetts State
Association of Spiritualists, Held in Tremont Temple,
Boston, Mass., January 9th and 10th, 1867." *Boston
Banner of Light,* 19 January: 4.

1867b   "Second Annual Convention of the Massachusetts State
Association of Spiritualists." *Boston Banner of Light,* 26
January: 3.

Denton, William,   *The Soul of Things; or, Psychometric Researches and Dis-
and Elizabeth M. F.   coveries.* 7th rev. ed. Wellesley, MA: Denton Publish-
1884   ing Co.

Deveney, John Patrick   *Paschal Beverly Randolph: A Nineteenth-Century Black
1997   American Spiritualist, Rosicrucian, and Sex Magician.*
Albany: State University of New York Press.

Dixon, Joseph   "A Criticism." *Boston Banner of Light,* 16 February: 2.
1867

Dods, John Bovee 1850 — *The Philosophy of Electrical Psychology: In a Course of Twelve Lectures.* New York: Fowler and Wells.

Farnham, Eliza Woodson Burhans 1864 — *Woman and Her Era.* New York: A. J. Davis.

Foote, Edward Bliss 1876 — *The Physical Improvement of Humanity.* New York: Murray Hill Publishing.

Fourier, Charles 1857 — *The Social Destiny of Man; or, Theory of the Four Movements by Charles Fourier. Translated by Henry Clapp, Jr. with a Treatise on the Functions of the Human Passions and an Outline of Fourier's System of Social Science, by Albert Brisbane.* New York: R. M. Dewitt.

Fowler, Orson Squire 1843 — *Hereditary Descent; Its Laws and Facts Illustrated and Applied to the Improvement of Mankind; with Hints to Woman; Including Directions for Forming Matrimonial Alliances So as to Produce in Offspring Whatever Physical, Mental or Moral Qualities Are Desired; Together with Preventives of Hereditary Tendencies.* New York: O. S. and L. N. Fowler.

Fowler, Samuel Theron [1882] 1921 — "Genesis: A New System of Learning." In *The Industrial Public: A Plan of Social Reconstruction in Line with Evolution.* Ed. by Horace N. Fowler. Reprint, Los Angeles: H. N. Fowler.

Gordon, Linda 1990 — *Woman's Body, Woman's Right: Birth Control in America.* Rev. ed. New York: Penguin Books.

Guarneri, Carl J. 1991 — *The Utopian Alternative: Fourierism in Nineteenth-Century America.* Ithaca, NY: Cornell University Press.

Hardinge (Britten), Emma 1867 — "The Marriage Relation." *Boston Banner of Light,* 2 March: 1.

1870 — *Modern American Spiritualism: A Twenty Years' Record of the Communion between Earth and the World of Spirits.* 2d ed. New York: Emma Hardinge (Britten).

1871 — "Spirit Art." In *The Year-Book of Spiritualism for 1871.* Ed. by Hudson Tuttle and James Martin Peebles. Boston: Banner of Light: 55–59.

Hawken, Frank 1928 — "Mrs. Henderson and Her Ectoplasmic Manifestations; the Phenomena in a Clear Red Light." *International Psychic Gazette* (London), December: 37–38.

Howitt, William   "The Mystic Crayon Drawings. A New Phase of Me-
1861   diumship." *Spiritual Magazine* (London), April: 173–
             180.

Hunt, Harriot Kesia   *Glances and Glimpses: or, Fifty Years Social, Including*
1856   *Twenty Years Professional Life.* Boston: John P. Jewitt
              and Co.

Jones, Stephens   "Extremisms." *Chicago Religio-Philosophical Journal,* 13
Sanborn   September: 2.
1873a

1873b   "Look at It, and Spurn It from Your Door." *Chicago
             Religio-Philosophical Journal,* 20 September: 2.

Keckeler, Temperance   *Thaleia: Woman, Her Physiology and Pathology, in Con-*
Hartman Kinsey   *nection with Maternity; with Hygienic and Medical Di-*
1869   *rections.* Cincinnati: Keckeler.

Laqueur, Thomas   "Orgasm, Generation and the Politics of Reproductive
1987   Biology." In *The Making of the Modern Body: Sexuality
              and Society in the Nineteenth Century.* Ed. by Catherine
              Gallagher and Thomas Laqueur. Berkeley: University of
              California Press.

Moore, R. Laurence   *In Search of White Crows: Spiritualism, Parapsychology*
1977   *and American Culture.* New York: Oxford University
              Press.

Moses, Stainton   "Researches in Spiritualism; by M. A. (Oxon), Spirit
1875   Photography—Chapter IV—(Continued) M. Buguet."
              Human Nature (London), February: 82.

Newton, Alonzo Eliot   "Convention in Buffalo." *Boston New-England Spiritu-*
1857   *alist,* 28 March.

1858   "Spiritualist Convention in Laona, N.Y." *New York
              Spiritual Age,* 30 October: 103.

1862   "Reserve—Its Uses." *Boston Banner of Light,* 24 May.

1863   "The Eucharist—Its Meaning and Value." *Spiritual
              Magazine* (London), October: 152.

1866   "Spiritualism in Religion—The Holy Spirit." *Spiritual
              Magazine* (London), July: 324.

1872   "The Limitations of True Freedom." *Boston Banner of
              Light,* 2 March: 1–2.

1875   *The Better Way: An Appeal to Men on Behalf of Human
              Culture through a Wiser Parentage.* New York: Wood
              and Holbrook.

1879   *Pre-Natal Culture: Suggestions to Parents Relative to Systematic Methods of Moulding the Tendencies of Off-spring before Birth.* Washington, DC: Moral Education Society of Washington.

Nichols, Thomas Low   *Esoteric Anthropology: A Comprehensive and Confiden-*
1853   *tial Treatise on the Structure, Functions, Passional Attractions and Perversions, True and False Physical and Social Conditions, and the Most Intimate Relations of Men and Women.* New York: Thomas Low Nichols.

Pancoast, Seth   *The Ladies' Medical Guide and Friend.* Philadelphia:
1871   Seth Pancoast.

Powell, William Byrd   *The Natural History of the Human Temperaments: Their*
1856   *Laws in Relation to Marriage, and the Fatal Consequences of Their Violation to Progeny, with the Indications of Vigorous Life and Longevity, Followed by a Fugitive Essay on the Protection of Society against Crime.* Cincinnati: A. T. and T. H. Keckeler.

Randolph, Paschal   *Sexual Magic.* Trans. and ed. by Robert North. New
Beverly   York: Magickal Childe Publishing.
1988

Sanger, Margaret   *Woman and the New Race.* New York: Brentano's
1920   Publishers.

Satter, Beryl   *Each Mind a Kingdom: American Women, Sexual Purity,*
1999   *and the New Thought Movement, 1875–1920.* Berkeley: University of California Press.

Saxon, Elizabeth Lyle   "Ante-Natal Impressions." *New York Brittan's Journal,*
1873   October: 531–533.

Sayles, Lita Barney   "Massachusetts Spiritualists' Association—'Integrality
1867   of Sexism.'" *Chicago Spiritual Republic,* 30 March: 196–197.

Schlesinger, Julia   *Workers in the Vineyard: A Review of the Progress of Spiri-*
1896   *tualism, Biographical Sketches, Lectures, Essays, and Poems.* San Francisco: Carrier Dove.

Sears, Hal D.   *The Sex Radicals: Free Love in High Victorian America.*
1977   Lawrence: Regents Press of Kansas.

Spear, John Murray   *The Educator: Being Suggestions, Theoretical and Prac-*
1857   *tical, Designed to Promote Man-Culture and Integral Reform, with a View to the Ultimate Establishment of a Divine Social State on Earth; Comprised in a Series of*

Revealments from Organized Associations in the Spirit-Life, through John Murray Spear. Ed. by Alonzo Eliot Newton. Boston: Office of Practical Spiritualists.

1858a "Birthology." Sheldon Papers, Darlington Memorial Library, University of Pittsburgh.

1858b "Human Chemistry—What Is It?" Sheldon Papers, Darlington Memorial Library, University of Pittsburgh.

1873 *Twenty Years on the Wing: Brief Narrative of My Travels and Labors as a Missionary Sent Forth and Sustained by the Association of Beneficents in Spirit Land.* Boston: William White and Co.

Spurlock, John C. *Free Love: Marriage and Middle-Class Radicalism in*
1988 *America, 1825–1860.* New York: New York University Press.

Stanton, Elizabeth "National Woman's Rights Convention, Cooper Insti-
Cady tute, 1856. Letter from Mrs. Stanton." In *History of*
1856 *Woman Suffrage,* vol. 1: 860–861. Ed. by Elizabeth Cady Stanton, Susan B. Anthony, and Matilda J. Gage. New York: Fowler and Wells.

Taves, Ann *Fits, Trances, and Visions: Experiencing Religion and*
1999 *Explaining Experience from Wesley to James.* Princeton: Princeton University Press.

Tuana, Nancy "The Weaker Seed: The Sexist Bias of Reproductive
1988 Theory." *Hypatia* 3 (spring): 35–60.

Wadsworth, "The Free Lusters." *Chicago Spiritual Republic,* 30
Frank L., ed. March: 196.
1867a

1867b "Massachusetts Spiritualists' Association." *Chicago Spiritual Republic,* 9 March: 152.

1867c "Massachusetts Spiritualists Association: Reply to E. S. Wheeler." *Chicago Spiritual Republic,* 4 May: 280.

Waisbrooker, Lois *From Generation to Regeneration: A Plain Guide to*
1875 *Naturalism.* Los Angeles: n.p.

Willard, Elizabeth *Sexology as the Philosophy of Life: Implying Social Orga-*
Osgood Goodrich *nization and Government.* Chicago: J. R. Walsh.
1867

Willis, Nathaniel "The Pencil of Nature; a New Discovery." *New York*
Parker *Corsair,* 13 April: 70–79.
1839

Woodhull (Martin),   "The Beecher-Tilton Scandal Case." *New York Wood-*
Victoria Claflin   *hull and Claflin's Weekly*, 2 November: 9–13.
1872

1873   *The Elixir of Life; or, Why Do We Die? An Oration De-livered before the Tenth Annual Convention of the Ameri-can Association of Spiritualists, at Grow's Opera House, Chicago, Ills., by Victoria C. Woodhull, September 18, 1873.* New York: Woodhull and Claflin.

Wright, Henry Clarke   *The Unwelcome Child: or, The Crime of an Undesigned*
1858   *and Undesired Maternity.* Boston: Bela Marsh.

1863   *The Empire of the Mother over the Character and Des-tiny of the Race.* Boston: Bela Marsh.

1867   "From H. C. Wright." *Chicago Spiritual Republic*, 2 March: 139.

 REVIEW ESSAY

Sacred Space in North America

Peter W. Williams

The Spiritual Traveler: New York City. The Guide to Sacred Spaces and Peaceful Places. By Edward F. Bergman. Hidden Spring (Paulist), 2001. 376 pages. $22.00.

Holy Personal: Looking for Small Private Places of Worship. By Laura Chester (photographs by Donna DeMari). Indiana University Press, 2000. 199 pages. $29.95.

American Sacred Space. Edited by David Chidester and Edward T. Linenthal. Indiana University Press, 1995. 352 pages. $19.95.

Shadowed Ground: America's Landscapes of Violence and Tragedy. By Kenneth E. Foote. University of Texas Press, 1997. 371 pages. $18.02.

The Hermeneutics of Sacred Architecture Experience, Interpretation, Comparison, vol. 1: Monumental Occasions: Reflections on the Eventfulness of Religious Architecture. By Lindsay Jones. Harvard University Center for the Study of World Religions/Harvard University Press, 2000. 326 pages. $22.00.

Peter W. Williams is Distinguished Professor of Comparative Religion and American Studies at Miami University, Oxford, OH 45056.

I would like to acknowledge direct and indirect contributions to this essay by Gary Ebersole, Paula M. Kane, Alan L. Miller, and Louis Nelson.

Journal of the American Academy of Religion September 2002, Vol. 70, No. 3, pp. 593–609.
© 2002 The American Academy of Religion

The Hermeneutics of Sacred Architecture Experience, Interpretation, Comparison, vol. 2: Hermeneutical Calisthenics: A Morphology of Ritual-Architectural Priorities. By Lindsay Jones. Harvard University Center for the Study of World Religions/Harvard University Press, 2000. 498 pages. $47.00.

Blessed Events: Religion and Home Birth in America. By Pamela E. Klassen. Princeton University Press, 2001. 316 pages. $18.95.

Preserving Memory: The Struggle to Create America's Holocaust Museum. By Edward T. Linenthal. Viking, 1995. 336 pages. $17.50.

Myths in Stone: Religious Dimensions of Washington, D.C. By Jeffrey F. Meyer. University of California Press, 2001. 343 pages. $35.00.

Gods of the City: Religion and the American Urban Landscape. Edited by Robert A. Orsi. Indiana University Press, 1999. 402 pages. $19.95.

THE EVENTS NOW universally known as "9/11," which took place at "Ground Zero," have been chronicled in the press and reacted to by untold Americans as events of extraordinary power and meaning. Although the term *hierophany* has not yet appeared in any account I have come across, the vocabulary of religion has from early on appeared in accounts of reactions of the victims' relatives; officials trying to devise an appropriate strategy for regulating the ruins; and artists, architects, and critics as well as local notables, such as New York City's mayor Rudolph Giuliani, speculating on what form an appropriate memorial might take and what balance it might strike with rebuilt commercial structures. Words and phrases such as *sacred place, sacred area,* and *shrine* recur frequently in this public discourse, as do activities such as cordoning off the area in which human remains were long intermingled with debris and the spontaneous fashioning of memorials to the dead. The student of religion in North America will naturally try to give an account of these events beyond a simple recording of who did and said what when. The problem then arises as to what sort of language and conceptual system over this transformation of American space is sufficiently precise for such a description and interpretation.

The following essay is an attempt to survey the state of the discussion of the general subject of "sacred space" in the North American context, from the viewpoint particularly of scholars who specialize in the post-Columbian history of that continent. Perhaps not surprisingly, part of the conclusion will be that the scope and meaning of the term *sacred space* in this context are by no means a matter of general agreement. In an effort to demonstrate the ways in which the term has been used both in recent scholarly and in more quotidian discourse, I will attempt to survey the relevant recent literature, discussing at some length those works especially that illustrate and advance the level of such discussion, that is, those books listed first above, with briefer references to a number of items listed in the accompanying references. I will first take a look at some recent works that directly address theoretical issues, followed by several more empirical areas of investigation, which I shall for convenience identify as "institutional," "ethnic," "public," and "domestic" sacred or religious places.

THEORY

A useful summary of the Eliadean approach to the issue is the entry on sacred space by Joel P. Brereton in *The Encyclopedia of Religion;* the latter closes with a useful bibliographical piece identifying salient texts by Eliade as well as a number of other, mainly more recent, contributions to the discussion. Although Brereton does not explicitly engage in criticism of Eliade, his concluding paragraph, which is worth citing, downplays the ontological nature of such space—an issue for which Eliade has encountered much criticism with regard to his alleged lack of clarity as to whether the "sacred" aspect of such space is such in ultimate reality or simply in the mind of the designator. Brereton stresses the social nature of such constructions:

> We began with the assumption that if a place is the location of ritual activity or its object, then it is sacred. To designate a place as sacred imposes no limit on its form or its meaning. It implies no particular aesthetic or religious response. But if sacred places lack a common content, they have a common role. To call a place sacred asserts that a place, its structure, and its symbols express fundamental cultural values and principles. By giving these visible form, the sacred place makes tangible the corporate identity of a people and their world. (534)

For some writers, such as Belden Lane, the ambiguously implicit theological formulations of Eliade's are not a problem. Lane, in his recently reissued *Landscapes of the Sacred,* presents a series of essays on particular instances of sacred spaces or religious landscapes in North America together with a set of categories for recognizing the phenomenon not only in a variety of religiocultural contexts but also in one's own personal experience. Lane leaves little doubt that such phenomena are in an important sense "real" rather than simply perceived to be such. For others—notably Lindsay Jones—Eliade's categories remain foundational for further exploration of the theme but need some recasting to be palatable to those who do not wish to enter into the realms of ontological speculation. In a two-volume attempt to bring about this reappraisal, Jones devotes his entire first volume to laying out his hermeneutical enterprise, relying heavily on the thought of Hans-Georg Gadamer. For those who are more interested in the interpretation of religious buildings themselves, Jones's major insight is that buildings can be an important source of evidence for the religious life not simply of the people who originally erect them but, rather, as the basis over time of what he identifies as "ritual-architectural events" (1: xxviii). Although knowledge of the intentions of the designers and sponsors of such structures is important evidence for such an understanding, Jones rejects the notion that such intentions are fully determinative of a religious building's "meaning." Rather, he invokes what he calls "ritual-architectural reception theory" as a methodology in which not only these sorts of data but also all evidence of the uses to which a building is put over time and the responses of all identifiable players in its use go to define the dialogical process that constitutes meaning (1: xxix). In developing the theoretical underpinnings of this method, Jones goes on to invoke a variety of scholars and theorists from a wide range of disciplines to reflect on its implications.

Volume 2 of Jones's opus resembles the first in a variety of ways. Each has copious endnotes and a lengthy bibliography, the latter of which is identical in each volume. Jones's prose is also noteworthy for its heavily Latinate character as well as the author's rather leisurely style, which results in considerable repetition (although, surprisingly, these works are not particularly difficult to read). The second volume begins with a summary of the first, an advantage for those who wish to cut to the proverbial chase rather than working through the *Grundrissen*. A lengthy appendix ("An Expanded Morphology of Ritual-Architectural Priorities" [2: 295–332]) contains what for many will be the work's most valuable feature: a detailed outline or checklist of categories against which any given religious building can be appraised and—a major emphasis for Jones—compared with other works, not primarily with regard to style, construction, or tradition but, rather, in terms of similar or differing religious/ritual purpose. He posits three broad interpretive categories: architecture seen respectively in terms of orientation, commemoration, and ritual context (2: 3). These are further broken down in the subsequent discussion and in the appendix into a complex set of elaborated subcategories, which he characterizes as "a kind of checklist, which enumerates an extended pattern of hermeneutical questioning, that students of sacred architecture can bring to bear on whatever specific ritual-architectural circumstance has captured their imagination" (2: 295). Jones stresses throughout that a major part of his task is the rescuing of the comparative method from the functional anarchism of contemporary thinkers like Michel Foucault, whom he also invokes frequently but far less approvingly.

The larger part of the second volume consists of a leisurely exploration of these comparative categories. The same advice might be given to a reader of Jones as has often been rendered to students assigned James's *The Varieties of Religious Experience* or Eliade's *Patterns in Comparative Religion:* skip the examples. Jones ranges widely over space and time for the latter, focusing frequently on his own area specialty of Mesoamerica. North Americanists will perhaps regret his scanting of post-Columbian developments in what are now the United States and Canada, although his methods of interpretation presumably apply equally well to more recent western phenomena as they do to traditional and archaic cultures. (Another common criticism of Eliade is that he dismisses modern culture as religiously thin and veritably exudes nostalgia for the archaic—the good old days when everyone attempted to live *in illo tempore.*)

Although the reader may wonder about the editorial decision to publish his work in two separate volumes, Jones's achievement is impressive and useful. While recognizing the value of Eliade's formulations as tools in identifying commonalities among religious traditions, he demythologizes the older thinker's work by putting metaphysical questions into brackets and emphasizing the dynamic character of religious rituals as acted out in significant physical settings, rather than focusing on the static qualities of unchanging structures without regard to the actual experience of those who interact with them over sometimes lengthy periods of time. Jones is also very clear as to what he sees as both the provisional and the pragmatic character of his work. In doing so, he indirectly calls attention to the tension that has from its beginnings as a disciplinary approach characterized the *religionswissenschaftlich* enterprise, namely, that between empirical description and analysis, on the one hand, and the impulse to make pronouncements on broader philosophical questions about the "essence" of religion, on the other. Although the temptation to play the sage and to give definitive answers to the "big" questions was greater for many of the pioneers of the enterprise—Freud, Durkheim, and Eliade himself come to mind—than for more recent generations, Jones makes what for many is the obvious leap in disowning interest in the latter and instead focuses on plausible descriptions and partial answers in the ongoing scholarly quest for making sense out of the inexhaustible data of human religious experience.

If Jones engages with Eliadean categories via a "hermeneutics of restoration"—a term coined by Giles Gunn which Jones favors—the editors of another important work on sacred space in the American context invoke instead a "hermeneutics of suspicion" (Jones, 1: 18). In their lengthy introduction to *American Sacred Space*, David Chidester and Edward T. Linenthal make clear that Foucault rather than Eliade is a more reliable guide to addressing the question of what might make a space "sacred," especially in the North American context. The editors begin by positing three attributes of sacred space: its ritual context, its significance in focusing central human questions, and its "inevitably contested" character (9–15). Although the first two of these in such general formulations would probably be acceptable to neo-Eliadeans such as Jones, the third most likely would not. The editors emphasize this putative unacceptability by making clear their own antipathy to Eliadean thought as productive of "easy pieties about sacred space as peaceful center and cosmic point of harmonial orientation" (a phrase employed by the series editors, Catherine Albanese and Stephen Stein, in describing the collective point of view of the volume's contributors [ix]) and "mystical theology" (18). Rather, the essays herein collected reject a focus on attempts by ruling elites to legitimize their hegemonic powers through the exploitation of popular nostalgia for ontological security by creating reassuring "sacred" places, which mask the trials of life in the mundane world of political and economic struggle and promise instead access for the compliant to an unchanging realm of supernatural well-being (18).

The essays that constitute this volume venture out in a number of directions, in the process bypassing such traditional spatial manifestations of institutional religion as churches, temples, and meetinghouses. Jacques Derrida is here invoked to legitimate the claim that "sacred meaning and significance, holy awe and desire, can coalesce in any place that becomes, even if only temporarily, a site for intensive interpretation." Examples of such sacralizable space might include "cities; homes; schools; cemeteries; hospitals; asylums, and prisons; tourist attractions; museums, and even shopping malls" (Chidester and Linenthal: 14). (Derrida's own example is post offices, apparently the occasion of an epiphany for him.) The essays in the body of this work are divided into three categories: land, built environments, and the United States itself as a mythic space (20–23). All of these in one way or another illustrate the themes that sacred space is not confined to buildings explicitly designed for the performance of the rituals of organized Euro-American religion and that each has been, or continues to be, the subject of contestation. (A clear illustration of the latter is Robert S. Michaelsen's "Dirt in the Courtroom: Indian Land Claims and American Property Rights" [Chidester and Linenthal: 43–98].)

It is clear that some of Jones's rhetorical strategy in his volume-long methodological prolegomenon is intended to defuse many of the criticisms here leveled at the Eliadean tradition by the editors and others writing in a similar vein; *American Sacred Space*, in fact, is practically the only volume on recent North America included in Jones's massive bibliographies. As suggested earlier, Jones argues for a neo-Eliadean approach that makes no claims to philosophical finality or theological definitiveness and which takes into account the responses and strategies of the politically weak as well as the empowered, thus accommodating the emphasis in much recent theoretical writing on strategies of subversion when overt opposition to oppressive rule is impractical. We will return to some of these issues at the end of this essay.

INSTITUTIONAL SPACE

Because I have written at some length elsewhere on the literature of North American religious architecture in the various Euro-American traditions, I will speak only briefly here on some of the issues involved in its study (Williams 1997a, 1997b). Until recently, there was little discussion of any sort on this subject, for it seemed to fall in the cracks between the expertise of architectural historians who knew little about religion and religious historians who knew little about architecture. Fortunately, more information on religious buildings as well as many other architectural genres is becoming accessible through such enterprises as the Buildings of America series, sponsored by the Society of Architectural Historians and published by Oxford University Press. To date, volumes have appeared on Alaska, Colorado, the District of Columbia, Iowa, Michigan, and Virginia (Tidewater and Piedmont), with plans for coverage of all fifty states plus the District. Although this series does not focus on religion, its inclusion of many religious buildings, such as the excellent essay on Russian Orthodox architecture in *Buildings of Alaska*, makes the task of surveying this material considerably more accessible (Hoagland).

More specialized monographic work on North American "mainline" religious buildings has been carried out primarily by younger scholars trained in American studies, American social and cultural history, or architectural history. Virtually all humanities scholars in recent years have had to come to terms with the challenges posed by cultural studies, poststructuralism, and other ideologically self-conscious movements to read texts (including material ones such as buildings) not simply in light of formal analysis or diachronic development but against the political and economic struggles underlying their creation. Thus, it is not surprising to find some of these concerns in more recent scholarship on religious buildings.

Similarly, History of Religions issues, especially the "sacred space" theme, occasionally appear in this scholarship. Harold Turner's *From*

Temple to Meeting House, a lengthy phenomenological study of the development primarily of Christian architecture in the West, is sometimes
cited in this literature. Turner provides a framework for understanding
the development of Christian and Jewish architecture in his ideal-type
opposition of temple (*domus dei*) and meetinghouse (*domus ecclesiae*), an
opposition that becomes heated in the wake of the Protestant Reforma-
tion(s) and the appearance of the "meetinghouse" as both place and term.
Although simplistic if taken too literally, this typology is heuristically useful
if employed with the caveat that real life phenomena are not usually so
easily classifiable. Turner acknowledges this in his theologically prescriptive ending.

On the whole, however, students of the built environments of Euro-
American religion have included such concerns as part of their broader
interpretive strategy without focusing on them to the exclusion of the more
traditional issues of architectural, cultural, and religious history. Such
works include Karla Goldman's study of the role of women in nineteenth-
century American Judaism, which devotes considerable attention to the
internal arrangements of temples and synagogues with an eye to gender
issues; Paul Eli Ivey's work on the early history of Christian Science churches
and their designers' attempts to identify with Progressive values in the
emergent American city; Gretchen Buggeln's study of church building in
Connecticut in the early republic; and Jeanne Halgren Kilde's tracing of the
development of the auditorium church in the nineteenth century with an
eye to the hierarchical implications of internal spatial arrangements.

ETHNIC SPACE

Like many others, the word *ethnic* has undergone a major shift in meaning during the past few decades. At one time it referred primarily to sub-
cultures within the United States that were constituted by the immigration
of Europeans (and, to a lesser extent, Chinese and other Asians) who lived
"betwixt and between" their old worlds and the English-speaking American mainstream. More recently, *ethnic* and *racial* have become conflated,
with the former frequently used to describe those social and cultural groups
that deliberately or otherwise stand apart from the (rapidly decreasing)
"Anglo" majority. This includes Native Americans, African Americans,
Latinos, and Asian Americans. The literature on Native American culture,
which has often included descriptions of the distinctive construal of space
as part of cultural systems, is simply too large to tackle here; let me simply
mention Michaelsen's above-cited essay as representative of a growing body
of literature treating current matters of legal dispute over land possession,
use, and desecration, which have roots in the long-standing cultural oppo-

sitions between Native and Euro-Americans in construing and inhabiting land.

The literature on Hispanic religion in North America is considerable, including both scholarly and more popular studies of shrines and churches in Mexico and the Spanish borderlands of the United States (see Williams 1997b: ch. 6, bibliography). That which attempts to bring analytic categories from the history of religions (as opposed to church history and architectural history) is considerably more limited. Notable among such literature is Thomas Tweed's study of what he calls the diasporic religion of Cuban exiles in southern Florida, as exemplified in La Ermita, the shrine built on the Miami shore that invokes La Virgen de la Cobre de Caridad, the patroness of Cuba. Similar studies of the cult of the Virgin of Guadalupe among Mexican Americans, as well as of Mexican American shrines in the Southwest or, for that matter, even the Spanish missions during the late colonial era, still await definitive scholarly attention. A good beginning, however, is James S. Griffith's *Beliefs and Holy Places*, which bears the intriguing and descriptive subtitle *A Spiritual Geography of the Pimería Alta*. Griffith takes as his subject the interactions among the "Anglo," Hispanic, and indigenous peoples (primarily the Tohono O'odham and Yaqui) in the central Arizona–Sonora borderlands. Particularly interesting from the point of view of the religious construal of space are his treatments of roadside shrines (which have become a more frequent feature of the broader U.S. landscape in recent years, with a considerable boost from the events of 9/11), as well as the remarkable shrine in downtown Tucson to El Tiradito, an unfortunate young man shot when engaged in adultery and eventually the subject of a National Historic Landmark designation indicating that his is "the only shrine in the United States dedicated to the soul of a sinner buried in unconsecrated ground" (105).

If there is a superabundance of literature on Native American conceptions of sacred space, the opposite is true with regard to African Americans. One of the few volumes to treat this topic is entitled simply *Sacred Space* and consists primarily of a collection of photographs by Tom Rankin of black churches, their interiors and furnishings, burial grounds, and the clientele who make use of them in the Mississippi Delta. Brief introductory essays by southern historian Charles Reagan Wilson and by the photographer himself present, respectively, an Eliadean reading of the churches and their settings and a local minister's narrative of his experience of what might be called a hierophany.

The most recent influx of immigration, precipitated by the Hart-Cellar Act of 1965, has been that of Asians, whose presence in the United States had been highly restricted by previous governmental policies. Although the recent proliferation of Islamic, Buddhist, and Hindu houses of worship has been duly noted, there has not yet been an extensive literature of description and analysis. An important exception is Joanne Punzo Waghorne's article on a Hindu temple in Robert Orsi's *Gods of the City* (103–130), a rich collection of essays on contemporary American ethnic communities, many of which contain provocative analyses of the spatial dimensions of religious life. Waghorne analyzes the Sri Siva–Vishnu temple recently built in the suburbs of Washington, D.C., by a community of immigrants from a variety of regions in India. Like many other American Hindu temples, this represents a compromise, focusing not on one Hindu deity, as would usually be the case in India, but, as the name indicates, on at least two, reflecting the manifold origins of the constituents. Waghorne also gives a sensitive treatment of the notion of sacred space in this context: "The 'space' of the . . . Temple exists somewhere amid the concreteness of the traditional temple, the ethereal space of 'traditional' India, the newer creation of an ideological motherland, and the shifting space of the everywhere/nowhere/everybody's/nobody's split-level world of the migrating international middle class" (110–111). (Other essays in the Orsi volume deal with Haitian Vodou, Jews, Italians, Japanese, Cubans, and the Salvation Army.)

PUBLIC SPACE

Thus far, most of the literature we have surveyed has dealt with structures and places that are readily identified as religious space, whether associated with institutionalized religious activity or not. Recently, a considerable literature has been developing that employs the phrase "sacred space" with reference to a wider range of public spaces. A good example of such a work, written by a geographer, published by a Roman Catholic house, and presumably intended for a broad, nonspecialist audience, is Edward F. Bergman's *The Spiritual Traveler: New York City*, the second volume in Paulist Press's The Spiritual Traveler series. A Publisher's Weekly blurb on the back cover is illuminating: "This is the first series to cater to the growing market for spiritual travel books." A series of excerpts from the author's introduction is also illuminating:

> Some form of spirituality is essential to human life, and city dwellers follow many paths to find spiritual peace and strength. . . . Our story is not just of the sacred spaces, but of the spirituality that created them. . . . Additionally, this book introduces some of the city's vibrant new spiritual centers. . . . Many natural sites invoke spiritual repose or reflection. Our city parks are not technically consecrated, but Americans have long found a spiritual consecration in nature, and New York's oldest trees or most restful oases of calm take their place in this book. . . . [B]otanical gardens in the outer boroughs feature traditional Asian landscape designs

and plantings in which the contemplation of nature is interpreted as a
form of worshipful meditation. . . . [T]his book also draws your attention to some sites of historical events that evoke spiritual reflection, great
sacrifices, or monuments for human welfare: memorials to firefighters
and police officers who gave their lives, war memorials, homes of writers
of spiritual masterpieces, and locations where new initiatives in social
service were launched. (1–2)

Bergman's use of the terms *sacred* and *spiritual* is certainly far-rang-
ing (if not rigorous) and is a good indication of the turn such terms have
taken in the everyday American vocabulary, reflecting the deep penetration of New Age ideas of "spirituality" into the culture. Whatever one
might think of the author's conceptual scheme and analytic vocabulary,
however, this is a very useful book for exploring New York with an eye to
its religious landscape. Bergman provides an excellent glossary of architectural terms, including those relevant not only to Christian building but
to Jewish, Muslim, Hindu, Buddhist, and Sikh traditions as well. He also
notes—echoing New Yorker cartoons to the same effect—that "buildings
in New York have hired feng-shui consultants to guarantee propitious
alignment of design features, including doors and windows, mirrors, foun-
tains, and paintings" (49).

Bergman is certainly not the only geographer to turn his hand to the
issues of religious space. Americanists especially should be cognizant of
the usefulness of John Stilgoe's *Common Landscape of America, 1580 to
1845*. Especially in the early sections, which deal with traditional European landscapes as well as those created by settlers in colonial New Mexico,
New England, and the southern Tidewater and Piedmont regions, Stilgoe
is clearly working within an Eliadean paradigm, even though that scholar's
name appears explicitly only in one bibliographical citation. More recently,
geographers have turned their attention to landscapes of calamity, with
the events of Oklahoma City and 9/11 bringing such concerns into even
sharper focus. Yi-fu Tuan's *Landscapes of Fear* is frequently cited by those
offering descriptive typologies for the human spatial response to such
events.

A more recent geographical work is relevant in this context. In *Shadowed Ground: America's Landscapes of Violence and Tragedy*, written post–
Oklahoma City but pre-9/11, Kenneth Foote presents a fourfold typology
for understanding public responses to physical sites that have been the
scene of large-scale or notorious calamitous events, usually involving
multiple deaths. These include sanctification, which usually involves the
erection of a memorial or monument to preserve a positive lesson generated by the event; designation, a similar process but usually initiated by a
minority group to preserve the memory of an event neglected in public

recognition; rectification, in which the site of a tragedy, usually acciden-
tal, is simply reused without public note; and obliteration, a fate reserved
for the homes of serial killers and the like whose memory is an embarrassment to the community (Foote: 7). Foote's comments on the first of these
is of particular interest: "'Sanctification' involves the creation of what geographers term a 'sacred' place—a site set apart from its surroundings and
dedicated to the memory of an event, person or group. Sanctification almost always involves the construction of a durable marker . . . to be maintained in perpetuity" (8). The term *sacred*, moreover, is reserved in this
discourse for sites that are "publicly consecrated or widely venerated rather
than those owned or maintained by a religious group"; furthermore, they
are bounded, marked, and publicly maintained and are thus "transformed
into monuments that serve as reminders or warnings" (Foote: 8).

Among these sites that serve a public memorial function are those
connected with the "civil religion," to use a term no longer as widely used
in the post-Vietnam era as it once had been. Jeffrey F. Meyer's *Myths in
Stone* (2001) is a study, as the subtitle indicates, of the "religious dimensions of Washington, D.C.," a subject previously explored at least in general outlines in the writings of Robert Bellah and others on the "American
civil religion." The book is arranged in the form of a pilgrimage through
the city, with a historical and descriptive account of the major architectural
and artistic monuments of the Federal City built around the Mall. Meyer,
who has previously published *The Dragons of Tiananmen: Beijing as a Sacred City* (1991), not too surprisingly draws heavily on Paul Wheatley's
analysis of the symbolic dimensions of the city and invokes an essentially
Eliadean vocabulary of myth, symbol, and ritual, emphasizing especially
the symbolism of the center. Washington, he argues, is "a myth in stone,
whose meaning is not fixed but has continually changed in the two centuries since its founding" (2001: 50).

When discussing memorial space, one must, of course, refer to the
copious and insightful work of Edward T. Linenthal, whose editorial contribution has already been noted. Linenthal's most recent monograph is
a study of the Holocaust Museum in Washington, D.C., one of the newer
and more controversial additions to the "Mallscape." (Actually, virtually
all new proposals for memorials on the Mall have excited considerable
controversy since at least the time of Maya Lin's Vietnam Veterans' Memorial.) Unlike his earlier major work, *Sacred Ground: Americans and
Their Battlefields*, which begins with an introductory discussion of the
nature of sacred space, the later volume focuses on what in fact is the
methodological approach throughout the body of the first, that is, a historical analysis of the debates over the designation, design, and interpretation of the sites of significant historical conflict. Linenthal does include

a sensitive discussion of the emergence both of the architectural plan of the Holocaust Museum and its exhibits and notes that, to achieve the desired effect, "visitors had to be removed from American ground on elevators, and introduced to Holocaust space that would both house the experience and suggest with what kind of spirit they should approach it. Visitors were to take this journey with a heart and soul 'heavy and dark,' like the space itself" (170).

DOMESTIC SPACE

Another venue that a significant numbers of Americans invest with sacrality is their own homes. My earlier allusion to *feng shui* might introduce the topic, in the context of an Asian ritual import that has become part of the broader eclectic vocabulary of ritual forms that middle-class Americans have at their disposal simply through a visit to their favorite shopping mall Border's or Barnes and Noble, where they can find both *The Complete Idiot's Guide to Feng Shui* (Moran) and *Feng Shui for Dummies* (Kennedy). Anthony Lawler, an architect, broadens the scope of such potential transcultural borrowings in his *The Temple in the House*, in which he draws on examples from a wide variety of cultures as well as an at times explicitly Eliadean vocabulary to suggest the potential symbolic import of many architectural features found in the home or otherwise not specifically religious venues.

In a different vein, feminist scholars and practitioners have found in the reality of the house and the idea of the home a very different venue for sacred activity. Colleen McDannell, a pioneer in the investigation of the material culture of religion, has in her essay in the Chidester and Linenthal collection presented an account of the home schooling movement among American evangelicals. McDannell begins with the notion of the Christian home as a sort of domestic shrine promoted by Catharine Beecher and Harriet Beecher Stowe in the nineteenth century (188). The recent home schooling movement, although by no means confined to evangelicals, flourishes especially among religious conservatives who see themselves at war with the secular world. McDannell's treatment of the issue of what sort of space such homes thus become is summarized neatly in two statements:

> For domestic Christians the division is not between the sacred and the profane but between good and evil. The home is sacred space when it is a space where people act in accordance with God's laws. Sacrality is accomplished through behavior and not through the intrinsic meaning of an object. . . . Home as sacred space . . . is a domain of purity in a defiling environment. It is a place of empowerment in a disempowering world. (208, 214)

McDannell thus touches deftly on several important issues of definition: sacred space as empowering and as a zone of purity resisting defilement. She also implicitly points up the ambiguity in the Eliadean concept of the profane, rejecting the term in favor of the more straightforward *evil*.

Another noteworthy recent work is Pamela E. Klassen's *Blessed Events: Religion and Home Birth in America*. Klassen conducted interviews with women from a wide variety of religious and ideological backgrounds who have rejected the institutions of organized medicine in favor of birth at home. Her study neatly dovetails with McDannell's, which she cites, in its analysis of historical changes in religious attitudes toward the home. A century or so ago, a newly empowered medical profession rejected mid-wife-assisted home birth on the grounds that "the home was no longer considered pure, but instead was a host of contagion, amateurism, and danger. Home-birthing families, since the 1970s, have been working to invert the purity/pollution one more time" (Klassen: 112). Klassen goes on to characterize home-birth events as "domestic epiphanies," carried out in homes where "the sacred can surprise them, or simply come when entreated" (113–114). She goes on to discuss in some detail how such women and their families revivify aspects of their own religious traditions or invent new rituals for the occasion. (Laura Chester, in her lushly illustrated *Holy Personal*, begins her story of her search throughout the United States for examples of "small private chapel[s] built from the heart," as "an American story" of individuals, often in private rebellion against the impersonality and commercialism of traditional religion, adapting elements of their own traditions to craft "a small space that allows the imagination free reign, perhaps because of the safe feeling of the small container" [xviiii, 3]).

SOME CONCLUDING THOUGHTS

From this (partial) survey of the literature, it is certainly clear enough that interest in the significance of "sacred space" and "place" is widespread today, both in the academy, in an transdisciplinary way, and among the broader public, especially those involved in New Age activity, and others who are not entirely happy with the offerings of traditional religious groups, as well as those who invoke it in defense of a traditional but endangered way of life. However, it is less clear from this literature that the term *sacred space* itself, hallowed as its usage may have become, is still academically usable. Because the phrase now has become inextricably entwined with notions of power commanded or experienced by the individual or group that invokes it, it has become politicized to the point at which it loses its value as an analytical category. To insist, as do Chidester and Linenthal, that for space to be sacred it must first be contested recognizes the indubitable fact of contemporary widespread contestation but is too restrictive to describe all sorts of spaces that have been consecrated for ritual use. (Presumably many Americans regard the spaces at which they attend weekly worship to be part of the ordinary patterns of their lives rather than the objects or symbols of conflicts with their neighbors.) The fact, however, that the term *sacred space* (or some close variant) is widely used by all sorts and conditions of folk is an empirical datum that can and should be recorded and described.

Although there is probably no definition of *sacred space* that would satisfy everyone—just as, in our postmodern age, everyone has the right to designate whatever space they choose as "sacred"—there might be some semantic solutions that would facilitate an end run on the whole issue. If to designate a space as sacred is to make a political statement, let us relegate the term to nonacademic usage. Rather, we might instead talk about "ritual space" as a broader category that would include sites utilized not only for Catholic masses or Aztec sacrifices but also for civic parades, football games, living rooms, or any place in which ritual performance can be identified, and devise finer categories to sort out significantly different forms of ritual from one another. A religious scholar might still advise the courts as to whether a particular group, such as a Native American people, has traditionally regarded particular places as integral to their own belief and ritual systems—that is, as "sacred" by their own definition—and that such places therefore should be protected from the depredations of outsiders. However, for us as scholars of religion to continue to employ the term as one of formal classification and analysis simply gets us deeper into the inextricable morasses of debate as to who controls the term *sacred* by expanding or contracting its meaning to their own specifications.

REFERENCES

Brereton, Joel P. "Sacred Space." In *Encyclopedia of Religion*, vol. 12: 526–
1987 535. Ed. by Mircea Eliade. New York: Macmillan.

Buggeln, Gretchen T. *Saved by Grace: The Material Transformation of Con-*
forthcoming *necticut's Churches, 1790–1840.* Hanover, NH: University Press of New England.

Eliade, Mircea. *Patterns in Comparative Religion.* New York: Sheed and
1958 Ward.

Goldman, Karla *Beyond the Synagogue Gallery: Finding a Place for Women*
2000 *in American Judaism.* Cambridge: Harvard University Press.

Griffith, James S.   *Beliefs and Holy Places: A Spiritual Geography of the*
1992   *Pimería Alta.* Tucson: University of Arizona Press.

Hoagland, Alice   *Buildings of Alaska.* New York: Oxford University Press.
1993

Ivey, Paul Eli   *Prayers in Stone: Christian Science Architecture in the*
1999   *United States, 1894–1930.* Urbana: University of Illinois
              Press.

James, William   *The Varieties of Religious Experience: A Study in Human*
1902   *Nature.* London: Longmans, Green.

Kennedy, David D.   *Feng Shui for Dummies.* Foster City, CA: IDG Books
2001   Worldwide.

Kilde, Jeanne Halgren   *When Church Became Theatre: The Transformation of*
2002   *Evangelical Architecture and Worship in Nineteenth-*
              Century America. New York: Oxford University Press.

Lane, Belden   *Landscapes of the Sacred.* Baltimore: Johns Hopkins Uni-
2002   versity Press.

Lawler, Anthony   *The Temple in the House: Finding the Sacred in Every-*
1994   *day Architecture.* New York: G. P. Putnam's Sons.

Linenthal, Edward   *Sacred Ground: Americans and Their Battlefields.* Ur-
Tabor   bana: University of Illinois Press.
1991

Meyer, Jeffrey F.   *The Dragons of Tiananmen: Beijing as a Sacred City.*
1991   Columbia: University of South Carolina Press.

Moran, Elizabeth   *The Complete Idiot's Guide to Feng Shui.* New York:
1999   Alpha Books.

Rankin, Tom   *Sacred Space: Photographs from the Mississippi Delta.*
1993   Jackson: University Press of Mississippi.

Stilgoe, John R.   *Common Landscape of America, 1580 to 1845.* New Haven:
1982   Yale University Press.

Tuan, Yi-fu   *Landscapes of Fear.* Minneapolis: University of Minne-
1979   sota Press.

Turner, Harold   *From Temple to Meeting House: The Phenomenology and*
1979   *Theology of Places of Worship.* The Hague: Mouton.

Tweed, Thomas A.   *Our Lady of the Exile: Diasporic Religion at a Cuban*
1997   *Catholic Shrine in Miami.* New York: Oxford Univer-
              sity Press.

Wheatley, Paul   *The Pivot of the Four Quarters: A Preliminary Enquiry*
1971   *into the Origins and Character of the Ancient Chinese City.* Chicago: Aldine.

Williams, Peter W.   "The Built Environment of American Religion: The
1997a   State of the Art." *Material History of American Religion Project Newsletter* (fall). Available at http://www.materialreligion.org/journal/archbiblio.html.

1997b   *Houses of God: Region, Religion, and Architecture in the United States.* Urbana: University of Illinois Press.

AAR RESPONSES AND REJOINDERS

Myth and Politics: A Response to Robert Ellwood

IN HIS CAREFUL and balanced review of Bruce Lincoln's *Theorizing Myth* and my *Theorizing about Myth,* Robert Ellwood raises the key question of the political nature of myth. Ellwood shares with Lincoln the conviction that myth is political, as the title of Ellwood's own recent book, *The Politics of Myth* (1999), evinces. I part company with both Ellwood and Lincoln on this point. For me, some theories of myth are entirely apolitical. A theory could loosely be labeled political because the theorist holds political opinions but could tightly be so labeled because the theory itself views myth as a political vehicle. In deeming myth political, Ellwood shifts from one sense of political to another, though recognizing the shift. He considers the political opinions of William Jones, Nietzsche, Dumézil, Eliade, and Campbell but also asks "to what extent can the political views—and sins—of a mythological scholar . . . be said to stain all the scholar's work?" (2001: 679).

In my own efforts at organizing the array of theories of myth, I have distinguished between rationalist and romantic approaches. In *Work on Myth* Hans Blumenberg makes a similar distinction. Ellwood, too, uses this distinction but always emphasizes that both rationalists and romantics politicize myth, albeit in different ways: "Let us look again at Segal's division of myth interpretation into the rationalist and the romantic styles. It is important to realize that both can have baleful consequences as justifications for colonialism and racist nationalism" (2001: 680).

For rationalists, myth is the wholly "primitive" counterpart to science, which is exclusively modern. Myth and science are not merely redundant but outright incompatible: myth invokes the wills of gods to account for events in the world; science appeals to impersonal processes like those of

Journal of the American Academy of Religion September 2002, Vol. 70, No. 3, pp. 611–620.
© 2002 The American Academy of Religion

atoms. Because both purport to give direct accounts of events, one cannot stack a mythological account atop a scientific one. The rain god does not manipulate meteorological processes but, say, collects buckets of water and dumps them on a chosen spot. For rationalists, there can be no "modern myths," and the phrase is self-contradictory. Any lingering myths are sheer relics. For Ellwood (see 1999: 171) as well as for me, the epitome of a rationalist is the Victorian anthropologist Edward Tylor, to whom I devote the first chapter of my book.

Just what is political about a rationalist approach to myth? According to Ellwood, myths for rationalists "represent premodern, prescientific ways of looking at the world that have now been superseded"; science has "emancipated" us from "the shackles of ignorance, superstition, and despotism" (2001: 680). Progress means not only the replacement of personal explanations of the world by impersonal ones but also the replacement of particularistic explanations by generalizations: "This knowledge that emancipates is found through the generalized, abstract, rational ways of thinking characteristic of science and social science. . . . [T]he particular is subordinated to the abstract category; . . . the local submits to the universal" (Ellwood 2001: 680–681).

How fully does this characterization of rationalism fit Tylor? While Tylor clearly associates myth with primitives and associates science with moderns, the similarities rather than the differences between myth and science grab him. Like science, myth arises from observation and hypothesis. Myth is consummately rational, even if false. Primitives concoct myth rather than science only because they take the first explanation at hand: they analogize from their own behavior to invent humanlike agents to account for events in the world. Primitives are uncritical but hardly "superstitious." Myths "rest upon a broad philosophy of nature, early and crude indeed, but thoughtful, consistent, and quite really and seriously meant" (Tylor: vol. 1, 285). Primitives harbor the same intellectual curiosity as moderns (see Tylor: vol. 1, 368–369). Not to emotion but "to the human intellect" "may be assigned the origin and first development of myth" (Tylor: vol. 1, 284).

For Tylor, myth is as generalizable as science: whenever it rains, the same god has decided to send rain and for the same reason. Each kind of event in the world may be attributed to a different god with a different myth, but taken collectively myths offer a uniform account of all physical events. Each culture may have its own, "local" mythology, but Tylor's insistence on a comparative approach "makes it possible to trace in mythology [worldwide] the operation of imaginative processes recurring with the evident regularity of mental law" (vol. 1, 282). Myths are similar because imagination is tethered to reason. Asks Tylor rhetorically, "What would be popularly [but incorrectly] thought more indefinite and uncontrolled than the products of the imagination, in myths and fables?" (vol. 1, 18).

Here Tylor anticipates Claude Lévi-Strauss, the grandest twentieth-century reviver of a rationalist approach to myth. Like Tylor, Lévi-Strauss observes that although "it would seem that in the course of a myth anything is likely to happen," in fact "this apparent arbitrariness is belied by the astounding similarity between myths collected in widely different regions" (1965: 83). For both Tylor and Lévi-Strauss, the demonstration of uniformity in myth, the seemingly least orderly of artifacts, proves that not only it but also its primitive creators are scrupulously rational. Lévi-Strauss ventures beyond Tylor to argue that mythic thinking is itself scientific, simply the science of the concrete. Abstractions get expressed *through* the concrete (see Lévi-Strauss 1966: chap. 1).

Ellwood—or Lincoln—could rightly reply that for all of Tylor's respect for myth, it remains for him wholly primitive, inferior to science, incompatible with science, and superseded by science. Tylor may not be contemptuous, but he is patronizing. To fill in a line of his already quoted in part, "to the human intellect *in its early childlike state* may be assigned the origin and first development of myth" (vol. 1, 284, emphasis added). Paternalism, it could be argued, provides sufficient "justifications for colonialism and racist nationalism."

In response, I would simply note that for Tylor myth comes very close to science, so close that it is not even easy to figure out why it fails to be scientific (see Segal 1999: 7–10). Certainly Tylor does not regard primitives as incapable of advancing beyond myth to science. Moreover, because there were no moderns until there was science, it can only be the last generation of primitives that created science. Juxtapose to Tylor his antirationalist critic Lucien Lévy-Bruhl, for whom primitives are driven by emotion rather than intellect, are incapable of recognizing even the law of noncontradiction, and use myth not to explain anything but to re-create the fading experience of mystical oneness with the world (see Lévy-Bruhl: chap. 9).

Furthermore, myth for Tylor is hopelessly apolitical. For it is almost entirely about the physical world. Myth explains why it rains, not why marriage exists. Myth is the counterpart to natural science, not to social science.

Some rationalist theorists do tie myth to politics. James Frazer, whom Ellwood (see 1999: 171), like me, also considers a leading rationalist, parallels intellectual change to political change. Magicians become kings and "gradually rise to wealth and power" (Frazer: 104). Priests succeed magicians and themselves become kings, initially merely human but eventually divine, and "no class of the community has benefited so much as kings by this belief in the possible incarnation of a god in human form" (Frazer:

105). Frazer even writes of "the great social revolution which thus begins with democracy and ends in despotism" (104). At the same time the key activity now is the killing and replacement of the king to ensure the health of the god of vegetation residing in the incumbent. Indeed, the chief event in the king's reign *is* his death, which is undertaken for the sake of the community. The Frazerian Lord Raglan thus singles out the loss of the throne as the heart of his mythic pattern and pronounces the king heroic exactly because the king dies for the communal good. Myths celebrate the selfless heroism of past kings and inspire emulation (see Raglan: pt. 2). Still, myth for Raglan does not quite justify regicide, and for Frazer the subject matter of myth is the death and rebirth of the god of vegetation, not the killing and replacement of the king (see Segal 1999: 39–41, 130–134).

The theorist for whom myth *would* justify ritualistic regicide is Bronislaw Malinowski, but ironically Malinowski scorns the rationalist approach. For Malinowski, primitives have myth not in place of science but alongside science: "There is no doubt that even the lowest savage communities have the beginnings of science, however rudimentary" (34). Primitives use science, together with magic, both to explain and to control the physical world. They turn to myth when the world proves uncontrollable. Myths about natural phenomena such as floods supplement primitive science. They serve no political function. Myths about social phenomena such as rituals serve the incontestably political function of giving these phenomena, which are anything but unavoidable, a hoary origin and thereby the clout of tradition. But these myths run askew to science, not, as in rationalism, contrary to science.

Among rationalists, the theorist most keenly attuned to myth as political is Ernst Cassirer, mentioned by neither Ellwood nor Lincoln. On the one hand, Cassirer places myth, or mythic thinking, within his main forms of knowledge—science being another. While he takes unabashedly from Lévy-Bruhl the conception of myth as primitive, as emotion laden, and as projective, he claims to be breaking with Lévy-Bruhl in asserting that mythic thinking, rather than "prelogical," has its own brand of logic and in asserting that mythic thinking, rather than inferior to science, is an autonomous brand of knowledge (see Cassirer 1955: 21). Myth so characterized can be studied philosophically.

On the other hand, Cassirer comes to see myth as not merely primitive but also modern. Now he turns to political myths, notably those of Nazism. Myth here amounts to ideology and very much fits Lincoln's provocative definition of all myth as "ideology in narrative form." Having previously concentrated on sublime, epistemological issues, Cassirer now turns to brute, social scientific ones: How do political myths take and keep hold? Having previously scorned Lévy-Bruhl's supposed stress on the irrationality of myth, Cassirer now embraces it: "In all critical moments of man's social life, the rational forces that resist the rise of the old mythical conceptions are no longer sure of themselves. In these moments the time for myth has come again" (1946: 280). Tying myth to magic and magic to a desperate effort to control the world—here the social, not the physical, world—Cassirer applies to modern myths Malinowski's analysis of primitive myths. Modern myths constitute an atavistic revival of, for Cassirer, primitivism.

Yet Cassirer still does not fit Ellwood's rationalist bill because, in deeming political myths irrational, he cuts them off from philosophy. Myth now is anything but a form of knowledge with a distinctive logic to be teased out. The marginalized role left philosophy is to challenge political myths: "It is beyond the power of philosophy to destroy the political myths. A myth . . . is impervious to rational arguments. . . . But philosophy can do us another important service. It can make us understand the adversary" (Cassirer 1946: 296).

To turn to the romantic theorists of myth, for them, myth, rather than merely primitive, is an eternal possession. Nothing can supersede it. Whereas for rationalists science better serves the explanatory *function* than myth, for romantics nothing duplicates the psychological or metaphysical *content* of myth. Whereas for rationalists science renders myth at once unnecessary and impossible for moderns, for romantics science and myth run askew, so that moderns can have and indeed must have myth. Whereas for rationalists the *function* served by myth may be indispensable, for romantics myth itself is indispensable to the serving of its function. Myth is revelatory. For me, and for Ellwood as well, the epitomes of a romantic approach to myth are C. G. Jung, Mircea Eliade, and Joseph Campbell. To the three of them Ellwood devotes his *Politics of Myth*.

As with rationalism, so with romanticism: What is political about this approach to myth? According to Ellwood, romanticism accords every race or nation "its own defining myth or 'myth cycle'": "One finds a rediscovery of founding myths and national heroes, an idealization of rural 'rootedness' located in peasants or pioneers, and a sense that the nation is not just a political entity but a spiritual reality as well" (2001: 682–683). Mythology serves the group, not the individual. This view might seem egalitarian, crediting the mythology of each culture with "still-valid messages from the timeless beginnings of humanity." But the mythology of one nation can be vaulted over others as that "of a superior people." Moreover, while some mythologies "were certainly brought into the service of legitimate independence movements and democratic reform" (Ellwood 2001: 682–683), others strove to revive a nondemocratic, idealized past. And outsiders could be targeted as aliens.

Ellwood maintains that Jung, Eliade, and Campbell, while conspicuously modern as academics, "can rightly be labeled antimodern," emphasizing as they do "the illness of the modern world, for which they contended myth could serve as sovereign elixir" (2001: 681). At the same time Ellwood divides the romantic camp into political activists, of whom the *locus classicus* is indisputably Georges Sorel, and "contemplatives," who in "gnostic" fashion sought escape from the flawed everyday world into "a dreamy escapist inner world" (2001: 684). Ellwood's trio falls here.

How well does this characterization of romanticism fit the three? Undeniably, modernity for Jung represents the triumph of rationalism and science over religion and myth, and Jung urges the recovery of myth. But that recovery is *not* to be at the price of modernity. Jung sees himself as *part* of the modern world and proudly dubs himself a "scientist" of the mind. Modernity marks progress, not degeneration. The aim is to continue forward, not go backward. Psychologically, modernity represents the attainment of ego consciousness or consciousness of the external world. The development of ego consciousness has necessarily required a break with the primordial unconscious. The goal now is to return to the unconscious—but as a means to forging a balance between it and ego consciousness. Modern consciousness is more, not less, advanced than that of primitives, who psychologically, as for Tylor intellectually, are childlike: "These considerations tempt us to draw a parallel between the mythological thinking of ancient man and the similar thinking found in children, primitives, and in dreams" (Jung: 22–23). Modernity properly involves the withdrawal of primitive projections of gods onto the world.

The Jungian aim is to live in the outer as well as the inner world—with the two simply kept distinct. The outer world is not evil. It is just not the only world. As the editor of *The Gnostic Jung*, I would never downplay Jung's fascination with gnosticism, but ironically Jung misinterprets gnosticism, as if it, like Jungian psychology, seeks to stay in the outer world rather than to escape from it (see Segal 1992b: 19–33). Because Jungian psychology stays tied to the outer world, it is open to political activism, as books like *Jung and Politics* and *The Political Psyche*, both cited by Ellwood, attest.

In *The Politics of Myth* Ellwood acknowledges some of these points. Commendably, he rejects the one-sided argument of Richard Noll in *The Jung Cult* and *The Aryan Christ* that Jung's psychology derives from avowedly nationalistic, neopagan, antiscientific, anti-Semitic cults that arose at the turn of the century in German-speaking lands (see Ellwood 1999: 184 n. 36; Segal 1995). But Ellwood still links Jung to a reactionary impulse and in so doing surveys the evidence of Jung's anti-Semitism.

What of the politics of myth? Jung does categorize mythologies along racial and national lines. But he categorizes myths in other ways as well, such as by the dominant archetypes. The fullest myths for him are personal ones, fitting most snugly the unique contour of each person's unconscious. Far from losing the individual in the group, Jung favors the individual, as Ellwood himself stresses. Primitive mentality is that of the herd.

I would characterize Jung's position on myth as romantic but not reactionary. Myth for romantic Jung is not merely primitive, is not about the physical word, and is not superseded by science. Moderns as well as primitives have and maybe must have myths: "Has mankind ever really got away from myths? . . . [I]f all the world's traditions were cut off at a single blow, the whole of mythology . . . would start all over again with the next generation" (Jung: 25; see also Segal 1998: 32–34 and chap. 8). Myth is a fount of wisdom. But the key to interpreting myth is twentieth-century psychology. Myth and modernity are thus allies, not antagonists.

When, in both his review essay and his book, Ellwood turns to Eliade, he considers the theorist at least as much as the theory. Unlike Jung, Eliade has frequently been charged with trucking not merely with anti-Semitic sentiments but with an anti-Semitic movement. Typically, Ellwood, while ever balanced, tends to be charitable. But what of the theory? Eliade fits Ellwood's reactionary romanticism more readily than Jung. Eliade vaunts primitives over moderns and the sacred past over the profane present. Like a magic carpet, myth functions to carry one back to primordial time and thereby to the gods. Myth is universal and indispensable. Primitives are superior to moderns, for they recognize their need for myth. Whereas the myths of primitives are public and conscious, those of moderns are private, camouflaged, and even degenerate: "In short, the majority of men 'without religion' still hold to pseudo religions and degenerated mythologies" (Eliade: 209). Unlike Jung, Eliade favors group myths over individual ones.

Like Jung, Eliade bemoans the one-sided character of moderns and, also like Jung, attributes that one-sidedness to the rise of science and the demise of religion. But Eliade is more extreme. Whereas Jung seeks to reconcile myth with modernity, Eliade seeks to topple modernity in the name of myth. Whereas Jung can reconcile myth with modernity because myth, read symbolically, is not about the outer world and so is not in conflict with science, Eliade cannot reconcile myth with modernity because he reads myth literally. Instead, he argues for the continuing presence of myth amid modernity and as more than a Tylorean relic or "survival." But myth and modernity remain at odds. If the sacred still exists in the modern profane, it does so paradoxically and defiantly. In his book Ellwood boldly suggests that Eliade actually embraces modernity in celebrating new mani-festations of the sacred (see 1999: 98, 119–120). But surely even those manifestations still exist paradoxically within modernity. Furthermore, Eliade's relentless opposition to the scientific study of religion evinces a rejection of modernity antithetical to Jung's participation in it. In short, Eliade is more reactionary for me than for Ellwood. Eliade's position is more dualistic and therefore more gnostic-like than Jung's, but in find-ing the sacred imbedded in the profane and not merely trapped in it, Eliade's dualism is less radical than the gnostic variety.

What of the politics of myth? Like Jung, Eliade clearly categorizes mythologies by nations, but also like Jung he characterizes myths in other ways as well, such as by religions. For Eliade, as for Malinowski, myth traces back the origin of present-day social phenomena and in that sense bol-sters them. Myth thus brings the sacred forward to the present. But surely myth also takes one out of the present and back to the past. Eliade thus interprets political hopes for future paradise, including that of staunchly atheistic Marxism, as really a hoped-for return to the prepolitical, prelap-sarian past (see 206–207).

When, in his book, Ellwood turns to Campbell, he again accords at least as much attention to the theorist as to the theory. In his review essay he notes that, despite my having documented elsewhere Campbell's anti-Semitism (see Segal 1992a), in my book I sidestep the issue. I do so because, despite Ellwood's efforts, I think it hard to tie Campbell's or other theorists' politi-cal positions to their positions on myth. In my book on Campbell (see Segal 1997) I trace Campbell's changing assessments of peoples. Over the course of his writings he variously touts the East over the West, the West over the East, hunters over farmers, farmers over hunters, primitives over moderns, and moderns over primitives. He takes no consistent line.

But what of Campbell's theory? For all his exasperatingly fluctuating views of the origin and function of myth (see Segal 1997: chaps. 10–11), he consistently maintains that all myth preaches a world-affirming rather than world-rejecting message. In *The Hero with a Thousand Faces* the protagonist, having ventured forth to a strange, divine world, returns home to discover that the divine world had been there all along, if only one had had the eyes to see it. The sacred does not merely exist dialecti-cally in the profane, as for Eliade, let alone lie trapped in the profane, as for gnosticism. The sacred *is* the profane (see Campbell: 217). Campbell espouses what W. T. Stace calls "extrovertive" mysticism. Campbell's own extrovertive quest for the sacred took the form not of meditation but of running and, later, swimming.

Whereas both Jung and Eliade seek to revive myth in the wake of the rise of science and the fall of religion, Campbell pits myth against religion—sometimes western religions, sometimes all religions. The fall of religion spells the salvation of myth. Whereas for Jung and Eliade moderns must scamper to create new myths, for Campbell myths get created almost spontaneously. Science itself spurs the creation of myths. Whereas for Jung modern psychology provides the grid for understanding myth, for Campbell primitives themselves have been psychologists. Only benighted moderns need Jung to decipher myth (see Campbell: vii). In these ways Campbell is even more antimodern than Jung or Eliade.

Seemingly, myth for Campbell contains a blatantly political message. For the hero, having set off for some personal reason, agrees to return from the divine world only for the sake of the community. But then Campbell's Jungian-like psychologizing of myths turns the heroic quest into a solipsistic quest for self-knowledge. The community disappears. The extrovertive Campbell does not turn away from the outer world in any gnostic-like manner, but the goal is personal, not collective.

Robert A. Segal
Lancaster University

REFERENCES

Blumenberg, Hans
1985

Work on Myth. Trans. by Robert M. Wallace. Cambridge: MIT Press.

Campbell, Joseph
1949

The Hero with a Thousand Faces. 1st ed. New York: Pantheon Books.

Cassirer, Ernst
1946

The Myth of the State. New Haven: Yale University Press.

1955

The Philosophy of Symbolic Forms, vol. 2: Mythical Thought. Trans. by Ralph Manheim. New Haven: Yale University Press.

Eliade, Mircea
[1959] 1968

The Sacred and the Profane. Trans. by Willard R. Trask. Reprint, New York: Harvest Books.

Ellwood, Robert
1999

The Politics of Myth. Albany: State University of New York Press.

2001

"Is Mythology Obsolete?" *Journal of the American Academy of Religion* 69/3: 673–686.

Frazer, James George
1922

The Golden Bough. Abridged ed. London: Macmillan.

Jung, C. G.   *Symbols of Transformation. Collected Works,* vol. 5. 2d
      1967   ed. Ed. by Sir Herbert Read, Michael Fordham, and
                    Gerhard Adler. Trans. by R. F. C. Hull et al. Princeton:
                    Princeton University Press.

Lévi-Strauss, Claude   "The Structural Study of Myth." In *Myth,* 81–106. Ed.
      [1955] 1965   by Thomas A. Sebeok. Reprint, Bloomington: Indiana
                         University Press.

      1966   *The Savage Mind.* Chicago: University of Chicago Press.

Lévy-Bruhl, Lucien   *How Natives Think.* Trans. by Lilian A. Clare. London:
      1926   Allen and Unwin.

Lincoln, Bruce   *Theorizing Myth.* Chicago: University of Chicago Press.
      1999

Malinowski, Bronislaw   "Magic, Science and Religion." In *Magic, Science and
      [1925] 1954   Religion and Other Essays,* 17–92. Reprint, Garden City,
                         NY: Doubleday Anchor Books.

Raglan, Lord   *The Hero.* London: Methuen.
      1936

Segal, Robert A.   "Joseph Campbell on Jews and Judaism." *Religion* 22:
      1992a   151–170.

      1995   "Critical Notice of Richard Noll, *The Jung Cult.*" *Jour-
                    nal of Analytical Psychology* 40/4: 597–608.

      1997   *Joseph Campbell: An Introduction.* Rev. ed. New York:
                    Penguin/Meridian Books.

      1999   *Theorizing about Myth.* Amherst: University of Massa-
                    chusetts Press.

Segal, Robert A., ed.   *The Gnostic Jung.* Princeton: Princeton University Press.
      1992b

      1998   *Jung on Mythology.* Princeton: Princeton University
                    Press.

Tylor, E. B.   *Primitive Culture.* 1st ed. London: Murray.
      1871

Rejoinder to Robert A. Segal

I AM VERY appreciative of Robert A. Segal's fine reply to my review essay, "Is Mythology Obsolete?" In tone and content it represents exactly what intellectual conversation in print ought to be. There is not too much left for me to say now because I find that by and large what Segal says is what I believe I said, or intended to say, in my essay and in my longer work on modern mythology, *The Politics of Myth*, which in effect he also reviews; he often, however, finds a nuance or perspective that brings the intent out more fully.

A couple of points, though, need to be clarified. I certainly agree that the creators of the "rationalist" approach to myth from Tyler to Cassirer and Lévi-Strauss, far more overall than the "romantics," perceived their work as nonpolitical. They no doubt thought of themselves as "value-free" scholars in the best modern sense, tacitly accepting scientific analysis as the ideal and intending no purpose beyond the enlargement of learning leading to the building of an enlightened, rational society. (Thus, E. B. Tylor accepted scientific knowledge as model and norm when he paid "primitives" the compliment of saying that they used ways of thinking congruent with science in their mythmaking, even though it is plain that their myths do not equal the modern laboratory in results.)

The issue, though, is what happens when this rationalist attitude toward myth trickles down to pundits, politicians, decision makers, and the person on the street for whom myth finally becomes what it is when someone today says, "That's just a myth." Then the interpretation of myth as premodern and outmoded science provides cover for those who wish to replace sacred kings with parliaments or, all too often, value-free dictators (as Frazer foresaw) and to clear-cut sacred groves in the name of "development." (But although this view stems from rationalism, it is certainly not all that scholars like Cassirer and Lévi-Strauss read in myth.)

Whether this upshot is good or bad is a far-reaching issue not to be resolved here in a few words. It is simply part of the modern package, a commodious box containing all sorts of positives and negatives for health of body, mind, and spirit. But it does seem evident that the rationalist approach to myth cannot be said to be without political consequences, intended or not—and most of the immense consequences of modern mythology were not completely and consciously intended.

Journal of the American Academy of Religion September 2002, Vol. 70, No. 3, pp. 621–622.

As to whether Jung, Eliade, and Campbell—the subjects of *The Politics of Myth*—were modern, antimodern, romantic, or reactionary, it seems to me that this debate has gotten to the point of a battle over words. Neither Segal nor myself, I believe, would deny that they all contained proportions of all these qualities. Possibly—I am not sure even of this—we would see the mix a little differently in each. The main thing, though, is that they, like many others, lived fully modern lives professionally and intellectually while criticizing important aspects of the modern world.

They were forward looking—in the case of Campbell, almost eschatological—and quite aware that the past cannot, and should not, be recovered whole. Yet they were conservative, if not reactionary, in the sense that they understood certain critical values of body-mind-spirit wholeness and "rootedness" desperately needed by the modern world to have been better exemplified in the simpler life of the past. These values are most accessible to us today in the recovery of ancient myth, and that is why they labored in season and out for its excavation.

In their romantic zeal for the task and its object, they made serious political mistakes, but in the end each came to realize that the restitution of roots and wholeness can only be personal and individual, not corporate—and then political only in the sense that individuals are, cumulatively, a political force. The results may be jumbled; one can see traces, intended and otherwise, of Jung, Eliade, and Campbell in causes ranging from ideological conservatism to the feminist and ecological movements. The predominant objective of post-1945 mythology and myth therapy, when not purely academic, may have been nonpolitical inner, subjective transformation. But as Jung, Eliade, and Campbell were well aware, history and societies are really just collections of subjectivities, and that hidden realm is the ultimate source of change, just as academic studies, if truly original and powerful, will not stay confined to the library. In the end I contend still that all mythology is political—in the sense that it can provide fuel for political fires—just as all politics are mythical.

Robert Ellwood
University of Southern California (emeritus)

 BOOK REVIEWS

The Architectural Setting of the Cult of Saints in the Early Christian West, c. 300–c. 1200. By John Crook. Clarendon Press, 2000. 308 pages. $85.00.

The Cult of Saints in Late Antiquity and the Early Middle Ages. Edited by James Howard-Johnston and Paul Antony Hayward. Oxford University Press, 1999. 298 pages. $74.00.

From early in the life of the church, veneration of the graves and physical remains of martyrs and other holy persons has been a central feature of Christian piety. The cult of the saints, as such veneration has come to be known, has revolted many, from ancient pagans (who thought living people should stay away from dead people) to modern historians (who see the cult of saints as essentially identical with pagan polytheism). This has not stopped Christians—ancient, modern, and in-between—from celebrating the Eucharist over the graves of martyrs, building altars over saints' graves and transporting relics to altars built elsewhere, arranging for their own burial near the tombs of saints, making pilgrimages to saints' graves in the belief that prayers said in proximity to holy relics are more likely to be heard and answered, moving and fragmenting saints' bodies to provide wider and more convenient access to the power of the saint's relics, building structures—crypts, shrines, and whole churches—to house such relics, and judging the saintliness of a deceased person by whether that person's body remains incorrupt or facilitates miracles of healing or exorcism.

Two recent books examine in detail different aspects of the Christian cult of saints. John Crook's *The Architectural Setting of the Cult of Saints in the Early Christian West, c. 300–c. 1200* discusses "the influence of the cult of saintly relics on the architecture of the early medieval churches of the West" (1)—by which Crook means Italy, the former Gaul, and Britain—and in particular on the crypts (rooms, either above or below ground) and shrines (freestanding structures within churches) that were built to house relics and to offer access to them by priests (who wished to celebrate the Eucharist in proximity to them) and laypeople (who wished to say their prayers in proximity to them). James Howard-Johnston and Paul Antony Hayward's edited volume *The Cult of Saints in Late Antiquity and*

Journal of the American Academy of Religion September 2002, Vol. 70, No. 3, pp. 623–684.
© 2002 The American Academy of Religion

the Early Middle Ages focuses on the process by which certain persons were recognized and venerated as saints in the late ancient and early medieval periods. This process required, among other things, the production of a written record of the person's life and deeds (a "saint's Life"). The essays in the book discuss the formation of these hagiographical texts, the role of such texts in promoting saints' cults, and the social forces that stood to gain from their promotion.

Howard-Johnston and Hayward's work is subtitled "Essays on the Contribution of Peter Brown." Peter Brown's essay "The Rise and Function of the Holy Man in Late Antiquity" (*Journal of Roman Studies*, 1971) and his book *The Cult of the Saints* (University of Chicago Press, 1981) played a key role in sparking interest among historians in the role of (living) holy people and (dead) saints throughout the history of both eastern and western Christianity. Several of the essays in Howard-Johnston and Hayward's book began as papers delivered at a seminar at Oxford marking the twenty-fifth anniversary of the publication of Brown's "Holy Man" article. All of the contributors to the work are either graduates of Oxford, former pupils of Peter Brown, or (in several cases) both.

Where Brown himself is concerned, the tone is alternately worshipful (he is referred to as "the Master" throughout Howard-Johnston's introductory essay), pointedly critical (coeditor Hayward's contribution, for example, is as much a critique of Brown as it is a positive case for an alternate understanding of the cult of saints), and defensive (in a postscript to his introduction, Howard-Johnston criticizes the recently published proceedings of another conference—this one in Berkeley—marking the quartercentenary of Brown's article, suggests that Brown's presence at the Berkeley conference may have "inhibited as well as enriched discussion" there, and claims that he knew secondhand of Brown's involvement in Kleinian analysis but was too tactful to make more than the "briefest and most allusive of hints" to this earlier in his remarks [24]). The effect of the introduction plus several of the more explicitly critical essays is to make the book seem a kind of evil twin of a festschrift.

The first two contributors to the book engage directly with Brown's work on the cult of saints. According to Averil Cameron, the focus of late antique historians has shifted from anthropology (thinking about people, which is what Brown did) to discourse (thinking about texts, which is what Cameron does). Cameron points out that a saint's Life is not a biography in any conventional sense, any more than the Gospels are biographies; they are, rather, examples of virtue and heroism constructed by an author. While Brown "avoided the deconstructive turn even in its milder forms" (36), Cameron is ready to take it. The qualities and activities—asceticism, for example—portrayed in late antique texts may never have operated in society; they may be purely intratextual phenomena. An appropriate focus for the historian is, thus, not the saint whose life the text purports to narrate but, rather, the text itself, its nature as discourse, and its use of rhetorical strategy.

Philip Rousseau, in his contribution, similarly criticizes Brown for having treated his sources as if they talked about things that really happened or people who really existed. Rousseau suspects that both the main character and the events portrayed in a saint's Life may be purely textual: "The circumstances of the central figure may be a mirage: they themselves appear only in the texts" (47). Brown had spoken of a "distance" between the holy man and his social context. According to Rousseau, "That distance is located in the texts, and was desired or achieved, therefore, more by their authors, perhaps, than by their subjects" (49). Rousseau knows this, he says, because he finds no such distance in those bits of text that appear "not calculated . . . or burnished with authorial intent" (49). (For all his postmodern sensibility, Rousseau sounds very much like an old-fashioned historical critic applying the criterion of dissimilarity: if it sounds like something a holy man might have said, the author or editor must have made it up.) For Rousseau, hagiography is fundamentally about power. He points out that most of the literary evidence about holy men was written by people who were themselves ascetics. Hagiography served to defend the holiness of holy men to a society skeptical of it and, thus, to further the interests of ascetics in their conflicts with bishops.

Parts 2–3 of the book treat the cult of saints in eastern and western Christendom, respectively. Claudia Rapp proposes that the primary function of the living holy man in the late antique period was not miracle working (a central feature of most saints' Lives) but intercession on behalf of devotees who requested prayers on the assumption that the saint's quest for spiritual perfection gave him special favor in heaven. She bases her discussion on "non-literary documents," namely, letters addressed to or written by holy men during their lifetimes. These letters, she thinks, "provide a corrective to the literary creations of hagiographers"; in fact, they reveal "the direct and largely unadulterated voice of the holy men and their correspondents" (67). (Rapp thus displays greater confidence in the sources than does Rousseau: of one of the same groups of documents, the letters of the early-sixth-century hermit Barsanuphius, Rousseau comments, "The letters, like all such collections, are in any case tendentious, and subject to editorial and interpretative influence" [50].)

Paul Magdalino, in the second essay in part 2, discusses hagiography as a vehicle for religious commentary and criticism. Saints' Lives can function in this way, he says, even when their subjects are purely fictional. In such cases, the text itself, rather than the person it purports to portray, is the historical agent, as, for example, in the case of the (fictional) Lives of Andrew the Fool and Basil the Younger, which served to shore up the authority of the religious establishment in tenth-century Constantinople.

In the opening essay of part 3 Hayward discusses the role of saints' Lives in promoting cults and associated vested interests. Most saints' Lives "were in reality a kind of propaganda" (124) that served to legitimize the authority of particular persons and groups. Gregory of Tours, for example, exaggerated the importance of saints' relics at the expense of other manifestations of the holy (stylites, hermits) because it suited Gregory's interests to promote the veneration of relics housed in his church and thus under his control. The cult of saints was not, as Brown would have it, a religious symbol system that led people to treat one another with justice and mercy. It was a "phenomenon of doubtful authenticity" (141), which was deliberately advanced by elites who saw it as a source of divine legitimation. As such, it was "deeply self-serving" (142).

Paul Fouracre doubts, with Hayward, that the cult of saints was really as pervasive and regulated in sixth-century Gaul as Gregory's writings imply. Only in the Carolingian period did bishops really come to have control over relics, as royal authorities set aside (local) aristocratic patronage of relic cults in favor of episcopal patronage. This served royal interests because the bishops who controlled the relics were themselves under the control of the monarchs. In this way Carolingian monarchs "tried to bring cults under their control, and to appropriate for themselves some of the politically potent qualities of the saint" (165).

Ian Wood, in the final essay in part 3, notes that the history of the evangelization of pagan peoples in Europe east of the Rhine is one that has to be constructed mostly from saints' Lives. The narrative delay between the life of a missionary saint and the writing of a hagiographical account of that life offered time for vested interests (rival monastic foundations or episcopal sees, for example) to rework history or for the writer of a Life to intrude his own interests (he may have himself been a missionary, for instance) into the account. In Wood's judgment, missionary hagiography offers significant insight into the inner life of the missionaries who were the authors (rather than the subjects) of such narratives.

Parts 4–5 of the book offer, by way of contrast and comparison, essays dealing with the cult of saints in medieval Russia and in Islam. Paul Hollingsworth discusses the cult of the Princes Boris and Gleb, who were murdered by their half brother, who wanted all the power for himself after their mutual father Volodimer died in 1015. The hagiographical narratives of their lives made them martyrs; their cult was advanced by churchmen in and around eleventh-century Kiev who wanted rulers to behave themselves instead of murdering each other. Richard Price looks at the way the Lives of missionary saints are similar through time and across large geographical distances. The late-fourteenth-century *Life of St. Stephen of Perm* shows remarkable similarities to much earlier Lives of Martin, Patrick, and Boniface, similarities that Price attributes in part to conscious imitation by later missionaries of the practices of earlier ones, as reported or misreported in the Lives.

Holy men and the shrines of saints became features of the Islamic world within two or three centuries of the life of Muhammad. Chase Robinson points out that Muhammad himself was not analogous to a Christian holy man. A holy man was a force of stability in an unstable era, whereas Muhammad was himself a destabilizing factor that made revelation and jihad the chief elements of the new faith. Josef Meri discusses the emergence of holy men in Islam in the ninth century. Some of these were mystics, although their claims to mediate revelation were opposed by the religious authorities. The teachings of the mystics came to be understood as inspired but not as revelatory in the strict sense, and some of the mystics were venerated as saints at their burial shrines. Veneration of Islamic saints (which implied their intercessory powers) was hard to square with Islamic monotheism, but such veneration became a central and vital feature of medieval Islam and continues to this day.

Whereas the interest of all the contributors to Howard-Johnston and Hayward's book is in the text as artifact, John Crook's interest is in buildings as artifacts. His book begins with a chapter focusing on literary evidence (early Patristic writings, the poems of late Latin authors, comments by sixteenth-century Reformers) concerning the cult of saints, especially as this touches on the architectural influence of relic cults. Crook notes that the cult of saints was both physical and practical: "It involved touching, even kissing, holy bones; crawling beneath shrines; creating contact relics; the fragmentation of saintly bodies; and burials *ad sanctum*" (2), all in the belief, shared by learned and simple believers alike, "that advantage could be gained by proximity to the physical remains of those venerated as saints" (36).

The book proceeds in chronological fashion, with chapters treating the early Middle Ages, with a focus on late antique Rome and Merovingian Francia (chapter 2); the Carolingian renaissance and its revival of architectural patterns derived from the Rome of Gregory the Great (3); the development of Carolingian shrine crypts—that is, crypts designed to accommodate the veneration of a saint or saints (4); Anglo-Norman relic cults in the tenth and eleventh centuries (5); and further relic-related architectural developments in twelfth-century England (6). A final chapter discusses shrines—monuments provided to house relics within their architectural environment—and the ways in which shrines functioned both to protect relics and to allow access to them.

Crook points out that the veneration of holy bones had physical requirements. People needed to be able to get close to relics, ideally to touch them. The primary arrangement, from which others evolved, was the construction of a church over a martyr's grave, ideally with the altar located over the grave itself. Sometimes bodies were moved to place them under the altar; later, purpose-built chambers (crypts) superseded the original graves. Crypts were sometimes above ground, for ease of access. Crypts below ground were equipped with staircases and, sometimes, with relic shafts (*cataractae*), which were like speaking tubes and allowed communication with the dead saint. As the church expanded to areas where there were no martyr's graves, older relics were brought—whole or in fragments—to be housed within the altars of new churches. Local saints were buried in the crypts of such churches or—increasingly—in tomb shrines located within the church itself and designed to permit access by clergy and laity alike.

Much of the evidence for the early practice of the cult of saints is literary. Architecture related to the cult of saints survives beginning in the eighth and ninth centuries. Crook's book is illustrated throughout with black-and-white photographs, floor plans, and other drawings. The author has made use of computer technology to emend existing base plans in light of photographs and measurements of actual buildings or their remains. His book will prove invaluable to the specialist and enlightening to anyone who has ever visited a medieval church and wondered why all those coffins are up on pillars (so pilgrims can crawl underneath).

Margaret Kim Peterson
Eastern College

Genetic Dilemmas: Reproductive Technology, Parental Choices, and Children's Futures. By Dena S. Davis. Routledge, 2001. 153 pages. $22.95.

Each year nearly four million births occur in the United States. A small but growing number of these infants exist by virtue of new reproductive technologies that enable the identification and selection (or rejection) of embryos based on their particular genetic profiles. In vitro fertilization, preimplantation genetic diagnosis, and sperm sorting, among other technologies, serve to multiply parents' reproductive decisions. *Genetic Dilemmas* focuses on the ethics of reproductive choices that have the potential to affect children's future life options. In making these reproductive choices, says Dena Davis, neither parents nor the health care professionals working with them give sufficient priority to the future child's potential autonomy. So begins chapters 1, which, with chapter 2, develops the moral principle of "a child's right to an open future." Chapters 4–6 introduce this constructive work to current ethical discussions surrounding specific reproductive and genetic dilemmas.

Genetic counseling typically embraces strong respect for client (parental) autonomy and is challenged by some ethicists to temper this autonomy with more beneficence, understood as greater concern for the future child's welfare. Davis rejects this competing values debate and reframes the conflict as one between competing autonomies, arguing that parental autonomy is overvalued while a weightier autonomy, the child's potential autonomy or "right to an open future," is undervalued. The child's right to an open future, elaborated by philosopher Joel Feinberg, is the sum of children's "rights-in-trust," that is, rights "*saved* for the child until he is an adult" (24). Protection of these rights enables the child to exercise them in adulthood: to sterilize a child would be to violate his or her right to reproduce and, thus, to an open future. The key normative implication of this right for reproductive decision making is that "parents ought not to make decisions about their children that severely and irreversibly restrict their right to an open future" (27). Jehovah's Witness parents who reject a life-saving blood transfusion for their child and Amish parents who withdraw their children from school after the eighth grade are examples of nonreproductive violations of the children's right to an open future. Furthermore, in conversation with Galston, Nussbaum, and Mill, Davis argues that liberal states should serve to protect individual autonomy, including the child's right to an open future, over parental, familial, or community autonomy.

Can we speak of moral harm to as-yet-unborn or not-yet-conceived children? Is harm done if a child is born deaf and the deafness was avoidable through technological intervention? Who is harmed? Chapter 2 sketches the "wrongful life" debate with Green, Cohen, Robertson, Steinbock, and Brock; affirms "our universal moral intuition that to avoid suffering is a good thing"; and charges parents with moral wrongdoing when they "deliberately or out of negligence, bring into the world children in a less than optimal state when they could easily have done otherwise" (47).

Many parents desire to raise children like themselves, and this holds true for parents who are deaf or achondroplastic (congenital dwarfs). "Choosing for disability" (the title of chapter3), understood to mean the intentional creation of children with disabilities, violates the child's right to an open future and does moral harm because these children will live with limited life choices. Deafness, understood either as a disability or a cultural identity, constrains possibilities: as a disability, deafness "substantively narrows a child's career, marriage, and cultural options" (based on empirical data demonstrating the relative low income and education levels of deaf persons); as a cultural identity, children participating in Deaf culture "will have only limited options to move outside of that culture" (64). Accordingly, genetic counselors are implored to abandon their value-neutral respect for parental autonomy and to reject such parental choices. Davis refrains from naming intentional achondroplasia as a moral harm given the lack of empirical data, despite its irreversibility, and states, "It does not seem that momentous pieces of his adult life will be foreclosed by that decision" (66).

Genetic counselors are also advised to resist parental requests to test their children for particular genetic traits. Chapter 4 argues that childhood testing—whether for late-onset diseases for which there is no treatment or cure, like Huntington's disease, or for carrier status of a recessive genetic disease such as Tay-Sachs—forecloses the child's future autonomy as an adult to decide whether to be tested and thus violates the child's right to an open future. Moreover, such childhood testing infringes on the child's right to privacy regarding the test results.

Is sex selection inherently morally wrong? If abortion were unnecessary (because of effective sperm sorting) and if female and male children were equally desired (as Davis believes will soon be the case in North America), would sex selection infringe a child's right to an open future? Yes, she argues in chapter 5, because sex selection "promotes gender role stereotyping and encourages parents to invest heavily in having certain types of children" and "makes it more difficult for the child to grow and develop in ways that are different than, perhaps even in conflict with, parental expectations" (106).

In the final chapter, future parental motivations for cloning a child are explored through the lens of a child's right to an open future. Parents who would choose cloning to produce "any" genetically linked child because they have deemed other reproductive choices unacceptable are said to have "logistical" motivations. Parents who would clone to produce a child with particular characteristics, such as tall height for playing basketball or "spare parts" such as bone marrow for saving a dying sibling, have "duplicative" motivations. Logistically motivated cloning is morally permissible because (it is assumed) these children would be valued like other children—cloning itself would not limit the child's life options. However, duplicatively motivated cloning that involves strong parental expectations that the child follow a particular life path would transgress the child's right to an open future. One morally permissible duplicative motivation would be cloning for "spare parts" if the child were primarily valued as his or her own person and only secondarily valued as instrumental to the good of another person. Health care professionals are called to evaluate parental motivations for cloning and to make the technology available accordingly.

The book's most significant contribution is its articulation and application of the moral principle of a child's right to an open future in the complex ethical context of genetic and reproductive technologies. Reflective of the embrace of autonomy and liberal individualism by U.S. bioethics, as well as its considerable attention to genetics, this book thoughtfully extends these subjects to children. Religion plays a minor role at best: religious communities understood to violate a child's right to an open future are discussed briefly (the Amish and Jehovah's Witnesses), as are a few handfuls of Jewish ethical sources.

Certain concepts in this work deserve greater critical examination, such as "an open future," which is referred to simply as "a wide variety of life choices" and "the greatest possible latitude of choice." The criteria that violate the right to an open future—irreversibility of decision and severely restricted options— weaken in the face of inconsistent application across different ethical and tech- nological contexts. For example, intentionally creating a child with achondroplasia is irreversible but does not violate the child's right to an open future, whereas childhood testing for Huntington's disease, also irreversible, does. Similarly, the morally permissible cloning of a child for "spare parts" allows for parental ex- pectations and investment in a particular child, but the parental expectations and investment involved with sex selection are, by definition, a violation of a child's right to an open future.

Individual autonomy is invested with the power to trump (all?) related claims of social collectivities including the family, religious communities, and the state. Little evidence emerges of a willingness to balance, for example, parental repro- ductive rights with a child's right to an open future. Also, the state must play a sizeable role beyond legal protection of autonomy in order to make possible a child's open future. Health care professions are granted substantial responsibil- ity for ensuring these rights, but whether they can or will remains to be seen.

Accessibly written, largely free of technical language, and sprinkled with the author's personal insights and experiences, this book is best suited to nonspe- cialists wanting broad exposure to the ethical argumentation surrounding repro- ductive and genetic technologies. Davis stresses, "It is crucial that as many people as possible begin to educate themselves about these issues and start to wrestle with the questions they pose" (7). *Genetic Dilemmas* succeeds notably in contributing to these goals.

Charlene A. Galarneau
Tufts University

Religion and the Continental Congress, 1774–1789: Contributions to Origi- nal Intent. By Derek H. Davis. Oxford University Press, 2000. 309 pages. $39.95.

Derek Davis sets out to get behind the federal Constitution and the Bill of Rights to examine what the Continental Congress had in mind when it had to face the difficult question of the new confederation's relationship to religion. Davis's perspective is that of an older-style Protestant evangelicalism that histori- cally championed a "strict separationist" view of church–state relations. That view flowed naturally from an old alliance that had driven, for example, Baptist assaults on the Anglican/Episcopal establishment of Virginia while yoked to liberal Deist allies. Such alliances changed in the 1980s, however, when a more "activist" conviction emerged among many evangelicals who believed that "strict separation" in the hands of an increasingly aggressive secularist elite was determined to eradicate the memory of how often government had "accommodated" nominally Christian cultural customs ranging from chaplaincies to national days of religious observance.

Davis nicely locates and summarizes the roots of such customs in the work of the Continental Congress. Like most Americans vaguely influenced at some cultural level by the history of Protestant evangelicalism, he concludes that "separationism, provided it remains sensitive to longstanding accommodationist practices, is . . . the best course for the future of America" (229).

The book provides a useful survey of the controversial claims made for "original intent" and argues that, in the end, the Continental Congress worried about the practicality of "securing an adequate government," not over adopting or prescribing either a "wall of separation" or an "accommodationist" theory of church–state relations (135). Just so, the Framers of the federal Constitution inherited that pragmatism, interested more in getting their document ratified by states they knew to be suspicious and hostile. They left the details of separating or accommodating religious matters to the police powers of the states (203–209). In surveying the colonial and revolutionary commitments of both "pietist" Protestants and liberal-rational Deists of various hues, Davis overstates the ecumenical perspective of the latter. Their confidence that "every religion" subscribed to their reductionist vision of what Robert Bellah has identified as a "civil religion" never imagined Muslims or Orthodox Jews in such a landscape and ignored contemporary Native American religious beliefs some of them knew to be quite different from their own. They were children of western Protestant Christianity, and when they assailed *tyranny* they almost universally employed the term from their perspective of an inherited and unrepentant anti-Catholic prejudice they shared with their evangelical allies.

Given this background, future debates over religion and the state promise to remain controverted. Davis concludes with legal scholar Steven Smith that the incorporation by the U.S. Supreme Court of the Civil War amendments in the 1940s to strike down accommodations of religious exercise and liberty historically left to the states has created a largely unusable past (22–24, 132–135).

Despite the largely evenhanded treatment of his subject, Davis at times falls into contradiction or fails to tease out some of the more troubling implications of his findings. Thus, for example, in speaking of the eventual omission of the rights of conscience from the wording of the First Amendment, he does not notice the significance of Congress's refusal to endorse that provision in the context of contemporary Roman Catholic doctrine. According to most Church theologians at the time, Catholics were bound in conscience to concede the superiority of an officially Catholic state. That the nationalists who had constructed a fragile federal government would not concede even more potent attacks on its claims within a dual sovereignty to those seeking the cover of religious conscience should be explored more carefully. If the founders were allergic to real or perceived threats emanating from the Roman Catholic version of Christianity, the ominous twenty-first-century rise in groups more than ready to appeal to religious conviction as justification for acts of subversion or terror suggests that such appeal to private religious conscience as the basis for "free exercise" was wisely rejected as the nation's leaders struggled over the wording of the First Amendment. That such a rejection sat oddly with the thrust of the late-eighteenth-century conviction that religion should be thought of solely in terms of private conviction deserves more analysis than Davis is willing to provide.

At times Davis strains to complicate terms or insights that eighteenth-century North Americans probably found unproblematic. The term *establishment* clearly referenced state constitutions and colonial charters where various Protestant churches were "by law established." Disestablishment was not identical to a commitment to "religious liberty," as evidenced by the persistence of oaths of office that even in liberal Pennsylvania demanded a testimony to the revealed nature of the Christian Old and New Testaments. It is correct to conclude that the Federal Convention's determination to avoid test oaths reflected a commitment to liberty of conscience. But regulating that liberty was left to the states. At times Davis seems to believe that "religious despotism" was familiar to the founders because of colonial or state establishments (9); elsewhere (110), he concurs with most experts that those establishments were relatively benign by early modern standards, however constricted they appear in hindsight.

The experiment in making religion and state independent to avoid the wars of the "age of conscience" does in fact summarize what "disestablishment" consisted of (64). But such discussions left to state control the deeper level of cultural and religious convictions held by the majority of Protestant Americans at the time. Davis agrees that appealing to that standard is nearly as impenetrable as a measure of "intent" as is the search for the founders' varied objectives. But he concludes that we have no choice but to attend to such democratic standards of reception, even as incorporationist tendencies of the modern federal courts continue to trump all counterclaims by local and state jurisdictions.

If migration from Latin America and East Asia continues at its present rate, concern over "accommodating" non-Christian minorities' sensibilities will only intensify, for most demographers project a distinctly Christian (Catholic or Pentecostal) character to the new immigration. Although Davis purports to be concerned about non-Protestant minorities (228–229), the future of religion in North America looks less likely to be determined by "Mormons, Jehovah's Witnesses, Hare Krishnas, Buddhists, Muslims, Hindus, Christian Scientists, and a host of other minority religions" (229) than by a burgeoning Catholic presence and the much less organized Pentecostal groups. To that mix, the rise of an aggressive Islamicist dissent from either separationism or accommodationism threatens the fragile compromises inherited from this distant, evangelical Protestant and Deist past that Davis does such an admirable job of summarizing. The rising tensions between an emerging Christian majority of non-European origins that will dominate democratic religious culture in the United States and the legal-constitutional guardians of "separationism" who still represent that fading Enlightenment world may prove to be the greatest test yet for the experiment in attempting to create independent realms for religion and the state in North America.

A. G. Roeber
Pennsylvania State University

The Academic Study of Religion during the Cold War: East and West. Edited by Iva Doležalová, Luther H. Martin, and Dalibor Papoušek. Peter Lang, 2001. 336 pages. $59.95.

In a recent review of Robert Ellwood's *The Politics of Myth* (State University of New York Press, 1999) I drew on the example of a public lecture on myth that I attended in the early 1990s in which the Soviet launch of Sputnik, on 4 October 1957, and the U.S. response of increasing funding throughout the university were used as a model for the sort of investments the U.S. government once again ought to be making in the humanities. Perhaps more surprising than hearing Sputnik mentioned in a lecture on myth was that this rhetoric seemed not to strike those attending the lecture as odd or out of place. It was therefore fascinating not just to see how easily one could connect the Cold War rhetoric of crisis to the presumption of the deep, enduring, even salvific knowledge provided by humanistic scholarship but to see this done in the 1990s. That making just this connection among myth, religion, the humanities, and democracy had a practical payoff—after all, more investment in the humanities means more prominence for our field, our departments, and our publications, and maybe even our salary woes might go away—should not go unnoticed.

Although a Cold War footing was given up some time ago (though there are those who would argue that the resources were simply shifted in the 1990s to such things as the War on Drugs and now the War on Terrorism), if this casual aside at a public lecture is any indication, presumptions basic to that stance still seem to inform some work carried out in our field. *The Academic Study of Religion during the Cold War: East and West*, therefore, is a much needed volume. Its international contributors very nicely complicate the dominant notion of the Cold War that circulates on this side of the Atlantic. More than likely, visions of Kennedy proclaiming to his German audience that he, too, was a Berliner, or Reagan informing Gorbachev to tear down this wall, represent the popular conception, but it is representative of but one view. Because it was in Europe, and not in North America, that much of the drama of the Cold War actually played itself out, the chapters on the situation in Poland and the former Czechoslovakia add much to our understanding of how this conflict impacted the study (as opposed to the practice) of religion.

The volume collects twenty-one essays from a 1999 conference of the International Association for the History of Religions (IAHR), held at Marsaryk University in Brno, the Czech Republic, that was cosponsored by the Czech Society for the Study of Religion (created in the wake of the dissolution of the former Czechoslovakia) and the North American Association for the Study of Religion.

The authors are from thirteen different nations: Canada, China, the Czech Republic, Estonia, Germany, the United Kingdom, Luxembourg, the Netherlands, Poland, Russia, Slovakia, Switzerland, and the United States. Whereas some draw on anecdotal or archival evidence to focus on the state of the art in their respective national settings between the years 1949 and 1989, others use the work of a particular writer prominent during this era as their point of entry (somewhat reminiscent of Donald Lopez's edited volume, *Curators of the Buddha* [University of Chicago Press, 1995]), and yet others tackle the problem of why the Cold War history of our field has yet to be written. The volume is the twenty-seventh in Lang's Toronto Studies in Religion series edited by Donald Wiebe. The series, whose aim is to publish both descriptive and explanatory studies of religion, has previously published books by such writers as Robert D. Baird, Thomas Ryba, Robert Segal, and Frits Staal, as well as the late Ninian Smart's festschrift, *Aspects of Religion* (1994).

Although some of the contributors are likely new to many North American readers—though many of these writers are well known in European circles, have appeared in other international essay collections, and are active in various North American professional societies—those acquainted with the recent study of religion on the international scene will surely be familiar with the work of such writers as Michael Pye (longtime member of the IAHR executive), Jacques Waardenburg (also well known for his edited *Classical Approaches to the Study of Religion* [Mouton de Gruyter, 1973 and 1999], along with his work in Islam), and such North American contributors as Gustavo Benavides, Gary Lease, Luther Martin, William Paden, and Donald Wiebe. These last few writers have been very active on the international scene; along with Robert Bellah and William James, Lease, Martin, Paden, and Wiebe are the only North Americans included in a new Czech anthology on the history of *Religionswissenschaft, Djiny religionistiky: Antologie* (Břestislav Horyna and Helena Pavlincová, eds., Nakladatelství Olomouc, 2001). For those interested in learning more about what some of our international peers are up to, this volume is one place to start.

Although the essays vary somewhat—from brief chapters that reflect the original conference setting of the papers, to some that are surveys of literature that might be little known to *JAAR* readers, and to yet others that are extended and well-researched essays—taken together they constitute an extremely important contribution to what may, in fact, be the most important phase in our field's history (second only to the colonial context of its nineteenth-century inception). The inability of European scholars, working in onetime Communist countries, to study religion in a nonideological fashion is a theme of many chapters, as in Dmitriy Mikulskiy's on Soviet research on the beliefs of native Central Asians and in BYetislav Horyna's chapter. Of interest is Josef Kandert's brief chapter on the ways in which overt ideology was sometimes less of an issue to scholars than were the plain old bureaucratic obstacles they faced. His thoughts on the practical techniques scholars used to overcome the former, such as inserting the appropriate propaganda into introductions and conclusions, help to account for how the field did not die out entirely in the former Eastern Europe. Lest one think that the volume merely celebrates the so-called freedom that swept over the study of religion when the Berlin Wall fell, Karel Werner's chapter presses an issue familiar to *JAAR* readers: the need to include the philosophy of religion in our methodological toolbox so as to address the degree to which all forms of materialist scholarship "deny even the possibility of a meaningful conceptual exploration of the sphere of the transcendent which is of central concern in all religions" (203). Whether or not this is a central concern of all religions, many in the field have yet to be persuaded of what exactly a meaningful conceptual exploration of the sphere of the transcendent would actually look like and how it would differ from what the various religions' learneds are already in the business of doing. And the complexity of studying such a thing as ideology and its interaction with scholarly work is nicely summed up by Halina Grzymala-Moszczyńska when, to her own question, "Does ideology matter for the psychology of religion?" she replies: "yes," "no," and "it depends."

Some of the more detailed chapters in the final section of the book (notably Martin's and Wiebe's) tackle the question of whether the North American field's rebirth in the late 1950s and early 1960s merely coincided with the peak of the Cold War or if the publicly funded, humanistic study of religion was intended as but one more way to defeat the "godless Communists." As Wiebe rightly points out, "There is no direct evidence that any direct support, whether from government agency or private foundation, is responsible for the entry of religious studies into the curriculum of college and universities in North America in the 1960s and no evidence that its research agendas were influenced to any great degree by specific Cold War values" (280). But there is considerable circumstantial or structural evidence to prompt further studies of what the Cold War setting of such things as the police action in Korea, the war in Vietnam, changing U.S. immigration policies in the mid-1960s, the antigovernment backlash among a younger generation, large-scale private funding of scholarship on religion from such sources as the politically liberal Pew Charitable Trusts (originating in 1948 and aiming to assist "America's will to protect democracy in Europe and the world," as described by the trusts' own history, its religion program awarded over $20 million in grants in 2001), and so forth all had to do with the sharp rise of interest in studying religion—and not just *being* religious—on college campuses. Such structural issues hardly amount to a direct cause, of course, but we might be mistaken if we study social systems by looking for smoking guns in the hands of intentional agents. I am therefore inclined to agree with Martin, who concludes that "the study of religion which was developed in the United States during this period must be seen as being in some way legitimated by the religio-political obsessions of that time, certainly in the selection of Asian and Third World 'religions' for its dominant subject matter" (220).

Although it is only a start at investigating these admittedly complex issues, *The Academic Study of Religion during the Cold War: East and West* is an important step in the right direction. The next step will be to press Martin's thesis and determine in which ways and to what extent geopolitics impacted the academy. Although this has begun in our field with works such as Steven Wasserstrom's *Religion after Religion* (Princeton University Press, 1999 [see, in particular, chapter 8]), there is still some distance to go before closing this chapter in our recent history. For example, the degree to which "ideology" in many of these essays is often juxtaposed to the value-neutral or objective study of religion—"ideology" being the thing that hampers serious scholarship—might be one area for future work. Depending on what one means by *ideology*, it can either be the rationale of an enemy's political system (where it works by means of propaganda) or the technique whereby any political system is justified to, and promoted by, its participants (thus making our "sharing of information" and "twenty-four-hour news coverage" instances of domestic propaganda). If complicated in just this manner, then, for example, the psychology of religion might very well be among the ideological effects of our current social system (an insight made possible by Foucault's work). If we approach the matter in this way, then perhaps it is not so much that, with the fall of the Berlin Wall, we are now able to draw "on intellectual traditions which are older and broader than the categories of both sides of the Cold War" (328) but, rather, that we are now able to proceed unimpeded with the assumptions, traditions, and techniques of the side that was left standing when the thaw eventually arrived.

Russell T. McCutcheon
University of Alabama

Constantine and the Bishops: The Politics of Intolerance. By Harold A. Drake. Johns Hopkins University Press, 2000. 609 pages. $68.00.

Harold Drake argues that Constantine had no particular animus against paganism and that imperial policy during his reign did not take any definite stand against traditional cults in the Roman Empire. To the contrary, Constantine was tolerant of other cults, promoted a latitudinarian kind of monotheism, and tried to ameliorate Christian militancy. But his policy was frustrated by the bishops' distinct and increasingly intolerant agenda. The bishops, we are told, gave rise to religious intolerance by attacking dissent in the church and eventually extending their hostility to other cults too. Drake, let it be known, does not neatly argue that bishops "caused" any of this, and less that Constantine "caused" any of this, but he argues that within the sinuous context of political behavior divergent trends and policies emerge among both emperors and bishops, a point argued in minute detail and with many journalistic analogies to recent presidents and such. You will gather that I think the latter detracts from the book. His argument continues: After Julian's brief reign, the bishops became very intolerant indeed. Insofar as a turning point toward imperial–Christian intolerance appears in the book, the honor seems to fall to Julian, who galvanized the bishops against paganism, and Theodosius I. This portrait of Constantine and his legacy is interesting, worthwhile, and controversial.

I doubt that too many people will take issue with Drake's conviction about the importance of political behavior in the religion of emperors or with the point that Constantine's conversion makes no sense apart from the demands of rule. A companion argument is more important. Constantine's view of Christianity,

Drake says, was essentially philosophical and learned from Lactantius. It roughly coincided with philosophical monotheism among pagan intellectuals, the very pagan–Platonist trend that excited so much interest and adaptation among fourth-century Christian writers, mostly bishops—and they were a diverse lot. Three and more generations after Constantine's conversion, they included the amazing neo-Platonist bishop of Ptolemais, Synesios of Cyrene (in spite of his office, it is easiest to think of him as a typical pagan intellectual of the late fourth/early fifth century), and the pugnacious bishop of Milan, Ambrose—more on him in a moment. As a ruler, by this account, the emperor was converted not merely to a religion that reinforced his own special kind of dictatorship, as I for one have been inclined to think, but to a religion the social ideals of which were especially useful to rulership after the debacle of Diocletian and the Tetrarchy—if the Tetrarchy really was a debacle. Drake's Constantine converted to a religiosity that embraced pagan and Christian alike.

Was the Tetrarchy a debacle? It seems so, in Lactantius's mind, whose *On the Death of the Persecutors* tries to prove the point in gory detail (in so doing, Lactantius gives us the best account of Diocletian's reign and its aftermath). Historians have been more generous, seeing Diocletian's reorganization of imperial government, together with his campaign against Christian and Manichaean "atheism" (that is, the opposition to traditional cults), as a sensible response to the growing instability of imperial government over the previous century. Diocletian's administrative divisions and his new ways of collecting money were left largely in place for the century to come and beyond, after all. Diocletian's reassertion of paganism gave the impression, at least, of a return to ancient values—even if the rule of Diocletian and his co-regents seems in retrospect a new thing, more despotic, even more Persian. By contrast, in Drake's account the Tetrarchy appears as something of a gambit, a failed gambit. Constantine, he argues, was "one of a number of younger players who realized the need for a more flexible and imaginative approach to 'the Christian question' than the traditional policy of periodic pogrom allowed" (157) or than the new policy of aggressive persecution allowed. He turned to a tolerant, philosophical Christianity during his contests against Maximin and Maxentius (even Maxentius had reached out to Christians, experimenting with a new solution to the religious problem before abdicating his office to his son [165–178]). The turn should serve a distinctly political end: It should unify the empire. The point is reinforced by an anonymous pagan oration given before the emperor that *could* be dated to 313, by Constantine's *To the Assembly of the Saints*, and by Eusebius of Caesarea's *In Praise of Constantine*, taken by Drake to represent Constantine's views more than Eusebius's own (380–390). Drake can easily argue that any such imperial ambition for unity around the Christian cult should and did at once get muddled by the Donatist and Arian controversies. For Constantine came quickly to depend on bishops for support and advice, as Augustus had once depended on senators (a provocative analogy [276, 467]); but bishops cared more for their own divisions than for the empire, and through the prolonged Arian controversy, the crevices dividing bishops deepened, widened, and moved about. Constantine's subsequent erratic course is described as a consistent attempt to ameliorate conflict. How else to reconcile the shifts in imperial policy toward anti-Arians like Athanasius and anti-Athanasians like Eusebius of Nicomedia? Emperors will be emperors, after all.

The ideal of imperial unity reinforced by Christian worship was a solidly Lactantian ideal. Lactantius develops it in his *Divine Institutes*, his own attempt to co-opt the apparent cultural traditionalism of the Tetrarchy's rulers. Drake, following his student Elizabeth Digeser, believes that Lactantius delivered the *Divine Institutes* as lectures at the emperor's court before Constantine's conversion (207). But whatever the source of Constantine's views, the association of Christianity and tolerance survived, we are told, among the irenic bishop-intellectuals of the later fourth century—like Synesios and Pegasios of Troy—and among the unambivalently orthodox who opposed coercion—like Gregory of Nazianzus and John Chrysostom (405–407). Even the pugnacious Ambrose, famous for the pressure he exerted on Theodosius I to support the church in two famous conflicts, learned through the conflict over the destruction of the synagogue at Callinicum to persuade emperors, not to condemn them. In Drake's review of Ambrose's relation to Theodosius, Theodosius's penance over the massacre at Thessalonica appears less remarkable; the bishop, less heroic; and the evolution of political behavior among bishops, more natural than the popular image of Ambrose driving Theodosius to his knees could ever hope to grasp.

Did Constantine occasion a "Constantinian consensus" that embraced pagan and Christian alike? A handful of imperial laws and actions clearly favored Christianity, and they would seem to contradict the idea that this consensus was built on tolerance. Of these, one law from late in Constantine's reign (333), known as the first Sirmondian Constitution, stands out as especially problematic. It granted the bishops and their Christian adherents an unbelievable right to interfere in pagan society. It was the right given to the *episcopalis audientia*, the bishop's court, to claim precedence in any case brought to it by either party in a suit, whether plaintiff or defendant. Presumably Christians involved in suits with pagans would wish to take special advantage of this. Perhaps it had the benefit of keeping Christians from having to perform religiously problematic oaths or rites before pagan judges. As one would expect, this law was a powerful tool in the hands of bishops later in the century, as the bishops' aggression against heresy and paganism grew, by the early fifth century reinforced by growing support in the regional administration of the empire. If Constantine did not want to tip the bishops' hand so decisively, whatever was he trying to do? According to Drake, he merely wanted to prevent injustice against the poor. The point is supported by a handful of phrases about such injustice tagged onto the decree and by a smattering of Constantinian complaints about the judicial abuse of poor people. If so, Constantine's remedy seems drastically overdone. Drake believes it was so nonetheless, suggesting that in Constantine's view of Christianity, who better than a bishop to uphold justice? Could Constantine have mistaken the bishops' monotheism for his own so late in his reign? Had he learned so little from the behavior of bishops in the controversies over Arius and Athanasius? If Constantine's monotheism proved by his late reign to be distinct from that of many bishops, it is hard to imagine how he could have made these mistakes.

Of course, it is still possible and not very controversial to see Constantine's eminently political behavior as reinforced by a Lactantian ideal of social unity. Drake calls our attention to how much the culture of pagan intellectuals changed in the fourth century (this is what the Emperor Julian really teaches us) and how much an emperor could identify the cultural matrix of an old world empire and a present pagan one with his new religion. That leaves the emperor just as Drake and others have described him: a man less interested in the world of bishops than Eusebius might have us believe. But an emperor, like a bishop, need not advocate religious tolerance to appropriate an image of pagan culture in the interests of Christian empire. Both Lactantius and Eusebius, as well as any number of bishops, had hoped to teach him just that.

Christopher Ocker
Graduate Theological Union and San Francisco Theological Seminary

Reenchantment without Supernaturalism: A Process Philosophy of Religion. By David Ray Griffin. Cornell University Press, 2001. 426 pages. $55.00; $24.95 paper.

In this ambitious book David Ray Griffin develops a naturalistic theism that he hopes can both transform the philosophy of religion and help to reverse the modern disenchantment of the world. Written with deep knowledge of both Whitehead's oeuvre and the contemporary issues in philosophy, it is the clearest and most comprehensive statement of what philosophy of religion looks like from a process perspective.

Though the basic premise of process theism may be widely known, neither of the two most significant moves in this book is that God is in process. The first is Griffin's distinction between two senses of naturalism. One form, which he endorses, is simply the rejection of supernaturalism; that is, it denies that divine beings do or even could interrupt the natural causal processes of the world. The other form, which Griffin rejects, is a naturalism that includes an atheistic and materialist worldview and an epistemology based solely on sensory data. By developing a religious philosophy that is naturalistic only in the first sense, Griffin shows that philosophers of religion are not required to choose either materialistic atheism or supernaturalistic theism. Though largely ignored by philosophers, this third option can be equally congenial to scientists who stay true to their own principles and to religious practitioners who stay true to theirs. It is as a version of religious naturalism, then, that Griffin develops his own "prehensive-panentheistic-panexperientialist" position.

The second significant move is that Griffin argues that the primary criterion for any theory is that it do justice to what he calls our "hard-core commonsense" notions. Such notions are the inevitable presuppositions of practice, notions at play in action as such. Because such notions are presupposed by every action, even the act of denying them requires them, and so they cannot be denied without self-contradiction. A philosophy is irrational, then, to the extent that it denies these pragmatically necessary ideas. This idea of a "pragmatic metaphysics" (31n, 51n) deserves a broader hearing in philosophy, though I was not always happy with the way that Griffin expresses it. For example, he suggests that philosophers should restrict their fallibilism in order to exclude the hard-core commonsense notions from criticism (33n, cf. 361). A better approach, I think, would be to argue that a putative hard-core commonsense notion is, like any other notion, fallible even while insisting that the nonrestricted scope of the notion means that if it is true, it is implied even by its denial. Also, to challenge such notions it is not necessary empirically to "find someone" who truly lives without the presupposition (34). Rather, the opponent can either demonstrate that the notion is conceivably falsifiable (in which case it is not really a "hard-core" notion) or that the notion is incoherent (in which case it applies to none of our practices). These disagreements on the fine points, however, do not take away from the important point that Griffin is identifying a criterion for philosophy to which the majority of modern and postmodern criticisms of metaphysics do not apply.

The greater part of the book develops the idea of a nonsupernaturalistic God, a "Holy Reality" that does not intervene in natural processes but, rather, is continuously and directly experienced. The chapters serially show how this idea transforms the basic topics in the philosophy of religion. Griffin argues, for example, that this naturalistic theism can serve to reconcile belief in God and the theory of evolution, that it (dis)solves the problem of evil, and that it provides a morality-supporting cosmology. Process thinkers have made some of these arguments before, but many of the chapters advance the issues in original directions. For example, though Griffin has claimed in the past that natural theology is not essential to process theism, he now holds that a process philosophy of religion not only presents a credible idea of God but also provides strong reasons for believing in God's existence. He also argues that a naturalistic theism like this one can not only reconcile science and religion but also account for the idea of evolutionary saltations without appealing to miracles. Third, Griffin argues that Whitehead's distinction between God and creativity makes possible a new answer to the problem of religious diversity. Griffin proposes that different religions seek to refer to and experience not the same ultimate reality but, rather, two different features of reality, both of which are ultimate, though in different senses. One feature is the personal ultimate reality, the ultimate agent, and the other is the impersonal ultimate reality, agency as such. Griffin then defends a pluralism in which two basic types of religious belief and experience can be valid. Fourth, he is concerned to argue that his naturalistic theism does not necessarily deny the possibility of life after death. He argues that Whitehead and Hartshorne do not deny that life after death is possible and that the evidence of telepathy and out-of-body experiences makes the idea of life after death plausible. Moreover, he argues that we have a psychic need for life after death, a need that includes the longing for more life or for an ideal mode of existence as well as the Kantian sense that those who live morally do not often in this life get the happiness they deserve, so life without an afterlife would be unfair.

Not everyone will find all of these new directions equally persuasive. For example, the alleged psychic need for life after death is not evidence, nor is this need exceptionless enough to call it "a permanent feature of human existence as such" (233). And even if one agrees that we have *nonsensory* perceptions, it does not follow that there can be *nonembodied* perceptions. And however one weighs the paranormal evidence, Hartshorne emphasized the fact that existence always involves a tragic dimension and even the best life cannot realize incompossible goods. In this light, Griffin's claims that we need an afterlife to provide enough time for souls "to actualize all their potentialities" (240), to become "perfect" (236), sound escapist. Coherent dreams of wholeness and integrity will aspire to less.

In the end, however, these are again disagreements about details. The book as a whole succeeds in its central goal to show that the philosophy of religion is ignoring a third option between atheistic materialism and supernaturalistic theism, a form of naturalism that is not a priori opposed to religion. And Griffin is correct that such a position has the potential not only to reorient the philosophy of religion but also to reconcile the truths of science with the truths of religion and thereby to point the way to a reenchanted worldview.

Kevin Schilbrack
Wesleyan College

God Is a Conservative: Religion, Politics, and Morality in Contemporary America. By Kenneth J. Heineman. New York University Press, 1998. 342 pages. $26.95.

The title of this work is misleading. Its actual focus, from beginning to end, is presidential election politics. There are eight chapters, each devoted to an election analysis, beginning with Nixon's success in 1968 and concluding with Clinton's 1996 victory. In a substantial epilogue, Kenneth Heineman summarizes trends he has detected in these three decades of U.S. politics and states his preference for a yet unrealized combination of economic populism and social conservatism. A major disappointment for the reader, however, is that there is little moral or philosophical argumentation even in the epilogue, and there is no theological argumentation anywhere in the book. It does not make the crucial argument, for instance, that religious conservatives are right on the public issues of the period; and although the author applauds religious involvement in the political order through voter guides distributed at churches and crusades organized by powerful pulpiteers, he nowhere engages the arguments based in theories of public reason that would deny the legitimacy of such political activity. Heineman does show that religious conservatives constitute an increasingly significant, though seldom determinative, voting bloc and that it is beneficial for campaigns to accommodate their concerns to be successful. At the same time, he argues convincingly that their influence is felt more strongly at the polls than in the actual determination of public policy in any administration. In light of the work's actual content, then, its catchy title must mean simply that conservative religion played a somewhat stronger role in American election politics toward the end of the twentieth century than it did earlier.

Heineman's writing style is lively and engaging. The comprehensive treatments of each presidential term are packed with information yet also laced with wonderful anecdotes, quotes, and occasional sarcastic and comical asides by the author. He has been able to incorporate the oral style of informed and entertaining classroom instruction into a literary format.

There is one feature of his presentation, however, that is distracting to academic readers and damaging to the credibility of his accounts. Although there are fifty-six pages of notation at the end, and many endnotes contain multiple references, there is no narrative content whatever in the notes. The problem is exacerbated by the fact that Heineman writes with his references occurring only at the conclusion of each paragraph. What the reader is typically given, then, is a paragraph with several pieces of empirical data, various generalizations, and a comical aside. The note provided may reference one work or a long list of works, but there is no effort to correlate any particular reference with actual claims in the text. Without considerable work as a literary sleuth, the reader is often lost as to whose voice is speaking, that of Heineman or one of his sources.

These problems are complicated even further by the author's penchant for hyperbole and hasty generalizations. For instance, he uses the inflated figure of 18 million Southern Baptists in discussion of their famous threat to boycott Disney (264), recounts that "hundreds of Pentecostal churches in Brooklyn mobilized their Puerto Rican flocks to combat crime" (52), and reveals that in the 1992 election "almost without exception, every southern white who clung to the Democratic Party was a senior citizen who believed Clinton when he warned that the Republicans would abolish Social Security" (206). Heineman ridicules social and religious liberals throughout, portraying activist pro-choice and gay rights groups, 1960s protesters who are now liberal humanities professors, the ubiquitous "liberal media," and mainstream Protestant denominations whose numbers are forever dwindling as simply out of touch with reality.

The chief merit of the book is its display of the deep divisions between liberals and conservatives that are at work in both the Democratic and Republican Parties and, further, the rifts among liberals and conservatives themselves within each party. Of particular interest in this regard is Heineman's perceptive analysis of the tension generated between religious conservatives and libertarians in the Republican Party, the former willing and the latter unwilling to accommodate government encouragement of a moral social order through restrictions on Big Business and personal freedoms.

Heineman also provides a penetrating account of the continual cycle of hopes and frustrations experienced by religious conservatives in the last three decades. They saw in Jimmy Carter, for instance, the first national political figure in modern American history who would speak openly of being "born again," but then were disappointed by his liberal and progressive social ethics. Jerry Falwell's "Moral Majority" rallied behind Ronald Reagan, who could "endorse" them though they could not endorse him, only to discover that Reagan's administration cared mainly for their votes, not their actual programs. Pat Robinson and then Ralph Reed marshaled Christian Coalition voters to support George Bush only to be frustrated again by an administration that carried forward the Reagan infatuation with Big Business but had even less real interest than did its predecessor in conservative moral concerns such as abortion. The greatest victory for religious conservatives was in the 1994 midterm election that gave Republicans control of both houses of Congress in an act of political rebellion against the Clinton administration. Here again, however, after their initial success slashing National Endowment for the Arts and National Endowment for the Humanities funding, religious conservatives found themselves trumped by Clinton's centrist economic policy, welfare reform, and other programs forged out of alliance with Republican liberals.

At this point in our history, Heineman argues, the future of religious conservatism as a political movement in America is uncertain. Before resigning his role in the Christian Coalition, Ralph Reed recommended a focus on local rather than national elections. Cal Thomas recommends pulling out of the political arena altogether, and religious leaders are giving much attention to the construction of a Christian counterculture. Though some notables dream of a third political party, the intractable obstacle to a political future for religious conservatives, in Heineman's view, is lack of funds. Organizations such as the Christian Coalition just "do not have the financial resources to take on either social liberals or libertarians" (263).

This may be, but Heineman likely underestimates the ability and willingness of churches all across America as well as their political arms such as the Christian Coalition and Focus on the Family to generate funds for their causes. Conservatives in control of the Southern Baptist Convention are now in position to use its considerable resources to support events with obvious political implications such as Sanctity of Life services. The Catholic Church outspent all liberal sources combined in the physician-assisted suicide battles in Oregon, and there seems to be no limit to the amount of money that can be raised by televangelists. It may be that the real problem for conservatives is not lack of money but lack of support, that is, the majority of Americans oppose their views.

Heineman hopes for a resurrection of something like the position maintained early in the twentieth century by silver-tongued orator William Jennings Bryan, a populist progressive with conservative moral commitments based in religion. Throughout the book, for instance, Heineman is concerned that problems of blue-collar labor, especially the white ethnic populations of traditional industrial centers, are not being met by either majority party. He worries about the black underclass, mired in poverty and trapped in inner-city war zones, ignored by country club Republicans and victimized, in his view, by Democratic welfare liberalism. He writes with approval of conservative political figures who have taken on Big Business and with strong endorsement of pro-life forces working against both abortion and physician-assisted suicide. The positions, though not the political ability, of Pat Buchanan are invoked as the most reasonable option on most issues. In a wistful comment toward the end of the book, Heineman states his recipe for the "moral populism" that is our hope: "If the social conservatives could ally with economic populists—and, in the process, create a new style of orthodox Protestantism that looked more favorably upon some degree of federal regulation of the marketplace—their rivals would be overwhelmed. Pat Buchanan has pointed the way toward such a future" (263).

Such an alliance is doubtful, as Heineman knows. More importantly, it is not clear on either a historical or a philosophical basis that moral populism is our hope. Heineman needs to answer the arguments of writers such as Richard Rorty in *Achieving Our Country* that the crucial human rights movements of twentieth-century American history were vigorously supported by social and religious liberals and opposed by social conservatives every step of the way; and he needs to argue, not simply assert, that U.S. democracy grounded in Protestant orthodoxy, or any other religious view, is preferable to a pluralistic future in which politics and religion are disentangled.

David McKenzie
Berry College

Becoming Divine: Towards a Feminist Philosophy of Religion. By Grace M. Jantzen. Indiana University Press, 1999. 296 pages. $24.95.

Do the inevitabilities of birth, materiality, immanence of mind, and related ethics of flourishing constitute a more primary, real, and compelling aim for feminist philosophies of religion than the inevitable "gifts" of death, radical otherness, conceptualizations of ideal ontostases (or heroic despair of ever having such), and related ethics of culpability? For those scholars engaged in various forms of feminist, womanist, and ecological work in religion, the answer is often a clear yes. This has been true ever since Mary Daly challenged the whole existentialist obsession with nonbeing and being-toward-death, denouncing it as unnecessary and fundamentally necrophilic. And it remains true as Alice Walker, Nelle Morton, Chung Hyun Kyung, Ivone Gebara, Sallie McFague, Starhawk, and so many others insist that the flourishing of the particular (whether animal, floral, mineral, communal, or individual) *in relation to* the whole is closer to what divinity means and intends than anything else.

Indeed, Grace Jantzen is well aware that the aim of natality (and flourishing) is not new to Anglo- or Euro-American feminist thought, for she focuses on Hannah Arendt's early development of the concept and gives a (cursory) nod to Daly's extensive work on it as well. She points out quite rightly, however, that many feminist theological projects tend to work uncritically with inherited frameworks and doctrinal commitments that undergird exclusion even as they try to invoke new visions. And they tend to confuse accounts of experiences of oppression with claims about divinity as if the two describe each other adequately. So what she is offering here is not necessarily a new aim for feminism but, rather, the beginnings of a solid philosophical foundation and set of warrants for claiming that aim.

Using primarily the ideas of Irigaray (and so French poststructuralism and the psychoanalytic theories of Lacan) Jantzen argues that the deeply masculinist roots of western culture and its long history of conceptual and material domination of women, marginalized and colonized peoples, and the earth is most fruitfully explained (and so deconstructed) via Freudian/Lacanian psychoanalytic theories of the cultural "Symbolic" that shapes individual and corporate imaginations and horizons of possibility. What is more, when this dominant, cultural symbolic is given a proper "double reading" (via Derrida) it reveals a bedrock "aim" of necrophilia that in turn shapes western philosophies of religion (and theology). Because this aim serves masculinist supremacy at the deepest levels of philosophical inquiry and as such is not properly necessary to that inquiry, Jantzen proposes natality and flourishing as a more appropriate aim, not only for feminist philosophies of religion but for theology and, presumably, western thought in general.

This is a hugely ambitious, important book, one that begins a comprehensive linkage among the spectacularly (and mutually) disrupting insights of French feminism (Irigaray in particular), Lacanian cultural psychoanalysis, complex theories of interlocking domination (such as Collins and McClintock have provided), Derridean deconstruction, Levinasian ethics, pragmatic western political feminism, and feminist theology with the goal of providing a rigorous philosophical foundation for turning the *Titanic* of western philosophies of religion onto a different course altogether. More modestly, Jantzen's goal is to serve feminist philosophers and theologians who stand with her at the crumbling limits of western thought with a glimpse of new ground as the "western masculinist symbolic" morphs from taken-for-granted reality into the desperate Oz curtain that it is.

By "thinking differently" (the name of her third chapter) Jantzen attempts to chart a deconstructive reading of this necrophilic symbolic such that its own dependence on the repressed Other (most specifically the female but also all of the repressed "others" that make possible the masculinist, totalistic assertion of the One) comes into focus, much like a simple change of lighting on a theatrical scrim can reveal what was invisible behind it. In so doing, Jantzen is confident that all of these deconstructive and political theories taken together can open pathways into the repressed background, which is the utter primacy of embodied, world-imbricated birth.

The aim of natality, Jantzen argues, is familiar because it is our repressed reality as living beings; we are natals constantly experiencing rebirth out of and into the matter of the world. Yet natality is radical for thought and remains largely untheorized precisely because of its power to disrupt the masculinist doctrines of the Rule of the (One) Father. If we were to start from here, from the primary necessity of birth and the secondary dependence of death on natality, we then open our theological imaginings into a landscape just coherent enough to follow but not so coherent that we remap the same system back onto it—and ourselves. Jantzen runs the risk of setting up another oppositional category here (between birth and death), but that may be only because she is working so hard to deconstruct the repression of birth, on which, she persuasively argues, the necrophilic symbolic depends.

Where Jantzen succeeds in this huge project is in opening doors for further critical work on natality. She also models use of *multiple* theories of domination, subjectivity, becoming, and materiality, none of which can be dropped at any point or employed serially. (Indeed, the brilliant work of Patricia Hill Collins, Anne McClintock, Evelyn Hammonds, Ellen Armour, and others like them has made serial theory wholly inadequate in the face of deep oppression.)

Its ambition is this book's Achilles heel. The demand that Jantzen makes—that we think about the masculinist symbolic in comprehensive terms of psychoanalysis, ethics, political theory, textual deconstruction, identity theory, and theology—leads her often into repetition and a sometimes heavy-handed slogging toward her proximal points, while the larger point, becoming divine, ever recedes. This is perhaps a cost of making fast all of the lines for a truly new comprehensive argument. Jantzen has to make large leaps between discourses, moves that yield important fruit but are not yet adequately developed. Her treatment of philosophers, not surprisingly, is more satisfying than her treatment of theologians. The choice to limit an in-depth analysis of feminist theology, for example, to Rosemary Ruether and Elisabeth Schüssler Fiorenza is understandable given their stature, but it is negligent given the current state of the field(s). There are a number of theologians who are answering Jantzen's concerns about feminist theology in provocative and potentially helpful ways. Catherine Keller, Delores Williams, Nancy Victorin-Vangerud, and Kathleen Sands come to mind as examples.

Becoming Divine is not primarily a theological text and should not be judged as one, although the distinction may be spurious (and Jantzen herself is interested in the power dynamics at play in disciplining such boundaries). Nevertheless, there are ways in which Jantzen's philosophical rigor falters up against the very theological matter of the book—divinity. The final chapter, curiously entitled "A God according to Our Gender," does not take up the problematics of the very term *god*; nor does Jantzen adequately define or make clear her use of the term *divine*. Given her method of double reading and the development of her argument, this is a curious omission. What is more, the bulk of this final chapter introduces yet another theory, this time Whiteheadian process thought, fruitful for a theology of natality but also requiring significant deconstruction. The theological result is fragmentary but suggestive, an undeveloped conclusion that pantheism and "sensible transcendence" are avenues toward divinity or at least toward becoming divine, which is "symbolic of outrage, imagination and desire, and compassionate action, not the detached and objective intellectual stance which traditional philosophers of religion assume and which they take also to be characteristic of God" (263). But, if convinced of the problem, don't we need more about this divinity we are urged to become?

Given this question, Jantzen does make a tantalizing but frustratingly incomplete suggestion, based on her reading of Irigaray, that an aim of natality leads us more clearly to a developmental notion of divinity as a process of achieving subjectivity, and so voice, and so flourishing. Divinity, in other words, "in the face of natals is a horizon of becoming, a process of divinity ever new, just as natality is the possibility of new beginnings" (254). Is this an answer? She might respond that it is an opening, and perhaps she is right. Over and over Jantzen argues that truth claims about divine existence miss the point and reveal masculinist commitments. But that may not always be the case. These are difficult theological problems, and the philosopher or theologian who takes up divinity *and* world cannot evade truth claims about either, both within and outside of contexts of communal experience. Jantzen does not deny this, and thus her work tantalizes even as it exhausts. To end a book with fragmentary suggestions about the divine we become is by no means a bad thing if she intends to pick up the fragments in a next edition or in an additional volume. We can hope that she will. As it stands, however, some will find this book maddeningly incomplete. That is, perhaps, all to the good. An open door, with light cast such that what lies beyond is uncertain, can be like that.

Laurel C. Schneider
Chicago Theological Seminary

Singing to the Jinas: Jain Laywomen, Mandal Singing and the Negotiations of Jain Devotion. By M. Whitney Kelting. Oxford University Press, 2001. 268 pages. $49.95.

Nobody with even a passing familiarity with Protestant Christianity could underrate the importance of hymns as a source of imagery, theology, and exemplification for believers. From Lutheran chorale, to the compositions of evangelical Victorian hymnodists such as Moody and Sankey, to the vast number of contemporary examples that run the stylistic gamut from the sentimental to the hard edged, hymns have occupied a vital role among Christian congregations, fully acknowledged by academic observers, in focusing faith and providing a source of comfort and community.

Devotional poems enacted in some sort of performative context (for that is effectively what hymns are) have also been ubiquitous in all the major Indian religions, representing in their textual form a substantial literary genre (in Sanskrit variously styled *stuti, stotra,* and *stavana,* although these terms are not entirely synonymous) that was skillfully manipulated by Hindu, Buddhist, and Jain poets for centuries and gained a receptive audience keenly aware of the redemptive and often magical power embodied in such inspired creations. Yet Indological scholarship has been slow to grasp the significance of hymnody in South Asian religiosity and has been largely disdainful of what is often presented as little more than the tiresome and repetitive effusions of a popular or popular-oriented piety. Perhaps only the Sanskrit hymns of the Śaivas of Kashmir or the southerner Vedānta Deśika have escaped this judgment, no doubt because of their often high philosophical tone, whereas the famous *stotras* attributed to Śaṅkara seem to have been studied more for the light they can shed on the date of the theologian with whom they are associated rather than for any possible significance they might have in devotional Hinduism. Much analytical and interpretive work needs to be done in this area, by Sanskritists no less than by students of Indian religions.

Hymns of praise to the *tīrthaṅkaras,* the great teachers of Jainism, go back to near that tradition's origins. The *Sūtrakṛtāṅga Sūtra* (ca. fourth–third centuries C.E.) contains a *stuti* in honor of Mahāvīra and his many heroic qualities, and the second part of the liturgically central *Āvaśyaka Sūtra,* which crystallized at the beginning of the common era, is a hymn of homage to all twenty-four *tīrthaṅkaras.* Such is the celebrity of the most famous of all Jain hymns, the *Bhaktāmara Stotra* of Mānatuṅga (ca. fifth century C.E.), that this Sanskrit poem has become an object of devotion in its own right, attracting to itself an extensive mass of narrative, ritual, and esoteric interpretation. Throughout the middle ages, a substantial portion of the prestige of the great teachers of Śvetāmbara Jainism derived from the regular composition of hymns in classical and vernacular languages (in the later case composed in meters linked to popular song melodies) that both testified to and promoted a vast and ever expanding network of local images and cult spots. In the Digambara Jain sect Sanskrit hymns to the *tīrthaṅkaras* composed by monastic poets such as Samantabhadra served as a means of communicating some of the most complex philosophical ideas of intellectual Jainism.

To this day, hymns are deeply embedded in the performance of temple worship and fasting by Jains and represent a vital point of reference for gaining a direct experience of the religious culture of Jainism. Although laymen unquestionably composed hymns in the medieval period and still utilize them in devotional contexts, the role of deploying and perpetuating the rich culture of Jain hymnody is now very much vested in laywomen who organize themselves in "circles" (*maṇḍal*) for this purpose. In her remarkably original and informative book, *Singing to the Jinas*, Whitney Kelting investigates the dynamics involved in one such group of Śvetāmbara Jain *mūrtipūjak* (image worshiping) women, the *maṇḍal*, or, as she styles it, "performance singing collective" (viii), associated with the temple dedicated to the *tīrthaṅkara* Ajitanātha in the Śivajīnagar district of the city of Puṇe in Maharashtra.

The members of the *maṇḍal* described by Kelting are middle-class Gujaratis whose families have migrated to Maharashtra to trade, and their hymns (*stavan*), which are composed in Gujarati rather than the local Marathi, are expressions of both their ethnic and their religious identities. Kelting shows how participation in the creative and performative activities of the *maṇḍal* enables women, who are both economically dependent maintainers of households and inculcators of religious values in the young, to develop their own versions of Jain theology and also to compete with the male-centered public prestige practices of Jain ritual that largely involve financial donation. The authority that women gain within the Jain community in Puṇe and in the *maṇḍal* itself is thus shown to be linked to their practical ritual and devotional-artistic expertise.

The literary culture described in fine-grained detail by Kelting involves a blend of the oral and the written. Hymns are composed orally by women, and they circulate in that medium until they are eventually collected and copied in notebooks, a process that Kelting suggests is an extension of the time-honored pious activity of the transcription of sacred texts. Furthermore, in copying a *stavan* a woman is not simply recording it but internally re-encoding and appropriating it so that the hymn effectively becomes part of her, with its theology percolating into her everyday life and influencing the various behavioral choices she makes as a woman and a Jain. The huge repertoire built up in this way, effectively a vernacularization of Jain experience, communicates a devotional religiosity centering on worship of an immanent and loving savior, rather than of a dead and inaccessible ascetic renouncer, which would otherwise be anticipated on the basis of a familiarity with philosophical Jainism only. The *stavans* produced by the *maṇḍal* also celebrate the greatness of legendary Jain women who have attained spiritual deliverance in the past and so reconfirm the status of women as exemplifications of traditional Jain virtues within the community today.

Stavans are performed in a multidimensional idiom of music and dance that countenances elements of improvisation and the use of ready-made components such as folk melodies and film tunes. Here, however, the pervasive ideology of restraint and personal discipline that governs Jain ascetic and lay behavior remains in place. Although the *stavan* performances of devotional Hinduism frequently involve overt displays of intense emotionalism, sometimes culminating in possession by a deity, which reflects a theology of God's unconditioned "play" (*līlā*), the public adoption of such an idiom of abandonment would generally compromise the social standing of a Jain in a manner that would not pertain to a Hindu. As Kelting shows in chapter 4 of *Singing to the Jinas*, in an impressive taxonomy of the various categories of *stavan* through which she conveys how individuals dictate choice and style of delivery of a hymn, the poetics of Jain hymnody taps into the nine *rasa* or the "flavor" model first evolved in the context of Sanskrit dramaturgical analysis at the beginning of the common era and then subsequently applied to all artistic production. Understandably, a common *rasa* like the "amorous" (*śṛṅgāra*) is deployed only rarely, and the ninth *rasa*, the "calm" (*śānta*), which was of controversial status in medieval Indian aesthetics but apparently accepted by Jain poets relatively early, is the predominant means of vectoring that sense of inner stillness typical of Jain devotion.

Despite the avowedly calming nature of the literary genre being described, Kelting has written an exhilarating book that represents a model for any type of research involving both texts and field observation. The vividness of her descriptions, enhanced with photographs and English versions of *stavans* whose effectiveness is in no way diminished by translation, is such that on occasion I felt myself to be participating in an actual *maṇḍal* performance. At the same time, Kelting's clearheaded analysis continually demonstrates how the singing of hymns to the *tīrthaṅkaras* connects with both the ideology and the actualities of Jainism on many levels. The Śivajīnagar Jain community described in *Singing to the Jinas* is not sufficiently large or prosperous to support a resident mendicant group during the rainy period, so it does not participate in the regular lay–mendicant interaction that is a significant feature of Śvetāmbara Jain religiosity elsewhere. Thus, while not completely ignoring mendicant influence, Kelting's treatment is in accord with the general trend of recent Jain ethnography (in actuality, the only type of Jain ethnography!) that would regard the realm of values associated with the laity, that of well-being and auspiciousness, as complementary rather than subordinate to the male ascetic-centered interpretation of Jainism that earlier textually oriented scholarship has taken as central.

Singing to the Jinas is a further significant landmark in Jain ethnography, which with other recent sophisticated studies, such as John E. Cort's *Jains in the World: Religious Values and Ideology in India* (Oxford University Press, 2001) and James Laidlaw's *Riches and Renunciation: Religion, Economy and Society among the Jains*, (Clarendon Press, 1996), has finally come of age in the last decade. This fine book should appeal to a wide scholarly constituency: Those interested in ritual and the relationship between women and religion in South Asia in particular will find much to engage them. But, above all, it should be read as a salutary corrective by anybody tempted to think of Jainism as a religion lacking an overt devotional dimension and a poor relation amid India's rich culture of *bhakti*.

Paul Dundas
University of Edinburgh

Women Preachers and Prophets through Two Millennia of Christianity. Edited by Beverly Mayne Kienzle and Pamela J. Walker. University of California Press, 1998. 384 pages. $17.95.

The force of Pauline injunctions, centuries of ecclesiastical tradition, and sedimented cultural understandings of gender roles and expectations have made preaching and prophecy contested arenas for women. By opting for a broad understanding of the word *preaching*, the essays in this book open the subject to a number of devices, strategies, and subversions engaged by women to proclaim their faith, but they also run the risk of emptying it of that which made it contested in the first place. Is there an issue, for example, when women offer testimonies or expositions of biblical passages within the context of their own homes to an audience of women? Is any public Christian witness, whether on the street, in the market square, or in a teaching setting, all outside the ecclesiastical structure, to count as "preaching"? As many of the essays make clear, the more fundamental issues are often about authority, opportunities for women's religious leadership, the development of female voice in an often restrictive context, and the nature and character of communication within a religious community.

Elaine Lawless's introduction to the book would have worked better as a final essay in the historical sequence, I believe, because it focuses on two contemporary women's sermons, and Lawless makes claims about what women preachers do with these messages (e.g., claim authority from a personal call from God and question the authority of the lectionary texts, respectively). Despite vastly different contexts, they both represent rhetorical empowerment. As the introduction, however, it suggests that the essays to follow will address actual preaching, which they do not.

The two essays that deal with early Christianity address aspects of women's prophetic experience and that role within the religious community. Karen King takes up the *Gospel of Mary* (Magdalene) and illustrates how its understanding that the mind rather than the soul was the bearer of the divine vision, its rejection of the idea that prophecy was the penetration of the body by a spirit, and its rejection of the body as the location of the self all argue for "the ideal of a common humanity based on the transcendence of bodily distinctions" (32) and for Christian identity "apart from gender roles, sex, and childbearing" (33). While this contested both social and sexual understandings of prophetic experience, she notes, it did so at the cost of women's bodies. Karen Jo Torjesen explores the many visual representations of females praying, often anonymous and, within that category, universally female. They point, but only implicitly, to a wide range of liturgical activities, including prophetic instruction, singing, exhortation, and Eucharistic celebration, often through the offices of widow and virgin. By claiming to speak to and for God in a prophetic voice, a woman claimed divine rather than personal authority, and the congregations recognized that in a number of ways.

Most of the essays address topics in the Middle Ages, reflecting perhaps the extensive research on women's religious lives in this period. Although placed in the early church section, Katherine Ludwig Jansen's chapter studies the mainly medieval construction of Mary Magdalene as "apostle of the apostles," more specifically in terms of her alleged missionary work of bringing the Christian message to France. For fully 500 years, down to the Council of Trent, this image appeared in popular devotional literature, religious poetry and art, and sermons. In the face of frequent opposition to women's preaching in the early church, one question is whether the persistence of this view of Mary Magdalene meant that those who used it believed that the office of preaching had been given to both men and women. It appears as though she functioned both as the divinely chosen exception for extraordinary times and as a model for at least some women to take up their own ministries.

Coeditor Beverly Kienzle takes up the other side of women's preaching, the arguments of opponents, as she considers three critics of women's preaching among the Waldenses, whereas Anne Brenon for the same period describes the extensive religious activities ("perhaps even to preach" [120]) of the Good Women (a religious community) of the Cathar movement. Nicole Beriou investigates the thirteenth-century debate over who (especially whether women) can give religious instruction to persons after baptism, which soon involved the questions of whether teaching was a form of preaching and whether prophecy, being a product of divine inspiration, was permissible for women when preaching was not. In both the evolution and the refinement of the argument, women's position as religious instructors to their children continued but was increasingly subordinated and supervised. Not surprisingly, then, the final three essays in this section explore the main theme indirectly and as forms of contest with the dominant churchly view: through song as a form of teaching (and of preaching?), lives of saintly women (here, Rose of Viterbo) as public apostolates, and representations of women saints in late medieval Italian iconography in a variety of preaching contexts.

The period from the sixteenth to the twentieth century, although with a respectable balance of eight chapters, seems most slighted because of the essays' particularity and lack of connection to each other. John Foxe's martyrology is used by Edith Wilks Dolnikowski to show how women could be "exemplars for reform" in the English sixteenth century, that is, that testimony, service, and martyrdom were equal-opportunity vocations. It is not clear, however, how she finds "the preeminence of the authority of the individual Christian believer" to be one of the tenets of reformed theology (200, 208) or why she seems puzzled that, despite the book's popularity, women's "contributions to the church as teachers and preachers were marginalized" (208). The only Catholic topic in the period is that explored by Linda Lierheimer on strategies of seventeenth-century Ursulines "to create space for the female teacher of the Word of God" (213) in their mission work in France. Although the Ursulines often blurred the boundaries between their teaching activity and preaching, both clergy supporters and opponents often tried to distinguish the two, seeing preaching as public (which they were not to do) and teaching as private (which they did). By midcentury most Ursulines had accepted enclosure, and their speech had been confined, but this very adaptation gave opportunities for expanding their mission within the Church that established those boundaries.

The two eighteenth-century essays, by Peter Vogt on Moravians and Phyllis Mack on Quakers, are not so much about preaching as about women's voice, and each provides remarkable insight into the complex world of religious communities and their discourse. In the first, women preached not to the entire community but to their own gendered "choirs," thus creating a somewhat ambivalent stance that was moderated by Zinzendorf's ongoing reflection but then hardened again after his death. Because the Quakers had accepted women's spiritual equality with men (and their preaching, based on the inspiration of the Holy Spirit), Mack addresses the negotiation involved in moving from a foundation in prophecy (seventeenth century) to one of rationality (eighteenth century) and in dealing with the cultural constructions of "masculine" and "feminine" characteristics, especially in terms of how each might enable or retard a public voice and the political consciousness for women.

Four chapters offer limited glimpses of the modern period in two countries. For the United States there are essays by Judylyn Ryan on black women's literature (the writings of Maria Stewart and a character from the fiction of Toni Morrison), as illustrations of an Africa-centered spirituality best understood as an ethos of connectedness, and by Yvonne Chireau on the black spiritual churches conceived by Mother Leaf Anderson and established between 1919 and 1927 on a self-consciously female-centered foundation with a very eclectic spirituality. Each is about much more than preaching; the latter especially explores the variety of activities of women religious leaders and the multiple influences taken from other religious traditions. For England coeditor Pamela Walker takes up the work of Catherine Booth (in particular her 1859 pamphlet defending women's right to preach the gospel) and the role of women in the Salvation Army. Finally, Jacqueline deVries argues, against several scholars, that the "turn toward religion" by a number of English suffragists in the later years of the suffrage campaign did not represent a repudiation of their feminism but, rather, an extension and advancement of it.

Karen King's concluding chapter reflects on arguments used to support and oppose women's public speech and on the conditions that encourage or inhibit it, and she notes that much of the history of women's experience on this issue has involved transgressing social and institutional boundaries. The book would have been richer had the several contributors engaged in further such reflection, such that broader frameworks for understanding might have more easily emerged. One can see from some of the essays, for example, that new religious movements in liminal religious eras are usually more open to claims by women than the traditions they seek to reform or oppose. In addition, movements with a high regard for the authority of the Holy Spirit or personal experience are often more receptive to women's public speech than those that place a high value on the authority of tradition or Scripture. Most important, one observes how women's preaching and prophecy reveal other prominent and complex issues in the history of the church. This is not the comprehensive survey implied in the title, but the book is filled with insights that readers can use as they take up other topics within the main theme.

Dale A. Johnson
Vanderbilt University

Women and the Word: Contemporary Women Novelists and the Bible. By Jeannette King. Palgrave, 2000. 207 pages. $59.95.

Jeannette King's investigation of several contemporary women novelists who wrestle with and rewrite biblical stories as a way of challenging and reconstructing our understandings of gender is a project that deserves attention—and further engagement. It would be more than worthwhile for other scholars to analyze both the texts King has chosen and other contemporary novels in an effort not only to see how thoroughly our imaginations have been shaped by biblical paradigms but also to see how recent feminist criticism of the Bible has altered our interpretations of both biblical stories and their fictional analogues. Unfortunately, as interesting as King's project is, her execution is marred by her thorough embrace of scholarship—now widely discredited—that posits an ancient, peaceful, matriarchal, goddess-worshiping society that was destroyed by the rise of patriarchal religion (specifically Judaism). This flaw not only leads her away from mainstream religious scholarship that would have been of use to her project, it also ends up limiting her specifically literary analysis of some of the works she has chosen. I will examine the problems with her religious scholarship first and then the related problems that appear in her analysis of fiction.

King acknowledges that her main field of expertise is literary criticism not religion (ix), and her lack of familiarity with the study of religion is often evident. For example, biblical scholarship points to a text (better, a collection of texts) that is rich in voices and authors often telling and retelling the same story over and over again, yet King makes the odd claim that the Bible is a "monologic" text that lacks "different voices, different points of view" (122). Even more disturbing is her understanding of the transition from a supposedly matriarchal Golden Age to patriarchal forms of society. Relying on Julia Kristeva's account of religion and patriarchy, King claims that "the Hebraic patriarchal tradition . . . moved women to the margins of a culture of which they were once the centre" (33). There are two problems here: first, most archaeologists and historians agree that the evidence simply does not support the idea that early human history was dominated by a peaceful, woman-centered, goddess-worshiping social system that was eventually destroyed by patriarchy; and second, blaming the rise of the God of the Hebrews for the death of the Goddess seems to slip into the anti-Judaism that Katharina von Kellenbach warns feminists about in *Anti-Judaism in Feminist Religious Writings*. King demonstrates both a troubling anti-Judaism and a disturbing lack of understanding of the development of religious faith in general when she makes statements such as the following: "When the Hebrews attempted to develop a monotheistic religion that would stand apart from and ultimately defeat the pagan religions of the other Canaanite tribes, they incorporated as well as reacted against Canaanite mythology" (13). Although it is true that Yahwism and Canaanite worship existed in tension or even competition for some time, the opening phrase of this odd statement flatly misunderstands religion. King seems to be saying that Judaism was not born of specific experiences of and encounters with the Holy but, rather, of a conscious desire to construct an ideology that would "defeat" others. This failure to see religion as anything more than the conscious invention of patriarchy is perhaps why King ignores pathbreaking feminist religious scholars such as Elisabeth Schüssler Fiorenza, Rosemary Radford Ruether, Phyllis Trible, and Letty Russell in her discussions of women and religion (although all of these, oddly, appear in her bibliography) and relies instead on Riane Eisler (*The Chalice and the Blade*), Gerda Lerner (*The Creation of Patriarchy*), and Julia Kristeva (*About Chinese Women*), whose work focuses on the glory days of Goddess worship in contrast to the destructive misogyny of Judaism and Christianity.

King's reliance on scholars who tout the Goddess at the expense of Judaism and Christianity is more than a problem of religious scholarship: It also harms her ability critically to analyze women's fiction. King sets out a theoretical structure in which contemporary women novelists attack biblical stories and characters while creating positive, Goddess-inspired models for women to follow instead. The possibility that biblical stories can be critiqued from within a Christian or Jewish perspective is not considered. King appears unacquainted with the practice of midrash, in which biblical stories are rethought and retold in order to address new questions or fill in gaps, and thus sees any retelling simply as a rejection. Reflection on feminist midrash would have been especially useful in discussing the works of novelist Sara Maitland, whose Christian feminism is marked by an angry rejection of patriarchy conjoined with a passionate commitment to Christianity—not to the Goddess. However, King ignores the midrashic elements of Maitland's storytelling and focuses instead on her rejection of much of traditional (patriarchal) Christianity. Maitland's work is analyzed in chapter 3, "'*Stabat Mater*': Christianity and the Virgin Mother," and readers familiar with Maitland will soon realize that her complex relationship with Christianity is being completely overlooked. King opens the chapter with a portrait of Mary that emphasizes her passivity, submissiveness, and impossible-to-emulate status as virgin and mother. Although many feminists have made this critique, other feminist scholars have emphasized Mary's free choice for God, her role in Christ's miracle at Cana, and the liberatory power of her Magnificat. King ignores this portrayal of Mary—despite the fact that Maitland embraces it. Although the chapter sets out to examine the paradoxes and "contradictions inherent in the ideology surrounding the Virgin Mother" (64), it ends by simply contrasting the passive "religious" Mary to the strong, independent "fictional" Mary presented by Maitland. The fact that Maitland's ideas about Mary are grounded in current feminist religious scholarship is overlooked—and thus the more interesting analysis of how the paradoxes and contradictions of feminist Mary scholarship interact with the paradoxes and contradictions of more traditional understandings of the Virgin is left undone. Trapped in her understanding that Christianity is relentlessly patriarchal, King is unable to engage Maitland's portrayal of the very different contrasting things Mary can mean to different women or sometimes to an individual woman.

Similarly, at the end of chapter 2, "'Destructive Genesis': Old Testament Myths of Origin and Creation," King's focus on narrative as a method of combating patriarchy prevents her from critiquing what could be seen as a narrative failure on Maitland's part. In the three sections of the short story "Triptych," Maitland retells the story of Abraham, Sarah, and Hagar from each of their three very different perspectives—or, at least, the narrator tells Sarah's story and Hagar's story and then pointedly refuses to tell Abraham's. Quite deliberately, the narrator "refuses to enter into his point of view . . . [because] Abraham's story . . . is already available in Genesis" (60). King does not contest the narrator's choice, noting instead with approval (and without noting any distinction between Maitland and the narrator) that "Maitland in effect answers 'No' to those who have advised women to write from the 'neutral' or 'universal' perspective of myth. . . . Her identification with the victims prevents her from identifying with the oppressor" (60). But Maitland's story deserves a more critical approach: It is a complex piece, combining two overlapping first person fictional accounts with a section of biting, angry biblical criticism. What happened to the story? Is it still a story? Did Maitland the theologian take over from the narrator? How many voices are here? Is this a failure of the imagination, a failure of compassion, a triumph for the "victims," or something else entirely? Disappointingly, King never addresses these questions. It is especially puzzling that she does not do so in light of her stated aim for the book as a whole: to explore the preoccupation contemporary women novelists have with the Bible (ix). Here Maitland's struggle with the Bible has led to a severe rupture in her storytelling, a highly unusual event that cries out for serious literary analysis, and yet King seems to see it not as a literary question but as an appropriate sociological response to victimization.

Women and the Word engages several novelists other than Maitland: among them are Michele Roberts, Angela Carter, Toni Morrison, and Alice Walker. The novels chosen (including Maitland's) are fascinating, often troubling works whose reliance on and struggles with religion and biblical stories are central to their power. Those struggles need to be taken seriously, and the religious questions at the heart of those struggles cry out for the attention of appropriate religious scholarship. Again, the project King began is a good one, with the potential greatly to expand our understanding of gender and religion—and yet *Women and the Word* does not fulfill this promise; I only hope others take up the challenge.

Colleen Carpenter Cullinan
Augsburg College

Worlds of Difference: European Discourses of Toleration, c. 1100–c. 1550.
By Cary J. Nederman. Pennsylvania State University Press, 2000. 157 pages.
$18.95.

The totalizing discourse of western liberalism and political thought generated by the Enlightenment and European modernism over the past three centuries led to a profound misunderstanding of medieval modes of toleration and
interaction with people of other faiths. The popular assumption has been that
contemporary societies are both tolerant and accepting of ethnic and religious
diversity whereas our medieval forbears were both intolerant and oppressive toward the "eternal other" living within and on the periphery of Latin Christianity.
Issues of "toleration" and "diversity" have been buzzing around the academic,
corporate, and political arenas for quite some time. In the wake of the tragic events
of 11 September 2001, and given the present rift between Muslims and Christians as well as between Israelis and Palestinians, this book provides a forum for
both historical and contemporary reflection on the sociopolitical and religious
dimensions of toleration. Cary J. Nederman takes up a familiar problem in this
book, yet by challenging deeply entrenched stereotypes of the medieval Christian worldview his work makes a significant and lasting contribution to our understanding of European discourses of toleration.

Nederman's introduction and chapter 1 offer readers a useful overview of some
of the research and theoretical assumptions that have shaped the modern scholar's
view of a Christian Middle Ages characterized by intolerance and the absence of
dissenting voices. Nederman cites Robert I. Moore's important book, *The Formation of a Persecuting Society: Power and Deviance in Western Europe, 950–1250*
(Blackwell Publishers, 1987), but his concern is that Moore's work only "depicts part
of the terrain" (11). It is important to note that Nederman does not simply choose
a few medieval authors and then project an anachronistic picture of their ideas or
romanticize their pronouncements on toleration to support his departure from the
work of other modern medievalists. Throughout the book's seven chapters he repeatedly reminds readers that there is ample evidence from the period in question
attesting to the Roman Church's autocratic practice of inquisitorial trials and ex-
communication. He also identifies similar shortcomings in the feudal and early
modern state's less-than-tolerant dealings with ethnic and religious minorities such
as Jews, Muslims and Arabs, and the French Cathars. However, as Nederman summarizes, "it is simply incorrect to conflate the Church's war on heresy with the stifling of all religious dissent" (17). Thus, as the *Republica Christiana* sought to increase
its influence across Europe and began persecuting heretics, Christian thinkers and
authors began an interreligious dialogue that affected how the West eventually dealt
with religious outsiders and ethnic minorities. The rest of the book hinges on the
following passage: "Once writers confronted the inherent diversity of human life and
hence admitted the practical impossibility of narrowly enforced religious conformity, they naturally started to consider ways in which people with divergent beliefs
and practices could live together. Here may be found the germ of various theories of
tolerance generated in Europe from the twelfth to the sixteenth centuries" (23).

The first and second chapters weave together an intriguing combination of historical, theological, and philosophical data ranging from late antiquity to the late thirteenth century. Nederman begins building his case by citing examples from the life and work of Augustine of Hippo, who sharply criticized fellow Christians for persecuting heretics and who sought to borrow all that was best and wise from both pagan culture and Hebrew tradition. The section "Medieval Christianity and Non-Christians" provides an exceptionally concise yet accurate summary of relations between Islamic scholars and the great learning centers of Latin Christianity during the period of the Spanish *convivencia* (20–22), a term that signifies the "living together" of Muslims, Jews, and Christians in medieval Iberia. Nederman then takes up the role of intellectual debate and human reason that formed the basis for the scholastic synthesis of the Early and High Middle Ages. He incorporates theoretical insights gained from Jay Newman's *Foundations of Religious Tolerance* (University of Toronto Press, 1982) by juxtaposing what he terms a "dialogue of demonstration" with Newman's notion of a "dialogue of mutual edification." Broadly speaking, the former is characterized by didactic information and aims toward establishing "the absolute and final truth of a single dogma," whereas the latter approach is committed to "mutual respect and openness to learning through discourse" (27). Nederman demonstrates these concepts by describing the wide range of Christian authors who employed the principles of rational debate and dialectical reasoning to examine the theme of toleration and religious nonconformity. Specifically from the medieval dialogue genre, he discusses Anselm of Canterbury's *Disputatio inter Christianum et gentilem* (ca. 1100), Gilbert of Crispin's *Disputatio Judei et Christiani* (ca. 1092–93), Peter Abelard's *Dialogus inter philosophum, Judaeum, et Christianum* (ca. 1130), and Ramon Llull's *Liber de gentili et tribus sapientibus* (ca. 1275). Although postmodern literary criticism has viewed all such dialogues from Plato to Voltaire as contrived and suspicious, Nederman's way of unpacking these texts leads one to recognize the candor with which some medieval thinkers conceptualized intolerance.

A brief account of the contents of the rest of the book, beyond the first two largely theoretical chapters, will make evident the range of materials and authors surveyed. Chapter 3 examines the Ciceronian skepticism of John of Salisbury (ca. mid-1100s), whose principal writings on liberty and individual judgment were way ahead of such Renaissance and modern figures as Erasmus of Rotterdam and John Stuart Mill, respectively. As Nederman points out, the medieval search for truth in matters of philosophical and theological discourse generated a "skeptical spirit of free inquiry," which, while not identical with modern notions of individual rights, nonetheless "explicitly embraced the spirit" of those times (52). Chapter 4 extends the analysis to the medieval encounter between Latin Christendom and the Mongol Empire of Central Asia by way of the Franciscan William of Rubruck's travel narrative, which details his twelfth-century appraisal of a multicultural and multi-faith empire negotiating the social and political dynamics of toleration. Alongside William's views, Nederman includes Pope Innocent IV's stance on the principle of reciprocity between Christian Europe and regions governed by non-Christian yet tolerant rulers. In chapter 5 Nederman sifts through Marsiglio of Padua's

Defensor pacis (1324) and *Defensor minor* (1340) by focusing on his political philosophy and his unique conception of religious pluralism. The author highlights Marsiglio's emphasis on the principle of balancing the private and the public realms in the life of the state as well as in the lives of individuals and shows again how ideas typically regarded as post-Enlightenment constructs were conceptualized by medieval, Latin Christian thinkers.

Chapter 6 surveys Nicholas of Cusa's *De pace Fidei* (1453), which addresses issues of national and cultural identity and was composed in the wake of the collapse of the Byzantine Empire and the rising military might of the Ottoman Turks. Quoting Nicholas's well-known call for "one religion in a variety of rites" (87, 96), Nederman bolsters the book's argument that the alleged hegemonic Christian Middle Ages produced a surprising variety of discourses of toleration. The juxtaposition between issues of conformity and issues of diversity in Nicholas of Cusa's work offers thought-provoking parallels with contemporary debates concerning the construction of national and religious identity. In the book's seventh and final chapter Nederman presents the case of the famous Dominican bishop of Chiapas, Bartholomé de Las Casas, who also drew heavily on Ciceronian notions of reason, religion, and politics to formulate his stance on the dignity of the native peoples of the Americas. Las Casas also employed Aristotelian and Thomistic moral principles to critique the Spanish colonial administration's mistreatment of the Indians. Nederman points out the characteristically medieval approach advocated by Las Casas in the conversion of the Native Americans without either compulsion or coercion and facilitated by rational "dialogue between believers and nonbelievers" (114).

It will be important for readers not to lose sight of the subtle differences existing between the medieval and early modern discourses of toleration, which is the book's central focus, and our unexamined assumptions about the liberal, egalitarian societies we moderns call our own. None of the authors considered in the book ever discussed such modern ideas as individual natural rights theory or individual freedom of conscience, yet Nederman wonders "whether theorists today have anything to learn from these predecessors" (120). This book should be read by a wider audience than just specialists in medieval and early modern history, for it is neither a work of mere presentism nor a rehashing of antiquarian political thought. The overall value of Nederman's work is its relevance to the present world crisis between the West and the Arab world, between exclusion and toleration within pluralistic societies, and between modernity and religious tradition across the planet: "There is simply no future for any theoretical attempt to understand political life, whether in the West or globally, that does not appreciate and take seriously the past" (121).

Albert Hernández
Iliff School of Theology

Donors, Devotees, and Daughters of God: Temple Women in Medieval Tamilnadu. By Leslie C. Orr. Oxford University Press, 2000. 305 pages. $45.00.

During the reign of the Chola kings (ninth–thirteenth centuries), the political, economic, and cultural influence of the Tamil country in South India reached its zenith. This was the period of a great religious transformation, as hundreds of stone temples appeared throughout southern India while elaborate ritual systems oriented believers to the worship of Vishnu, Shiva, and the goddess—the culmination of devotional (*bhakti*) religiosity. A large mass of hagiographic and ritual literature provides access to the social and religious landscape of the Tamil country under the Cholas, but one of the peculiarities of the historical record is the survival of well over 10,000 inscriptions, mostly on the walls of religious institutions, describing eleemosynary grants. These epigraphs, copies of legal documents usually dated with kings' regnal years, are a treasure trove of information on the social environment of temples. Previous studies based on inscriptions have increased our understanding of the political geography, economy, and social systems oriented toward a male-dominated public life. Leslie Orr has focused on the epigraphic sources in order to reconstruct the social and religious world of women.

Unlike most literary sources, the corpus of inscriptions lends itself to strict controls over time and space, allowing the author to engage in detailed statistical analyses of records from specific geographic zones, organized within four subperiods. She scans the massive body of published and unpublished inscriptions for references to vocabulary describing the activities of women and then creates typologies for classifying their actions. The substantive chapters of this book revolve around a series of tables presenting descriptive statistics, demonstrating variability of terminology over time and space. Working with a data set of 820 inscriptions, the author concentrates primarily on 304 inscriptions that yield linguistic markers that indicate the activities of temple women. She has taken this methodology to the limit, teasing out from small samples support for subtle analyses that trace changes in social, economic, and cultural life. Along with 177 pages of text that include maps and tables, we have sixty-eight pages of notes and several appendixes that immerse the careful reader into a magisterial discussion of language, culture, and the lively theoretical debates that have emerged from the study of Tamil epigraphs. This work, therefore, operates at the highest levels of scholarship and regularly yields gems of insight on problems of South Indian historiography. The text of the substantive chapters clearly stands by itself, regularly summarizing arguments, making the work accessible to more general readers. I have already used its chapters successfully in advanced undergraduate and graduate seminars as examples of methodology, excursions into the history of women, and immersions in the analysis of religious institutions.

The author draws the reader into the study by framing it within a more familiar theme concerning the condition of the *devadasi*, or the "female slave of the god," who by the nineteenth century was attached to a temple, ostensibly to perform classical dances, and married to the deity but in practice was involved with male patrons of the temple in relationships little different from prostitution.

Reformers during the nineteenth and twentieth centuries pushed through legislation that outlawed this condition, although journalists in more recent times have continued to find instances of forcible recruitment of girls into roles that resemble those of the *devadasi*. Scholars have tended to project the more recent roles of these "temple women" into the past, linking references to the activities of women in Chola-period temples to their gender-based roles as dance specialists. This process of historical projection, which presents women's social roles as perpetually fixed within male-dominated institutions and sexual public personas, is precisely what the author wants to disassemble. She uses a detailed empirical study to eliminate the idea of a pan-Indian *devadasi* "tradition" along with the hackneyed idea that the mode of transmission for an earlier "classical" art form must have suffered decay or degeneration over time. Instead of symbolic feminine power, the author wants to reinsert agency, difference, and change in our vision of women in the past. She is looking for women in control of their lives, constructing worlds and worldviews, not merely victims.

Before she can access the target population of Chola-period temple women, the author meticulously examines other kinds of women who appear in the inscriptions. These include women acting within Jaina religious contexts, queens and female members of royal courts (who during early subperiods were quite active as donors within temple transactional networks), and women (including brahmanas) who appear primarily through kinship, usually with a man. Eliminating these many women from the analysis leaves a core group termed "servants (or slaves) of the god" (*tevaratiyar*), "daughters of the god" (*tevanar makal*), or "temple women" (*taliyilar* or *patiyilar*). During the 400 years of the Chola period, these temple women tended to become more individuated over time, more often identified through their personal names. Temple women controlled property (*kani*) and shares (*panku*) within property relations. They increasingly appeared as donors or the relatives of donors, concentrating on temples close to their homes and appearing often in low-profile or regional establishments instead of famous shrines like Chidambaram or Srirangam. They often made deals with temples, with gifts contingent on their long-term, honorable, public participation within prestigious rituals. Unlike temple men, who usually performed specified administrative or ritual actions within organizations that were becoming larger and more complex, temple women typically remained aloof from managerial or functional roles; only about 20 percent of the inscriptions describe temple women performing some kind of temple service, and only seven inscriptions (all later in date) refer to temple women as festival dancers (105, 126). There is no evidence that temple women were dedicated or married to the god, and only a small percentage of these women identified themselves as spouses of men. Instead—and here lies one of their more fascinating features—many identified themselves within female-focused family groups and matrilineages, with some inscriptions mentioning several generations connected to the same temples.

Orr is too good an epigraphist to jump from these fragmented data to some comprehensive portrait of temple women, and in fact she maddeningly suggests that "the individual and local nature of temple women's associations" precludes generalization (168). Perpetually embedded in legalistic situations, Orr's temple women still elude personification. Some conclusions do appear warranted. During the later Chola period, as temples became larger and more prominent as centers of ritual legitimacy, women as well as men gravitated to them in order to establish and confirm social status. While cultural convention severely (and perhaps increasingly) limited women's public roles, the title of temple woman allowed some to exchange economic resources for honorific titles and positions within highly visible ritual space, in a manner that did not directly compete with males. How did they gain access to these economic resources? The author claims that women apparently did not control property gained through inheritance (*stridhana*), which went to their husbands, but they could control wealth gained through marriage (e.g., through widowhood). I think that the impressive volume of references to transactions involving women is just the tip of an iceberg, so to speak, and that women during the Chola period were in charge of all kinds of agrarian and commercial property. Regardless of its original source, the connection of wealth with temple women introduces the possibility of a class analysis that views them as a relatively privileged group capable of manipulating their old or new wealth within the more refined levels of cultural performance. As the public profile of temple women grew over time alongside a decline in donations from the court, we see once again in the language of the inscriptions the traces of a general shift toward localized "lordship" and class-based individuation that marks the later Chola period.

In the conclusion the author returns from her close empirical reading to the *devadasi* problem, constructing an explanation of why the condition of temple women in the late thirteenth century should change into the situation in the nineteenth century. Max Weber's concept of bureaucratization is used to describe the progressive enmeshing of women within skill-based, hereditary positions while the courts of the later Nayakas promoted a more passive and instrumental vision of the feminine. This section reinforces the thesis that the thirteenth-century formation remains quite remote from the *devadasi*, requiring a shift from essentialist generalizations toward close historical analyses. It also provides tantalizing glimpses of a comparative project, through an excursion into women's religious donations in contemporaneous Europe (169–170) and a hint of parallels in Buddhist societies (166). The true value of this book lies not in historicism or comparison but in its portrait of women's agency within a "broader context of relationships" (35) during their own time. Now our task is to align these nonaffective epigraphic insights on women in public, legal moments with a critical understanding of ritual change and highly personalized hagiographies within the Chola period, questing for that "thick description" that is the basis for historical discussion.

James Heitzman
Georgia State University

Muscular Christianity: Manhood and Sports in Protestant America, 1880–1920. By Clifford Putney. Harvard University Press, 2001. 300 pages. $39.95.

"Muscular Christianities" have definitely been around for over 140 years, and muscularity in world religions has been present from the start, if more apparent at certain points in recent years. The history of sport certainly lends itself to an interdisciplinary effort as in the present book. However, the strength of this approach can also become a weakness if a particular scholar oversteps him- or herself. Clifford Putney's work is a clear illustration of this truth.

This work is the result of the author's revision of his doctoral dissertation at Brandeis University, vividly witnessed in 1,061 fine notes for 207 pages of text. Lest there be some confusion, let it be noted that this book has the same title (though the subtitle differs) as that published by Tony Ladd and James A. Mathisen in 1999. Interestingly, though Putney shows a thorough use of Ladd and Mathisen in many footnotes, he fails to refer to this work in his index. It is rather odd, too, for a scholarly work, that over three dozen notes carry the words *quoted in*, as the writer has been led by secondary sources to important and available primary sources. Nevertheless, Putney does succeed in his time period (1880–1920) in giving a legitimate survey of muscular Christianity in Protestant America.

Putney opens his survey by stating: "Between 1880 and 1920, American Protestants in many denominations witnessed the flourishing in their pulpits and seminaries of a strain of religiosity known, both admiringly and pejoratively, as 'muscular Christianity'" (1). The term itself had originated in England in the 1850s as a partial description of the novels of Thomas Hughes and Charles Kingsley, especially their criticism of Victorian Anglican Christianity as being far too effeminate and physically weak. Both writers issued a clarion call for more manliness in the expression of Christianity. The essence of their critique was imported into the United States and was received in a number of circles with great enthusiasm. Putney effectively rehearses the roles of Josiah Strong and the Social Gospel movement, G. Stanley Hall, and Theodore Roosevelt in their advocacy of a manly religion for the American scene especially in its urban setting.

The "Who's Who" list of advocates of muscular Christianity is an interesting cross section ranging from scholars and educators, to coaches, to popular preachers, to one president of the United States. Horace Bushnell, Charles W. Eliot, and Hall, among others, agitated on behalf of "all-around men." Amos Alonzo Stagg was the epitome of a manly coach, urged on by William R. Harper initially. Stagg actually studied theology under Harper at Yale prior to Harper enticing him to Chicago to develop muscular, successful, and Christian teams. Dwight L. Moody (though making room for women in ministry) and the athlete-turned-preacher Billy Sunday obviously rank first among those who preached the values of muscular Christianity. Of one important advocate Putney reflects: "One man who seemed to embody all the tenets of manly religion was Theodore Roosevelt" (77). A public and powerful layperson such as this president certainly advanced muscular Christianity by example and by words, though one is forced to wonder whether or not his use of sports rhetoric to communicate the gospel was often more important to him than the essence of the Christian gospel. This applies as well to the numerous popularizers of the movement.

Local, regional, and national movements and organizations gave muscular legs to this Protestant manly Christianity as well. Early on, none was more successful in blending sport and religion than the Businessmen's Awakening (late 1850s) and the Young Men's Christian Association (founded in England in 1844; the first YMCA in the United States was founded in 1851). By 1860 there were over 200 associations across the United States. Other groups and movements that advocated muscular Christianity as explored by Putney were Men and Religion Forward, the Boy Scouts, the Social Gospel, and the Student Volunteer Movement.

Putney, of course, feels that the "historical peak" of muscular Christianity appeared "roughly from 1880 to 1920." This is to be expected because it is the time period of his expertise and research. Those who address the topic from a broader historical approach might argue that a peak was reached after the re-engagement of muscular Christianity in the 1940s and 1950s. Ladd and Mathisen's book is far more useful in bringing the story up to the 1990s, whereas Putney only has hints and staccato statements in that direction.

The author is well aware of the search to fulfill emotional needs as one goal of muscular Christianity, but he also addresses other aims such as "'defeminizing' the clergy, 'masculinizing' religious imagery, and getting more men involved in the churches" (98). Interestingly, Putney's freshest and most creative additions to the Ladd and Mathisen presentation are in his chapters "Muscular Women" and "Christians in Khaki." In the first of these, white Protestant "jocks for Jesus" are joined by "jockettes for Jesus" by way of the Young Women's Christian Association, the Camp Fire Girls, and the Girl Scouts in their emphases on the strenuous life and Christianity's physical side.

"Christians in Khaki" is one of Putney's longest chapters (and his final chapter before his conclusion), in which he points out that during the Spanish–American War and World War I, "ministers wrapped themselves in the flag and championed war as a cure for effeminacy in men" (163). The terribly confusing scenario in relation to war and muscular Christianity is described by Putney as he points out that after each of the wars "ministers repudiated their support of war, embraced pacifism, and sought to cure effeminacy with 'moral equivalents of war,' such as boxing" (163). Putney clearly depicts pacifism and the peace movement and its tensions with governmental war supporters. He affirms that in the postwar periods there evolved a "disenchantment with ultra-militant muscular Christianity" (194). Among others, Sherwood Eddy, a muscular Christian, expressed strong regret for any support for war.

This deserving book points in numerous other directions for fresh research in the history of sport and religion. Putney's survey of white Protestant males committed to muscular Christianity calls for additional and more complete efforts directed to Protestant women. Muscularity in religion also deserves to be broadened in the directions of African Americans, Catholics, Jews, Muslims, and so on. Steven Riess did open one of these doors in 1998 with his edited *Sports and the American Jew* (Syracuse University Press).

Within his time frame (1880–1920), Putney makes a capable and instructive presentation. Outside this period he is at times superficial or simply in error. Two examples illustrate this point. He ventures briefly into the period of medieval sport and quotes a general survey done in 1971: "The Church also 'persistently suppressed many sports and games'" (51). This is true in part but also misleading. One need only consult the voluminous literature on chivalry, tournaments, and holy war. There one would find more than enough material on medieval muscular Christianity.

Then, in his presentation of fundamentalism he makes some critical errors. Putney actually never gives an acceptable definition of a fundamentalist as distinguished from an evangelical. The two words are definitely not synonyms. There are far more muscular Christian evangelicals than fundamentalists. Putney never refers to the excellent books by George Marsden on fundamentalism or to the mammoth Martin Marty multivolume series on the subject. On the matter of differentiating the two streams of thinking and commitment, Ladd and Mathisen's book does a far superior job.

As an American history dissertation piece reflecting an important topic within a specific time frame, this is an instructive work. It is hardly a corrective of "scholarly blindness," as the dust jacket affirms. That corrective began earlier than this book, though it is an important piece in the ongoing process of interpretation and presentation of muscular religion.

George H. Shriver
Georgia Southern University (emeritus)

Decolonizing Biblical Studies: A View from the Margins. By Fernando F. Segovia. Orbis Books, 2000. 177 pages. $24.00.

Composed of an introduction and eight previously written essays, this book reveals the growing impact of the voices of the nonwestern world on the discipline, interpretive strategies, and pedagogy of biblical studies. With two essays devoted to each of four thematic parts, the work is a theoretically sophisticated, geopolitically attentive, and personally revealing collection. As an analysis of the introduction and thematic parts will disclose, moreover, Fernando Segovia's essays (1) recount the evolution of biblical criticism, (2) elucidate the recent decolonizing influence of cultural studies and postcolonial studies on biblical criticism, and (3) chart the future of biblical criticism in the late twentieth and early twenty-first centuries.

Signaling the importance of *social location* for the entire collection, the introduction *contextualizes* the author, the book's essays, and the recent changes in biblical criticism. Segovia's own context includes his birth and primary socialization in Latin America (Cuba) along with his exile and secondary socialization in the United States. Honed in collaborative projects, his essays were initially written to plot the development of biblical criticism or to highlight some of the critical issues with which the changing face of biblical criticism has made it necessary to grapple, for example, decolonization and liberation or the role of nonwestern "personal voices." The context of the recent changes in biblical criticism and in all of the theological disciplines, moreover, is actually the expansion of earlier forms of liberation theology and the recent post-1980s "spread of the postcolonial program" (x).

Part 1 ("Grand Models and Strategies of Interpretation") has three concerns: (1) a brief plotting of the evolution of biblical criticism, (2) a description of the impact of cultural studies on biblical criticism, and (3) an analysis of the radical changes in the philosophical presuppositions of biblical studies as impacted by cultural studies. Segovia argues that biblical studies evolved in four stages with historical criticism as its first stage; literary criticism and (socio)cultural criticism as its second and third stages, respectively; and cultural studies, its present (and) fourth stage (11–29). With cultural studies, biblical criticism takes on a provisional mode of discourse and a multitude of voices and directions. The mode of discourse is provisional because of an explosion of methodological positions, resulting not in a consensus but in a state of "radical plurality" (37). The voices and directions are multiple because of the growth of nonmale and nonwestern individuals in the biblical profession. Critical to the radical changes that cultural studies commends for biblical criticism on several basic interpretive principles ("location of meaning, reading strategy, theoretical foundations, the role of the reader, theological presuppositions, and pedagogical implications" [42]), moreover, is the "situated and interested nature of all reading and interpretation" (39).

In part 2 ("Grand Models and Strategies of Pedagogy") Segovia initially explores pedagogical discourse (what is learned and practiced in biblical criticism) as treated by representative scholars of the initial three paradigms (historical criticism: Joseph A. Fitzmyer; literary criticism: Mark Allan Powell; [socio]cultural criticism: Bruce J. Malina) and several cultural studies proponents: W. H. Myers, P. J. Hartin, K. O'Brien Wicker, J. R. Levison and P. Pope-Levison, and B. K. Blount. Then, focusing exclusively on pedagogical discourse within cultural studies, Segovia endorses some of the principles of the cultural studies proponents, critiques a few others, and proffers his own constructive proposal. Segovia endorses (1) a radical appreciation for "the other"; (2) a broadening of "textuality" to cover (traditionally regarded) "texts" and interpreters; (3) an accentuation on readers throughout the world, not exclusively on those from the West; (4) the postmodernist antifoundationalist stance; (5) a high regard for multiple methods, not solely the traditional ones; and (6) a broadening of "biblical text" to include a social element as well as a religious one. Segovia's critiques include (1) a widening of the scope of examination to move beyond the canonical and extracanonical "texts" of antiquity, (2) a dismantling of the idea of stable meaning in a text, and (3) a serious regard for metatheory. Segovia's constructive proposal is grounded in a hermeneutics of otherness and critical engagement with two key concerns: a quest for diversity and an acknowledgment of the ineluctable reality of "empire." With respect to diversity, moreover, Segovia asks his audience to hear the cacophony of voices that could be heard, in principle if not always in praxis, when one becomes acutely cognizant of all the voices lodged in texts, readings, and readers. Accordingly, a quest for *diversity in texts* would be metacanonical in its explorations of ancient Judaism or early Christianity, extensive in its investigation of suppressed or discordant voices (beyond historical criticism's exposure of a text's sources), and holistic in its examination of *all* the differing religious expressions of antiquity's milieu. Likewise, a quest for *diversity in readings* would honor scholarly and nonscholarly readings, readings based on competing paradigms within scholarly traditions, and multiple types of readings within a particular scholarly paradigm. Furthermore, a quest for *diversity in readers* would commend both intratextual readers (i.e., reader constructs) and extratextual readers (i.e., real flesh-and-blood readers).

In part 3 ("Biblical Studies and Postcolonial Studies") Segovia links cultural studies with postcolonial studies, the latter of which he has "come to regard as a most appropriate, most enlightening, and most fruitful approach to biblical criticism" (120). He especially appreciates the model for the several roles that it allows a biblical scholar to play—biblical critic, constructive theologian, and cultural studies critic (120). After mapping his own history vis-à-vis colonialism, he then turns his postcolonial optic to ancient texts, modern readings, and ancient readers—all of which, he argues, are affected by the shadow of the empire and a series of binomials that are designed to subordinate persons on the margins. Moreover, only with such a thoroughgoing optic, avers Segovia, can a genuine transformation of society arise.

In part 3 Segovia also responds to questions posed to the postcolonial model. First, he acknowledges the problems of the term *postcolonial* for the ways that it and other related expressions "continue to view the reality and experience of the periphery . . . with reference to the center and hence in terms of external intervention, domination, and oppression" (134). Then, Segovia offers an apologetic for the Marxist critique of postcolonial studies, that is, that the postcolonial optic overlooks the differing modes of production between the present context and the ancient biblical one and thus is ahistorical. Segovia situates this critique in the context of a long-standing argument between Marxist and postcolonial critics with the former averring that "postcolonial critics deal with the superstructure of imperialism while bypassing the question of its material base" (136). Segovia relativizes all approaches as constructs, notes the importance of all models, and situates the Marxist concept of modes of production in the nineteenth century and thus its analytical focus as not something "demanded by the 'data' [of antiquity] for proper interpretation" (139). In short, he notes that the Marxist model itself is not indispensable, and, as he adds, "there is no self-evident project of resistance and emancipation for all in the periphery, although there may be quite self-evident projects for the various groups that comprise the periphery" (141).

In part 4 ("Voices from Outside") Segovia calls attention to both his own voice and the voices of other racial and ethnic minorities in the recent history of biblical criticism. In recounting his own voice, Segovia divulges three exchanges with other biblical scholars in which his personal voice, roughly over a twenty-year period, was first suppressed, then dismissed as partisan, and later simply ignored. In part, the exchanges reveal some of the constraining presuppositions of those who seek to deny the personal voice, namely, that objectivity is possible, that meaning is stable, and that good scholarship is the result of a "divestiture" of one's self (147–150). Thus, the work of anyone departing from these constraints, especially those who shift from historical criticism to cultural studies (as with Segovia), is dismissed as a "decline in standards and the anarchy of partisanship" (151). Or a departure from these constraints is judged as not even worthy of conversation, especially when the scope of one's work embraces the theoretical sophistication and the geopolitical scope of postcolonial studies (again, as with Segovia). In part, the exchanges (and Segovia's reflections on them) also reveal the evolution of a change in biblical criticism's attitude toward personal voice as proponents of literary criticism, sociocultural criticism, cultural studies, and postcolonial studies grew in number and created a *mercado* (marketplace) of competing paradigms (151).

In recounting the voices of other racial and ethnic minorities, Segovia reflects on the future of biblical studies. Initially, he notes how "children of the non-western world," largely through a process of "conscientization," have begun to see themselves as "subjects of history" (169), are ready to call "into question the dominant Western and modern myth of the impartial and objective observer," and are eager to appreciate their "own cultures and histories for grounding and inspiration" (170). Then, averring that the future of biblical criticism for racial and ethnic minorities will improve despite the present *lucha* (struggle), Segovia offers several remedies for a significant change in biblical studies: (1) more readings of the biblical text from a nonwestern focus; (2) a "poetics of construction," that is, an analysis of the power dynamics entailed in western presentations of Christianity throughout the centuries (175); (3) more geopolitical analyses of the connections between the development of the discipline of biblical criticism and the virtually simultaneous growth of "Western hegemony and colonialism" (176); (4) a dialogue on how the Bible should be read "in the aftermath of centuries of domination" (176); and (5) a self-generated and self-governed dialogue about the Bible among various nonwestern groups (176).

Although Segovia's collection lacks a conclusion and an index, it is a tour de force in the argument it develops on behalf of the marginalized in 177 pages. While some books on theory are inaccessible, incoherent, and even unconnected to the struggles of everyday people, these essays depart from works of that ilk. Written with lucid prose, an incisive command of theory, and a remarkable identification with a variety of subaltern communities, this work will inevitably become a *touchstone* across the theological disciplines for all persons interested in biblical criticism's role in the radical transformation of human society.

Abraham Smith
Andover Newton Theological School

Modernity's Wager: Authority, the Self, and Transcendence. By Adam B. Seligman. Princeton University Press, 2000. 177 pages. $27.95.

Adam Seligman is known for his sociological studies of the nature of civil society and the philosophical problem of trust within such a society, studies that have led him further and further into a philosophical and theological analysis of agency and personhood. *Modernity's Wager* consciously follows this same trajectory toward theology, although Seligman cautiously notes, "Just how far short of theology it falls I am not sure" (ix). It is certainly true that this is no theology text; the issues and idiom are those of sociology, and this emphasis sometimes presents difficulties for readers (like myself) who are outside that specialization. On the other hand, clear theological emphases abound and make this book as provocative for theologians and philosophers as it is for social scientists.

The central argument of the book is for "the need to take authority seriously in order to maintain a more rigorous and morally thick notion of autonomy" than the modern worldview normally allows (125). Genuine moral action presupposes some nonnegotiable locus of sacred authority. Yet modern thought affirms as well the intrinsic value of the autonomy of the moral actor, and it therefore rejects a transcendent locus of authority as too restrictive and burdensome. Instead, modernity—including "contemporary modern" thought, that is, postmodernism—opts for (in Kantian terms) a transcendental locus. The question is, Can an immanent, internalized, autonomous, transcendental reason provide an authoritative ground for moral action? Modernity answers yes—and this is precisely the "wager" that gives this book its title. According to Seligman, however, events in the twentieth century have made it increasingly uncertain that this wager can be won. It looks more and more as if a self whose only authority is its own autonomous moral will is a self bereft of enduring ethical moorings and, hence, a self that cannot stand as the foundation of civil society.

The overall strategy of the book is to present a sustained account of why this modern approach to selfhood and authority is, and was from the beginning, doomed to fail. The argument is straightforwardly organized into five chapters, which together make up a presentation that is surprisingly elegant for such a wide-ranging investigation. The first three chapters set up the crucial contrast. The modern, "instrumental" view of the self, so ubiquitous among social scientists that no alternative seems possible, cannot account for genuinely moral decision making because it reduces agency to mere power and reduces the agent to a mere preference calculator, construing the "self" (à la Thomas Hobbes) solely in terms of individual desires and interests. By contrast, the "constitutive" view of the self recognizes that for most people "I" is not an independently and self-referentially invented entity. Instead, to be "I" is in many respects to be a particular type of person constituted by certain external obligations, expectations, and relationships. This account explains why I might refrain from stealing a candy bar even in a context in which being caught and punished is unlikely or impossible (36). To steal the candy bar would violate an authoritative communal standard that I have internalized. It would make me a thief, which is not what "I" am.

Seligman uses simple examples like this one as well as complex analyses of phenomena such as shame, collective responsibility, "moral luck," and ritual symbolism to build an impressive case for the logically interdependent relationship among ideas of self, community, authority, and the sacred. Some form of sacred communal authority must constitute the self if that self is to be understood as a moral evaluator rather than simply as a bundle of desires. But whence comes such constitutive authority? On Seligman's account, it comes either from universal principles of civic virtue, from "primordial" identities dependent on kinship solidarity, or from transcendent dictates. The first is the modern referent for authority, which fails because the authority thus generated devolves into mere power because it rests epistemologically on a purely individualistic foundation. The second has often been the de facto principle of authority in modern politics, as the racism, anti-Semitism, ethnic barbarism, and gender conflict of the twentieth century have demonstrated all too clearly. The third is a locus of authority set aside by modernity but perhaps ready for recall in the twenty-first century, for it alone makes appeal to something external to self and community as a non-negotiable basis for the moral life of self and community.

If an external or "heteronomous" authority is the solution, then it is no surprise that the internalization of authority in the autonomous individual is a large part of the problem, and chapter 4 is Seligman's long and provocative study of how the modern western world came to internalize authority in this way. The major villain in this sad story is Christianity. According to Seligman, the Christian worldview, from its very inception, challenged the publicly expressed, ritually enacted transcendence espoused by Judaism and introduced in its stead a privately acknowledged, internally adopted transcendence. In a word, faith replaced obedience to law; questions of internal purity or fidelity were granted a special, privileged status, and all that is external came to be viewed with suspicion, thus weakening and ultimately undermining the external authority that alone can make "self" a morally coherent category. Of course, this road to ultimate incoherence is a long one, with many significant figures and movements along the way. Seligman devotes substantial attention to the apostle Paul, whom he sees as the (perhaps unwitting) origin of the dramatic distinction between internal and external; to Augustine, who made salvation a matter of personal, internal conversion rather than one of collective, external redemption; to the twelfth-century Renaissance, which granted wholesale cultural approval to the emphasis on individual identity and conscience; to Luther, whose stark contrast of law and grace has opened up "the possibility of a *principled* antinomianism" (106); to Calvin and the Puritans, who have attempted to establish a formal community based on internal "sincerity" rather than on external conformity, thereby giving rise to that category of externality unknown to the medieval world, the "secular"; and to later sectarian movements, which increasingly privatized religion, and thus removed any religious ground for corporate unity, and which therefore cry out for a secular, rational ground for unity. This complicated story leads inexorably to the paradoxical modern situation: Authority has been sensitively internalized and democratically dispersed, but when so internalized and dispersed "it is no longer authoritative" (120).

Seligman's concluding chapter attempts to point the way to a retrieval of authority—yet without the authoritarianism that the modern approach has rightly rejected. He calls his proposal a "skeptical toleration" (128)—not a toleration despite skepticism about alternative views but a toleration rooted in skepticism about one's own view. Noting the complicated interdependence of faith and reason, Seligman advocates an "epistemological modesty" that undermines strident claims of certitude by acknowledging the ultimately fideistic character of all beliefs and values. Indeed, Seligman briefly suggests that religious traditions themselves might be the best resource for developing such modesty—and this claim he is currently in the process of substantiating as director of the international research project known as the Tolerance Project (at Boston University's new Institute on Religion and World Affairs), which is designed to investigate the theological resources for tolerance and pluralism within Judaism, Christianity, and Islam.

One might voice a couple of complaints about *Modernity's Wager.* Seligman's impressive erudition sometimes keeps him from saying simply and directly what he means: Even sociologists may find the multitude of scholars he interacts with to be sometimes distracting rather than helpful. Also, as with all short but comprehensive investigations, one frequently feels that complicated issues have been addressed in a bit too summary a fashion. This is especially true of the sweeping historical survey in chapter 4, in which weighty theological issues are almost entirely ignored in the pursuit of a sociological agenda; the brief discussion in chapter 5 of the relationship between faith and reason is also rather thin. These are the places where theologians and philosophers are likely to find the book wanting. Still, these are relatively minor criticisms of a generally excellent book. The careful correlation of ideas (like *autonomy* and *authority*) often thought of in opposition to one another, the careful discrimination of ideas (like *power* and *authority*) too often conflated, the critical examination of assumptions rarely questioned or even recognized, the concrete attention to antimodern phenomena shown to be unmistakably relevant by the events of last 11 September—all of this makes *Modernity's Wager* a very valuable contribution to the sociological study of religion, with strong relevance to philosophy and theology as well. Any work that can connect such diverse domains deserves to be applauded.

Steven D. Boyer
Eastern University

God and Modernity: A New and Better Way to Do Theology. By Andrew Shanks. Routledge, 2000. 187 pages. $24.99.

When people write about a "new and better way to do theology," they set themselves up for tough going. Not that theology does not need continual critical reflection or that there may not be better ways of doing it; but the subject matter is so elusive. If theology's task is about the reality of the divine life (an assumption not altogether agreed on in academic circles), then Andrew Shanks is seeking its tracks in the contemporary landscape of the "third modernity." It is in this space that Shanks, an Anglican priest, believes that it is possible to do theology "quite directly, on the basis of the solidarity of the shaken" (15). Just who the shaken are and what solidarity with them might offer to theology constitute the novel theological proposal that Shanks offers.

He does so by a careful exegesis of numerous and disparate authors, seeking to employ or critique them regarding his own proposal. Drawing most heavily on Hegel but also on Augustine, John Milbank, Mark C. Taylor, Habermas,

Wilfred Cantwell Smith, and Joachim of Fiore (this is just a representative list), Shanks uses them as foils for sharpening his own proposal, which argues that "the sort of theology I envisage would simply be a systematic attempt to transform the pure solidarity of the shaken, which is otherwise just a reaction to oppression, into a constructive ritually-focused community-tradition" (15).

In this constructive enterprise Shanks makes a very interesting reading of history, heavily informed by his reading of Hegel, which offers the view that we are presently in the third stage of modernity. He states that the first stage of modernity really began with the grand narrative ethos carried on by a particular confessional community. Christendom, as exemplified in such writings as Augustine's *The City of God*, would stand as a prime example, but he also mentions the Islamic *umma* as another type of movement with a universalizing vision. These culture-shaping religions established the consciousness of a significant part of the world, unquestioned until the Enlightenment. Thus, we have the second stage of modernity, beginning with the secular reaction to the first modernity and resulting in a critical stance to its religious universalizing tendencies. The tensions resulting from the interaction between the first two stages of modernity led to Shank's third modernity. This third modernity is constituted by a number of factors that make it fruitful for theological exploration, according to Shanks, because the possibility now exists for societies to escape Hegel's "unhappy consciousness" and create transconfessional communities of solidarity with one another: "What is most significantly new about the possibility of third modernity is just that it represents the solidarity of the shaken as mediated through groups with a relatively far smaller degree of distorting self-interests" (23).

This sense of shakenness comes from those communities that have worked through the grand narratives and historical consciousness that shaped identities, systems, and cultures and have emerged on the other side of this process. Indeed, Shanks identifies divine revelation with the entire process of cultural shake-ups in general, seeing the action of God precisely in the emerging historical consciousness arising in moments of cultural upheaval. What stands after the consuming fires of these encounters constitutes theology's interpretive focus.

Thus, Shanks understands theology's task to be a faith-driven positive critique of all ideology, including those forms of ideology toward which a particular theology or confessional community is pulled. One of the great problems with religion in general and Christianity in particular is that theological reflection has erected walls of defense around dogma, doctrine, and liturgy, resulting in a certain closedness to the action of God in the world working outside the established structures. Shanks wants theology, in sensitivity to God's new thing in the world, to abandon its ideological ramparts against the moral claims made on it by the shaken communities of the world that call it into question.

And yet this is in some ways a too simple reading of Shanks's attempt at forging a different type of theology, for his analysis is intricate and complex, sometimes even frustrating. For instance, when he treats the issue of a postmetaphysical faith by means of advocating a world theology, he responds to the notion of religious pluralism by treating the tripartite structure of exclusivism, inclusivism, and pluralism. He breaks down the pluralist category by addressing the type of pluralism that would level all differences to a lowest common denominator, something he sees especially operative in John Hick. Employing Karl Barth, Wilfred Cantwell Smith, and John Cobb, Shanks argues for a position of critical faith that straddles the boundaries of confessional and transconfessional communities.

By doing so it seems that Shanks's hope is that the traditions can be approached in such a way that distinctions can be made between the Transcendent given in formulas and dogmas of the confessional traditions and the Transcendent that truly transcends all givenness in doctrine or liturgy. And this would seem to constitute one of the major difficulties facing Shanks's project. His criteria for teasing out the authentically Transcendent would come precisely from a theology's openness to the claims made on it by those who have been awakened from the slumber of unconscious acceptance of the systems and structures whereby society is constituted, be they religious, economic, political, or military. It is in this encounter with the other voices that faith (and culture) is able to transcend even itself, "but to speak of shakenness as the essence of the divine presence is at once to affirm it as the basis for true solidarity demanding positive religious articulation" (88).

But it is Shanks's definition of shakenness that makes for a difficult path. While he wants to locate the presence of God's action in such movements as feminism and the peace or green movements, he does not seem to consider how other communities can also be shaken in the encounter with the absorbing secularity of the second modernity. He has a nice chapter on Islam that, post–11 September, makes for an interesting analysis of how the Islamic world is struggling with the forces of secularizing modernity, but what about the shakenness of fundamentalist Christians in American culture who read the sign of God's action in response to this moment in far different ways than Shanks would? Would American culture's turn to the *libido dominandi* be interpreted as a sign of God's presence in the world? Although Shanks tries to safeguard the place of the shaken among those oppressed by structures of societal power, those who war against the secularity brought about by the second modernity see God very much involved in their struggle. Shanks's answer to this might be that authentic communities of transcendence move beyond the barriers of confessionalism, in whatever tradition, to embrace a new way, but it still seems thin for what theology currently faces.

At the book's heart Shanks gives voice to this when he raises a question asked by Helmut Peukert: "But what, then, of those whose voices are silenced by *death*? What, in particular, of those who die as victims of human wrong: how are we most authentically to hear their cries of protest—or perhaps their testimony to alternative ways of life, crushed by the oppressor?" (154). This shows the true stakes in any theological enterprise. Shanks envisions the future of theology resting in the engagement of practical solidarity building with communities that transcend confessional positions. But the suffering unleashed on the world in the name of God, national security, defense, or even such things as ethnic purity calls for commitments to something more profoundly rooted than the contemporary narratives of third modernity. These narratives are just as susceptible to projection and self-interests as those that have preceded them, and tying the future of theology to the vagaries of the moment, while important, does not offer the type of resistance to the systems of oppression that Shanks hopes will emerge from his new way of doing theology.

Jeffrey C. Pugh
Elon University

Why Religion Matters: The Fate of the Human Spirit in an Age of Disbelief. By Huston Smith. HarperSanFrancisco, 2001. 290 pages. $25.00.

Imagine two professors, both noted for their rhetorical powers and both so fascinated with ancient stories of heroes, warriors, saints, and sages that they speak movingly of the courage those men and women had. But one professor, while recognizing that courage entails standing his ground in the face of fear, had long ago and all too often "yielded" for career and other pragmatic concerns. And although his "retreats" did not lessen his fascination with the virtue of courage, still, for him, this virtue stood only as an idea. Courage remained at a safe distance from this scholar, thus allowing him a competent phenomenological study of how courageous people have acted at different times and in different cultures. Perhaps he even persuaded himself that this outsider's study of courage was necessary to derive "objective" and scientifically valid results.

Contrast this with the other professor who, after becoming fascinated with the stories of heroes, warriors, saints, and sages, decided to take them seriously. He understood that the virtues cannot be brought down on our terms; rather, the individual must make the effort to ascend to them on their terms. This professor, then, decided to inquire personally into what those individuals were saying and what they had become. When it came to the virtue of courage, he decided to test it out. He did not run. In time and with much diligence, no metaphysical gulf separated this professor from courage itself. As he stood his ground in the face of his fears, he *had become* courage. This professor, though just as scholarly as the other, now apprehended courage, not only intellectually and from a distance but in itself, from the inside. His study is not a phenomenological circumambulation of the subject matter but, rather, a penetration into it.

Huston Smith, over a long life of writing and teaching, has taken his stance with this second professor and urges others to follow such a path so that they too might grasp the subject matter of religion from the inside. Why? Why does Smith insist on the path of commitment in his approach to the study of religion over the "scientific" or phenomenological approach—and this in spite of the stiff academic winds blowing in his face? In his latest book, *Why Religion Matters,* he offers an answer that may explain: The very project of religion, Smith tells us, is one of "commitment to making people real" (231). Neither courage nor religion can "really" be known without an existential engagement.

"We are theomorphic creatures," Smith contends, "one whose *morphe* (form) is *theos*—God encased within it" (148). Thus created in the image of God, we all already have individual and unique "God-shaped vacuums" built into our hearts. The world's religions, according to Smith, serve to fill this emptiness and so "enable people to come as close as possible to God's infinite reality" (231).

But couldn't this becoming "as close as possible to God's infinite reality" be understood as merely a subjective or felt sense of completion? Couldn't it be just another psychological event with no causal connection to "objective" reality, let alone attributable to some transcendent spiritual being called God? If so, then Stephen Jay Gould is right to separate science from religion by giving to science the task of "document[ing] the factual character of the natural world" while leaving religion to "operate in the equally important, but utterly different, realm of human purposes, meanings, and values" (71).

Many in academia would accept this fact–value split as decisive for demarcating the line between science and religion. Not Smith. "The fundamental issue," he tells us, "is about facts, period. . . . Specifically here, it is about the standing of values in the objective world" (71). This point is crucial. It serves as the key insight of *Why Religion Matters*. Gould would have science deal with facts about the natural world and leave religion to human (notice he does not say "divine") purposes, meanings, and values. But who, then, is left, Smith asks, "to deal with the *factual* character of the nonnatural, supernatural world"? The answer is no one, for from Gould's point of view (not to mention the general bias of the scientific worldview), there only is the natural world of matter. The assumption that matter is the foundation of all reality, Smith contends, is a basic feature separating legitimate science from *scientism;* and for Smith, this "scientism" is the clear and ever present foe.

Smith uses a line from Freud dramatically to highlight the reductionist character of scientism. "Our science," Freud says, "is not illusion, but an illusion it would be to suppose that what science cannot give us we can get elsewhere" (60). Scientism has dismissed the Transcendentals of religion and now stands guard against their return, declaring a priori that formal and final causation exist only in human imagination. The effect of this modern worldview, Smith tells us, is to render the world "dis-qualified"; that is, it strips the world of quality and value: "We experience the corporal world decked with sounds, smells, and color, whereas science gives us only the quantifiable underpinnings of those sensations" (50).

In an explicit reference to Plato's allegory of the cave, Smith uses the image of a *tunnel* to dramatize the practical effect of this modern scientific worldview. He describes this tunnel as the place in which we find ourselves so restless because we are culturally and emotionally cut off from vital light. Subtly and skillfully, Smith weaves the imagery and pathos of modern man as prisoner in a world of his own inadvertent making. The first several chapters describe the construction and maintenance of our tunnel. Its floor is scientism itself. Its "left wall" is higher education, which teaches that relativism, reductionism, positivism, and determinism are the only scholarly (i.e., valid) methods for mining from nature her secrets. Our tunnel's "roof" is the media, whose secular worldview and cultural isolation allows it to ignore the 120 million people in America who regularly practice their religion. Its "right wall" is law and secular politics, which has tried mightily to expunge from public life all reference to God or any transcendent value that might imply the need for allegiance to something higher than social institutions and human law.

But *Why Religions Matters* also leads toward the "light at the tunnel's end." In the latter chapters Smith contrasts the traditional metaphysical view of things with the scientific worldview and suggests a framework within which a more fruitful dialogue between science and religion can occur. First, that which separates the scientific from the traditional worldview "as day from night" is the scientific assumption that qualities such as "life, sentience, and self-consciousness . . . can derive from the rearrangement of elements that themselves lack those qualities" (263). In short, the scientific worldview "assumes that the *more* derives from the *less*" (260). Smith contends just the opposite—that the greater is the source of the lesser, that the whole is prior in principle to the part. The religious view is that "spirit is fundamental and matter derivative," that the natural world and quality itself are both derived from a common spiritual source. This source is the single world in which we humans are no longer restless but, rather, finally "at home."

Second, because science is not its own measure and, as we saw in the last century, technological progress is not necessarily accompanied by moral progress, exiting the tunnel requires that science admit other ways of knowing. As Smith points out elsewhere, to use our empirical faculties alone to understand what transcends those faculties is analogous to a dog sniffing the pages of a book and concluding that grammar does not exist. In a similar way, the pillars of scientism—that scientific method alone reaches truth and that matter is the foundation of everything—are themselves "unscientific." The world is not only as the scientist describes but also as it is revealed to the poet, mystic, artisan, and person of sound common sense. It is *not* on the fact–value split that science and religion are to be distinguished. Rather, "science deals with the natural world and religion with the whole of things" (200).

Finally, Smith predicts that the "two worldviews, the traditional and the scientific, [will] compete for the mind of the third millennium." And, Smith reminds us, we do have a choice "because neither of [these worldviews] can be proved to be truer than the other" (193). The fact that a metaphysics of spirit is challenged by a metaphysics of matter is more a consequence of the times or mentality of the age then of logic or any scientific discovery. But, of course, the mentality of the age is nothing to be trifled with.

Still, Huston Smith continues to think against the times. The basic assumptions of neither the traditional nor the scientific worldviews can be proven empirically; and yet, as we see above with the example of courage and our two professors, such things can be verified existentially. In such a way is religion's aim "making people real": "The traditional worldview is preferable to the one that now encloses us because it allows for the fulfillment of the basic longing that lies in the depths of the human heart" (28).

Bruce K. Hanson
Fullerton College

Reason and Religion in Socratic Philosophy. Edited by Nicholas D. Smith
and Paul B. Woodruff. Oxford University Press, 2000. 226 pages. $45.00.

This book is an anthology containing some previously published and some
newly published material dealing with Socrates' religious views and the reasons
behind his conviction for impiety in 399 B.C.E. Although most of the nine selec-
tions are written by philosophers, one is written by a distinguished ancient historian (Robert Parker), and one is by a classicist (Stephen A. White). The tenth
selection is an edited version of correspondence between the late Gregory Vlastos
and Thomas C. Brickhouse, Nicholas D. Smith, and Mark L. McPherran. It does
not take long for the reader to see that the level of argument in this book is very
high and that new ground has been broken in several areas.

The traditional view is that Socrates was brought to trial for political reasons,
chiefly his association with discredited figures like Critias and Alcibiades, and the
subsequent claim that he corrupted the youth of Athens. On this reading, the
charge of impiety and the accusation of atheism were just a pretext to get him
into court and raise the prospect of death. In recent years the traditional view has
been called into question by several of the contributors to this book. They argue
that it is impossible to read the early dialogues without seeing that Socrates regarded himself as the servant of God, that he was willing to die rather than abandon that service, and that he claimed to have private revelatory experiences (a
certain *daimonion*) that warned him against doing the wrong thing.

Upon hearing that Socrates has been charged with impiety, Euthyphro's
immediate reaction (3b) is to say that the reason must be the *daimonion*, for surely
Socrates' loyalty to it amounts to a religious innovation and counts as evidence
that he did not recognize the gods of the state. But here the trouble starts. Does
recognize (*nomizein*) mean that Socrates did not believe in the gods' existence or
that he did not show them proper respect by participating in the required festivals? As anyone can see, this is a version of the old question about orthodoxy versus
orthopraxy. And what about the *daimonion* itself? Did it confirm the conclusions
Socrates reached on the basis of argument and refutation, or did it go beyond
argument and refutation and provide him with direct access to the will of God?

Asli Gocer reminds us that our knowledge of Greek religion is sketchy at best,
so it is difficult to say what Socrates' jurors would have regarded as normal or
how far they would have been willing to tolerate differences of opinion. Parker
and Richard Kraut both argue that other people were allowed to express unor-
thodox views or engage in novel practices without being sentenced to death. Thus,
politics cannot be completely disregarded. The question is: Where does politics
end and religion begin? In ancient Athens, as in modern America, there is no
simple answer.

The larger problem, as Kraut maintains, is that we will fall into the trap of
becoming "so dazzled by the dignity and innocence of Socrates and so critical of
a highly flawed Athens that we will miss the profound moral dilemma that lies
behind his trial and death" (22). More than 100 years ago Hegel pointed out that
there is a sense in which Socrates was guilty as charged: by substituting the inner

certainty of argument and refutation for the festivals and pronouncements of traditional religion, Socrates *did* introduce new gods or, as one might say, a new absolute.

These gods, it may be assumed, share his commitment to virtue, refuse to be bribed or cajoled, and take pleasure when someone with a false reputation for wisdom is shown to be ignorant. On this point, consider the words of Vlastos: "What would be left of her [Hera] and the other Olympians if they were required to observe the stringent norms of Socratic virtue which require every agent, human or divine, to act only to cause good to others, never evil, regardless of provocation? Required to meet these standards, the city's gods would have become unrecognizable. Their ethical transformation would be tantamount to the destruction of the old gods, the creation of new ones" (59). In short, reason requires a religious revolution, and Socrates is its leader.

Needless to say, others see things differently. According to McPherran, Vlastos is right to argue that the Socratic reform of traditional religion could have been seen as a threat to cult worship as the average Athenian understood it. But it does not follow that Socrates leaves no room for prayer, sacrifice, or other ritual. In McPherran's words, what Socrates objected to is not religion itself but "the narrow, self-aggrandizing *motivations* of many of its practitioners" (98). In the proper hands, prayer, sacrifice, or other ritual may perform a valuable service by reinforcing the right sentiments and stimulating the need to develop reason. According to Brickhouse and Smith, there is no reason to think that Socrates' contemporaries were troubled by his attempt to moralize religion, "however revolutionary that transformation may seem to us" (76). Rather, the reason for the prejudice that arose against him is exactly what he says: his practice of examining the knowledge claims of others.

To this it may be objected that Socrates did not just examine others; he claimed that doing so was a service to God and that he was closer to God than those who sat in judgment of him. As Callicles says to Socrates at *Gorgias* 481b–c: "If you're serious and what you say is actually true, won't human life have to be turned upside down? Everything we do, it seems, is exactly the opposite of what we ought to do." It seems to me that this reaction is as true in religion as in morals, politics, or anything else.

That brings us to Socrates' *daimonion*, the place where he not only accepts but appears to be guided by the supernatural. Does this experience confirm the conclusions to which a lifetime of questioning point? Is it an early version of what came to be known as the double faith theory—faith in reason *and* revelation—or does it show that there are places where Socrates was willing to put reason aside and trust in a revelation unique to him?

Again Vlastos notes: "So all he could claim to be getting from the *daimonion* at any given time is precisely what he calls the *daimonion* itself—a 'divine sign,' which allows, indeed requires, *unlimited scope for the development of his critical reason* to extract whatever truth it can from those monitions" (61). Again Brickhouse and Smith disagree, claiming that when Socrates maintains at *Apology* 40a that his *daimonion* speaks to him quite frequently even on small matters, we should take him literally. In their view the *daimonion* does not oppose Socrates when he is'pondering his next course of action but, rather, when he is about to take it. Moreover, it opposes him not just when he is about to act impulsively but when he is about to act with forethought. Socrates, then, is not the rationalist that later generations of philosophers took him to be. In the words of Brickhouse and Smith, the *daimonion* "trumps" reason (82).

As a rationalist myself, I find Brickhouse and Smith's interpretation hard to swallow. Can we really believe Socrates would have been willing to overturn years of rational inquiry because a voice he could not question told him to do so? I think not. Anyone who wishes to see how Brickhouse and Smith defend their view against Vlastos is invited to read the correspondence between them published in chapter 10. My own position is much closer to the one expressed by C. D. C. Reeve, who argues that Socrates trusts the *daimonion* precisely because he regards it as a manifestation of divine wisdom (35). This is true even though the information he receives from it may exceed the information he could acquire by use of reason alone.

Obviously, I cannot cover all of the essays or issues raised in this book. But there is no doubt that someone who wishes to pursue the nature of Socratic religion in detail not only will have to read it but must chew and digest its many valuable insights. In sum, it is a worthwhile contribution to an important subject.

Kenneth Seeskin
Northwestern University

Go and Do Likewise: Jesus and Ethics. By William C. Spohn. Continuum, 1999. 227 pages. $24.95.

Clearly and elegantly written, this study displays the pedagogy of a seasoned teacher and the precision of a moral theologian who is well aware of the broad range of problems that make it difficult to connect biblical texts and everyday life. This book is also marked by an uncommon understanding of the importance of Christian spirituality for moral formation. Indeed, one is struck over and over again by the ways William C. Spohn tries to connect features of Christian life that have tended to be compartmentalized within American Catholicism—before and after Vatican II—and in many non-Catholic communions as well.

Spohn is also alert to the discrepancies that too often surround the relationship of Jesus and ethics. Some Protestants talk or act as if Jesus totally determines ethics, little realizing the ways other factors play mediating roles that shape the way Christians appropriate Scripture. Others, including many Catholic moral theologians, remain skeptical that there can be much of a relationship at all. By contrast, Spohn aspires to provide a *via media:* Jesus is to be understood as playing "a normative role as a concrete universal for Christian ethics. Through faithful imagination his story becomes paradigmatic for moral perception, disposition, and identity" (2). Specifically, he integrates "three avenues of reflection: a) the New Testament story of Jesus, b) the ethics of virtue and character, and c) the practices of New Testament spirituality" (12).

Part 1 comprises three chapters. In the first Spohn offers an overview of this "threefold approach" and introduces his hermeneutical approach. Stressing the "complementarity" of these three sources, Spohn contends that moral theologians must *go beyond* the descriptive results of the historical method of biblical interpretation to explain what it means *morally* and *spiritually* for Christians to "imitate" Jesus. Practicing a "hermeneutics of appreciation" (5, 18), Spohn contends that participation in the "life, death and rising" of Jesus Christ (25) is the proper way to think about this matter. For this reason, Spohn stresses the "pedagogical role" played by practices of Christian spirituality in cultivating moral dispositions and habits. The second chapter explains why Spohn favors "an ethics of virtue and character" over deontological and consequentialist approaches to the moral life. There he also shows how a focus on *practices* can "link" spirituality and virtue. This aspect of the book is especially noteworthy because this is where Spohn makes a real contribution to the scholarly conversation about Jesus and ethics.

In the third chapter Spohn lays out his methodological proposal. Agreeing with David Tracy that "analogy enables the biblical text to mediate between the original generations of Christians and subsequent ones," he argues that it is the "analogical imagination" that serves as the bridge between "the moral reflection of Christians and the words and deeds of Jesus. It provides the cognitive content for obeying the command, 'Go and do likewise'" (50). By plunging "into the concrete details of the life of Jesus in order to become universal," Christians can gain normative guidance through the "discovery of patterns" (50). Spohn displays the results of this kind of analogical reasoning through an extensive commentary on the Johannine account of Jesus washing the disciples feet, which serves as a "test case" (51–54).

In part 2 Spohn explores the moral psychology of Christian transformation. While carefully explaining the differences among perception, emotion, dispositions, and identity, Spohn notes that the very features—that he distinguishes for "analytical purposes"—must be "integrated in walking the way of discipleship" (74). In the fourth chapter Spohn explores how the faculty of perception, which is "a function of character"(86), is shaped by Christian practices. But as chapter 5 makes clear, in order for Christians to learn to see life from the framework of the Kingdom of God, a "retooling" of imaginations is required to make sense of the "cosmic generosity" of God's grace (106). In this context he describes the role of spiritual practices, understood as the "means of grace," in sharpening or "correcting" moral perception (112–119). For example, intercessory prayer "trains the imagination to locate experience in the context of God" (115). Similarly, the "rich vocabulary" of the Psalter "tutors" the emotions and dispositions by "articulating fear, sadness, and abandonment and then leading them back into the presence of God" (123).

In chapter 6 Spohn discusses the ways in which the practice of meditation (*lectio divina*) can foster "a deepening familiarity with God, a growing friendship and intimacy, a greater openness to the divine life and direction of the Spirit" (140). The intuitive and deliberative aspects of the practice of Christian discernment are explicated in chapter 7. In the eighth chapter the practice of the Eucharist is shown to foster forgiveness and reconciliation, which make it possible for one's identity to be reoriented, thereby making solidarity with others possible (180). Some of Spohn's own most perceptive observations are offered in these chapters, in which he "spells out" the implications of the linkage between spirituality and virtue.

Issues of authority also float through this book, but they are handled unevenly. On the one hand, Spohn can be very candid about interpretive matters: "Scripture has authority over discernment but not the final word" (164). On the other hand, he is ambivalent at best about the nature of ecclesial authority in "tutoring" the analogical imagination. Such reticence about ecclesial authority might not be regarded as significant in a book on this topic, except that Spohn clearly states that the *locus* of this kind of moral formation and reflection "is not primarily an academic enterprise. The New Testament writings should be engaged by specific communities to discern what they call for in their situation" (187). In his conclusion Spohn notes that if space had permitted he would have examined "how communities of faith instruct, test, and inform the analogical imagination and keep it honest" (186). As difficult as this task would be, one hopes that in his next book Spohn follows through on this aspiration.

I question, however, whether Spohn's proposals for the "analogical imagination" can account for those communally specified enactments of discernment that display the strong imprint of tradition. Interestingly, Spohn makes it very clear that he agrees with Alasdair MacIntyre's contention that "the virtues in any tradition are narrative dependent" (128). What is *not so clear* is how Spohn regards the diverse kinds of enactments of spiritual practices, particularly as they exist in the separated Christian communions.

Such ambiguity or ambivalence extends to his own tradition. At points this Catholic moral theologian writes *as if* there is no functioning magisterium in matters moral. At other points his book reads as an "invitation" to episcopal leaders of the church to think of what they do (at their best) as exercising an analogical imagination. Clearly ambivalent about both the kinds of formalistic moral reasoning that disengage from "lived spirituality" and the kinds of pious moralism that fail to engage the analogical imagination, Spohn tries to chart a different course. As long as the "extremes" are in full view, advocates of a *via media* can appear to be prudent and wise. When internal tensions in a proposal become prominent, however, the "middle way" can become less persuasive.

One such set of tensions in Spohn's book surrounds the way he deals with the evident difference between the "dramatic and more gradual paths of conversion" displayed in the writings of Paul and the four Gospels. Although he certainly does not ignore the dramatic paradigm that informs much of Protestant spirituality, Spohn does focus attention on "the more pedestrian route of Peter and the other disciples. . . . Their blindness is not total and they do not recover their sight in a miraculous instant"(112). Although I tend to agree, this is one of several instances in which Spohn overplays David Tracy's misleading distinction between the "dialectical" and "analogical" imaginations. In the process a key presumption of Spohn's argument can easily be overlooked. Namely, he tends to presuppose *liturgical practices* of spiritual formation, which in turn means that his understanding of the *linkage* between spiritual practices—understood as "means of grace" (112–119)—and discernment also tends to be framed within a sacramental framework.

This need not have been a problem, in my judgment. Indeed, given the insightful way in which Spohn discusses the moral significance of the spiritual practices in question, one is inclined to think that he might have made as strong a case for a *liturgical* imagination as he tries to make for the "analogical imagination." Had he done so, I suspect Spohn's discussion of discernment would have worked even better because his discussion of this particular practice has been most strongly influenced by the Ignatian tradition along with the Catholic tradition of liturgy. Further exploration of how discernment is enacted in the wider diversity of Christian traditions would also have been illuminating. While the Quaker, Mennonite, and Wesleyan practices of discernment certainly share a "family resemblance" with the Ignatian tradition, the differences are not unimportant. Authority is located in different agencies, and Christian vocation is construed in divergent ways. Jesus and the Spirit are understood to be "present" in *different modes.* One might even say that each of these communions *orients* judgment about *which kinds of analogies* are to be sought.

To acknowledge this does not entail that we ignore shared practices where they exist. It is useful, however, to observe how the presence or absence of liturgical practices such as the Eucharist (or the sacrament of reconciliation) can *alter the focus* of what is to be discerned—by whom and for what purpose. The question that arises when we recognize this circumstance is, *How should we think about the disanalogies* between these practices as they exist within the historical Christian communities? For that task we need a *different kind* of criteria than the "analogical imagination" provides. In my judgment, the real value of *Go and Do Likewise* does not reside in its methodological proposal so much as in Spohn's insightful discussion of the linkage between spiritual practices and moral formation. For that reason, as well as others, this book should be read by Protestant and Catholic moral theologians alike.

Michael G. Cartwright
University of Indianapolis

Breaking the Fine Rain of Death: African-American Health Issues and a Womanist Ethic of Care. By Emilie M. Townes. Continuum, 1998. 214 pages. $24.95.

Arguing that gender-based understandings of moral reasoning are too narrow "to address an increasingly complex and distressed social order" (1), *Breaking the Fine Rain of Death* offers a "womanist ethic of care" that explores health and health care as social constructs, "compris[ing] a wide range of activities that foster healing and wholeness" (2). Emilie Townes says that U.S. health care is in crisis because it has become "overly individualistic," making persons health consumers in a for-profit industry. This situation reflects what she describes as a transgression for which society should repent and engage in "genuine lament."

Townes argues against narrow, static ideas about health and health care and contrasts "biomedical" and "cultural" models (the body as a machine to be maintained and repaired and the interrelationship of mind and body interacting with cultural contexts, respectively). Following Collins Airhihenbuwa, who says "health is a cultural production" (49) that involves adapting to social realities, the book advocates health care that draws on biomedical *and* cultural models to express "caring and hope." Townes distinguishes personal from social caring and encourages social caring as a "means [of] organizing institutional support for those who are in need [to] help people either adapt to or resist their health situations in structured ways" (163).

Using African Americans as a test case for a theory with "universal dimensions," Townes describes her methodology as praxeological and interdisciplinary. Written in prose and poetry, the book consists of three parts: chapters 1–3, exploring lament, fragmented U.S. health care, and general African American health and health care; chapters 4–6, looking more closely at health in black communities, including the notorious U.S. Public Health Service (PHS) Tuskegee syphilis study, black women's health, and HIV/AIDS and African Americans; and chapters 7 and 8, which give examples of cultural models of health care that support her constructive discussion.

Exploring the Hebrew tradition of lament in the Old Testament Book of Joel, Townes says Joel's "day of the Lord" sayings follow devastation and point to a deficiency for which the community should repent. "Day of the Lord" also announces God's imminent action of judgment or salvation. Townes calls for lamenting the nation's health care as means to both abide and address its consequences. "Communal lament, as a corporate experience of calling for healing, makes suffering bearable and manageable in the community," she writes: "We must name [the problems] as such and seek to repent. . . . It is only then that we can begin to heal" (24).

Townes lifts two causes for lament in U.S. society— the "fragmented" health care system and racialism in health quality and care. Her compelling catalog of deficiencies in the current system includes the difficulty of the working classes and the poor in finding affordable health care, figures for uninsured persons in 1996 at 42 million and growing, unemployment as insignificantly related to being uninsured, Medicare and Medicaid fraud and enrollment increases of 95 and 275 percent between 1967 and 1996, and various difficulties arising from managed care. Townes also notes the failure of national health plans presented by the Truman and Nixon administrations prior to the defeat of Clinton administration efforts.

Her discussion of African American health care begins by asserting that historic racialized conceptions of black bodies continue to influence black health. Townes cites research documenting the tendency by physicians to give African Americans "less-advanced treatment than Whites" (67) and "patterns [that] indicate that Black folks and poor folks receive less primary and preventive care than either White or more affluent beneficiaries" (76). Ironically, though poverty significantly influences health, regardless of African Americans' places "on the socioeconomic ladder, health problems have a greater impact on Blacks than on other Americans" (50).

Alongside racism, other considerations compound contemporary black health problems. Genetic factors such as higher lactose intolerance impact vitamin D deficiency; dietary practices and obesity foster diabetes and cardiovascular disease; and black smoking rates contribute to high incidence of lung cancer. Townes says that "crack cocaine addiction has exacerbated ongoing problems of crime, poverty, unemployment, and racism" (69) but quotes the National Institute on Drug Abuse indicating that "race/ethnicity was not a significant determinant" of drug usage. She calls drug abuse a national health problem, saying drug usage relates directly to poverty, hopelessness, and "the economics of our country" (70).

Townes's closer examination of African American health identifies deception as the major problem of the forty-year Tuskegee study. "PHS officials," Townes writes, "ignored the principle of the patient's right to know and withheld information that was crucial to the program's [original] goal of controlling syphilis in Macon County" (89). Beyond withholding information, the PHS intentionally misled study participants. Townes says that "protocol for the [research] was suspect just six years into the study" (95) and concludes that ultimately racism and classism contributed to the travesty.

Exploration of black women's health and health care begins with the picture of all U.S. women and health. Stereotyping similar to racialist theories also supports gendered medical perspectives, often referring to "gender weaknesses" and delicacy as causing health problems—although, as Townes notes, this understanding of women and "womanhood did not extend to slave, or working-class, or poor women" (107). Contrasting with the focus of biomedical ethics on reproduction, she considers the broader issue of women's absence from clinical trials and the dearth of trials focusing exclusively on women. She notes, for example, that "a Rockefeller University project that explored the impact of obesity on the development of breast or endometrial cancer used only men" (110). From this foundation of looking at all women, Townes says that even worse is the "gross under-representation of racial-ethnic women in clinical trials" (113) and the affect of racialized gender perceptions. Cancer diagnosis for black women comes later, making treatment less effective. She also notes that "racial-ethnic women have more difficult time gaining health insurance than white women, and they are disproportionately represented in the ranks of the uninsured" (117). African American women's health also is affected by environmental factors. Black women have almost "epidemic" incidences of diabetes, are overweight more often (more than 50 percent), and are less likely to quit smoking.

Breaking the Fine Rain of Death includes staggering statistics on HIV/AIDS infections among African Americans: in 1990 AIDS was the leading killer of black males ages thirty-five–forty-five, almost 75 percent of black people with AIDS are ages twenty–thirty-nine, in 1998 black women constituted 57 percent of new AIDS cases among adult women, and in 1997 black children were 58 percent of the reported pediatric AIDS cases. Race, economic standing, and gender also have bearing on treating persons with HIV/AIDS. A 1989 Brown University study found that in determining who could receive the drug AZT, "doctors were practicing a form of social Darwinism along with medicine, deciding who would get the drug based on the perceived 'social worth' of their patients. . . . [W]omen, who are also disproportionately represented among minority, drug-using, and uninsured groups, weren't seen as 'worthy' of treatment that might keep them alive longer" (137). Her meandering discussion of HIV/AIDS points to the need for considering issues of sexuality, drug abuse, and the role of black churches.

To construct her womanist ethic of care, Townes cites the PEN-3 model advocated by Airhihenbuwa as paradigmatic in its consideration of three interdependent dimensions: (a) the roles of individual persons, the extended family, and the neighborhood in informed health decision making; (b) the roles of perceptions, relationships, and enabling forces in lifestyle change; and (c) the significance of culturally appropriate health behavior. Other cultural models include such things as neighborhood access to health facilities; protests and activism; and small group gatherings for consciousness raising, education, and support. There also are two examples of religiously based community health care projects, including a black church HIV/AIDS ministry.

Townes calls for communal repentance and lament to attend to problems deriving from "rampant individualism." She argues for culturally empowering health programs integrated with asset-based health care strategies (looking at resources internal to communities). Developing these requires a sense of empathy and a reconfigured understanding of love. Empathy, Townes says, is "sharing and understanding emotions and social experiences of others and coming to see the world as they see it." From this view love means "moving in the direction of a commitment to deepen our understanding and respect for one another in our uniqueness and in our commonality without one overriding or subsuming the other" (175). Both derive from hope as the "expectation of a justice-filled future established on God's promise" (179) and the human commitment to struggle and risk demanded by having hope in God.

Townes's "social ethic" focuses on health policy concerns. In contrast to bioethicists who often relate medicine and health care to specific issues, individuals, and extraordinary cases, Townes attends to the millions of persons daily contending with how to secure routine medical treatment. She *re*focuses the discussion on distributive justice and quality of life issues for all. Among womanist religious literature, *Breaking the Fine Rain of Death* stands with Kelly Brown Douglass's *Sexuality and the Black Church* (Orbis Books, 1999) and Karen Baker Fletcher's environmentally focused *Sisters of Dust, Sisters of Spirit* (Fortress Press, 1998) as the first book-length treatment of a particular issue and is in this regard groundbreaking.

Rosetta E. Ross
United Theological Seminary of the Twin Cities

AAR BOOKS RECEIVED

Aviezer, Nathan, *Fossils and Faith: Understanding Torah and Science.* KTAV, 2001. 270 pages. $24.95.

Baltzer, Klaus, *Deutero-Isaiah: A Commentary of Isaiah 40–55.* Edited by Peter Machinist. Translated by Margaret Kohl. Fortress Press, 2001. 597 pages. $78.00.

Bataille, Georges, *The Unfinished System of NonKnowledge.* Edited by Stuart Kendall. Translated by Michelle Kendall and Stuart Kendall. University of Minnesota Press, 2001. 305 pages. $39.95.

Bergant, Dianne, *Berit Olam: Studies in Hebrew Narrative and Poetry. The Song of Songs.* Edited by David W. Cotter. Liturgical Press, 2001. 123 pages. $29.95.

Berrigan, Daniel, *Wisdom: The Feminine Face of God.* Sheed and Ward, 2001. 197 pages. $24.95.

Bill, James A., and John Alden Williams, *Roman Catholics and Shi'i Muslims: Prayer, Passion, and Politics.* University of North Carolina Press, 2002. 194 pages. $24.95.

Blowers, Paul M., Angela Russell Christman, David G. Hunter, and Robin Darling Young, eds., *In Dominico Eloquio—In Lordly Eloquence: Essays on Patristic Exegesis in Honor of Robert L. Wilken.* William B. Eerdmans, 2002. 438 pages. $45.00.

Bobrick, Benson, *Wide as Waters: The Story of the English Bible and the Revolution It Inspired.* Simon and Schuster, 2001. 379 pages. $26.00.

Brettler, Marc Zvi, *Biblical Hebrew for Students of Modern Israeli Hebrew.* Yale University Press, 2002. 355 pages. $40.00.

Burr, David, *The Spiritual Franciscans: From Protest to Persecution in the Century after Saint Francis.* Pennsylvania State University Press, 2001. 427 pages. $45.00.

Cabantous, Alain, *Blasphemy: Impious Speech in the West from the Seventeenth to the Nineteenth Century.* Translated by Eric Rauth. Columbia University Press, 2002. 288 pages. $29.50.

Caputo, John D., ed., *The Religious*. Blackwell Publishers, 2002. 322 pages. $64.95.

Caterine, Darryl V., *Conservative Catholicism and the Carmelites: Identity, Ethnicity, and Tradition in the Modern Church*. Indiana University Press, 2001. 155 pages. $29.95.

Chazelle, Celia, *The Crucified God in the Carolingian Era: Theology and Art of Christ's Passion*. Cambridge University Press, 2001. 338 pages. $70.00.

Chittick, William C., *The Heart of Islamic Philosophy: The Quest for Self-Knowledge in the Teachings of Afḍal al-Dīn Kāshānī*. Oxford University Press, 2001. 360 pages. $60.00.

Cleaveland, Timothy, *Becoming Walāta: A History of Saharan Social Formation and Transformation*. Heinemann, 2002. 232 pages. $67.95.

Clooney, Francis X., *Hindu God, Christian God: How Reason Helps Break Down the Boundaries between Religions*. Oxford University Press, 2001. 209 pages. $39.95.

Corrigan, John, *Business of the Heart: Religion and Emotion in the Nineteenth Century*. University of California Press, 2002. 389 pages. $40.00.

Cowling, Maurice, *Religion and Public Doctrine in Modern England, Vol. 3: Accommodations*. Cambridge University Press, 2001. 766 pages. $100.00.

Cummins, Stephen Anthony, *Paul and the Crucified Christ in Antioch: Maccabean Martyrdom and Galatians 1 and 2*. Cambridge University Press, 2001. 287 pages. $64.95.

Dandelet, Thomas James, *Spanish Rome, 1500–1700*. Yale University Press, 2001. 278 pages. $35.00.

Dawson, John David, *Christian Figural Reading and the Fashioning of Identity*. University of California Press, 2002. 302 pages. $50.00.

Faber, M. D., *The Magic of Prayer: An Introduction to the Psychology of Faith*. Praeger, 2002. 154 pages. $62.00.

Fox, William L., ed., *Valley of the Craftsmen: A Pictorial History. Scottish Rite Freemasonry in America's Southern Jurisdiction, 1801–2001*. University of South Carolina Press, 2001. 269 pages. $75.00.

Friesen, Steven J., *Imperial Cults and the Apocalypse of John: Reading Revelation in the Ruins*. Oxford University Press, 2001. 285 pages. $49.95.

Groves, Betsy McAlister, *Children Who See Too Much: Lessons from the Child Witness to Violence Project*. Beacon Press, 2002. 168 pages. $24.00.

Gunton, Colin E., *The Christian Faith: An Introduction to Christian Doctrine*. Blackwell Publishers, 2002. 198 pages. $57.95.

Hahn, Cynthia, *Portrayed on the Heart: Narrative Effect in Pictorial Lives of Saints from the Tenth through the Thirteenth Century.* University of California Press, 2001. 442 pages. $60.00.

Hanson, Mark J., ed., *Claiming Power over Life: Religion and Biotechnology Policy.* Georgetown University Press, 2001. 236 pages. $44.95.

Harries, Richard, and Henry Mayr-Harting, eds., *Christianity: Two Thousand Years.* Oxford University Press, 2001. 279 pages. $18.95.

Heyduck, Richard, *The Recovery of Doctrine in the Contemporary Church: An Essay in Philosophical Ecclesiology.* Baylor University Press, 2002. 239 pages. $34.95.

Holloway, Paul A., *Consolation in Philippians: Philosophical Sources and Rhetorical Strategy.* Cambridge University Press, 2001. 208 pages. $54.95.

Howell, Kenneth J., *God's Two Books: Copernican Cosmology and Biblical Interpretation in Early Modern Science.* University of Notre Dame Press, 2002. 319 pages. $39.95.

Johnson, Dale A., ed., *Vanderbilt Divinity School: Education, Contest, and Change.* Vanderbilt University Press, 2001. 420 pages. $49.95.

Jordan, Mark D., *The Silence of Sodom: Homosexuality in Modern Catholicism.* University of Chicago Press, 2000. 322 pages. $25.00.

Kabir, Ananya Jahanara, *Paradise, Death and Doomsday in Anglo-Saxon Literature.* Cambridge University Press, 2001. 210 pages. $70.00.

Karkov, Catherine E., *Text and Picture in Anglo-Saxon England: Narrative Strategies in the Junius II Manuscript.* Cambridge University Press, 2001. 225 pages. $69.95.

Kraushar, Alexandr, trans., *Jacob Frank: The End to the Sabbataian Heresy.* Edited by Herbert Levy. University Press of America, 2001. 555 pages. $64.00.

Levy, B. Barry, *Fixing God's Torah: The Accuracy of the Hebrew Bible Text in Jewish Law.* Oxford University Press, 2001. 237 pages. $49.95.

Lindsay, Stan A., *Revelation: The Human Drama.* Lehigh University Press, 2001. 216 pages. $42.50.

Long, Lynne, *Translating the Bible: From the 7th to the 17th Century.* Ashgate, 2001. 230 pages. $69.95.

Lupieri, Edmondo, *The Mandaeans: The Last Gnostics.* William B. Eerdmans, 2002. 273 pages. $25.00.

Mann, Gurinder Singh, Paul David Numrich, and Raymond B. Williams, *Buddhists, Hindus, and Sikhs in America.* Oxford University Press, 2001. 158 pages. $24.00.

Matthews, Scott, *Reason, Community and Religious Tradition: Anselm's Argument and the Friars.* Ashgate, 2001. 238 pages. $69.95.

Matthews, Shelly, *First Converts: Rich Pagan Women and the Rhetoric of Mission in Early Judaism and Christianity.* Stanford University Press, 2001. 164 pages. $49.50.

McGrath, Alister, *In the Beginning: The Story of the King James Bible and How It Changed a Nation, a Language, and a Culture.* Doubleday, 2001. 340 pages. $24.95.

McGrath, Alister E., *Scientific Theology, Vol. 1: Nature.* William B. Eerdmans, 2001. 325 pages. $40.00.

McMahan, Jeff, *The Ethics of Killing: Problems at the Margins of Life.* Oxford University Press, 2002. 540 pages. $39.95.

McMillen, Sally G., *To Raise Up the South: Sunday Schools in Black and White Churches, 1865–1915.* Louisiana State University Press, 2001. 297 pages. $54.95.

Mews, Constant J., ed., *Listen, Daughter: The Speculum Virginum and the Formation of Religious Women in the Middle Ages.* Palgrave, 2001. 306 pages. $49.95.

Moore, John A., *From Genesis to Genetics: The Case of Evolution and Creationism.* University of California Press, 2002. 223 pages. $27.50.

Nathanson, Paul, and Katherine K. Young, *Spreading Misandry: The Teaching of Contempt for Men in Popular Culture.* McGill-Queen's University Press, 2001. 370 pages. $39.95.

Newport, Kenneth G. C., *The Sermons of Charles Wesley: A Critical Edition with Introduction and Notes.* Oxford University Press, 2001. 407 pages. $105.00.

Perdue, Leo G., ed., *The Blackwell Companion to the Hebrew Bible.* Blackwell Publishers, 2001. 471 pages. $124.95.

Phiri, Isaac, *Proclaiming Political Pluralism: Churches and Political Transitions in Africa.* Praeger, 2001. 169 pages. $62.00.

Pike, Dana M., and Andrew C. Skinner, *Qumran Cave 4, Vol. 23: Unidentified Fragments.* Oxford University Press, 2001. 380 pages. $125.00.

Possenti, Vittorio, *Philosophy and Revelation: A Contribution to the Debate on Reason and Faith.* Translated by Emanuel L. Paparella. Ashgate, 2001. 88 pages. $59.95.

Rupp, Joyce, *The Cosmic Dance: An Invitation to Experience Our Oneness.* Art by Mary Southard. Orbis Books, 2002. 128 pages. $25.00.

Ryan, Maura A., *The Ethics and Economics of Assisted Reproduction: The Cost of Longing.* Georgetown University Press, 2001. 183 pages. $44.95.

Sack, Daniel, *Whitebread Protestants: Food and Religion in American Culture.* Palgrave, 2001. 262 pages. $18.95.

Sassi, Jonathan D., *A Republic of Righteousness: The Public Christianity of the Post-Revolutionary New England Clergy.* Oxford University Press, 2001. 298 pages. $49.95.

Satlow, Michael L., *Jewish Marriage in Antiquity.* Princeton University Press, 2001. 431 pages. $55.00.

Schmidt, Thomas, *A Scandalous Beauty: The Artistry of God and the Way of the Cross.* Brazos Press, 2002. 127 pages. $14.99.

Shakespeare, Steven, *Kierkegaard, Language and the Reality of God.* Ashgate, 2001. 252 pages. $69.95.

Sharf, Robert H., *Coming to Terms with Chinese Buddhism: A Reading of the "Treasure Store Treatise."* University of Hawaii Press, 2002. 400 pages. $47.00.

Sharma, Arvind, *To the Things Themselves: Essays on the Discourse and Practice of the Phenomenology of Religion.* Walter de Gruyter, 2001. 311 pages. $74.00.

Simons, Walter, *Cities of Ladies: Beguine Communities in the Medieval Low Countries, 1200–1565.* University of Pennsylvania Press, 2001. 335 pages. $65.00.

Smith, David M., and Vera C. M. London, eds., *The Heads of Religious Houses: England and Wales, II. 1216–1377.* Cambridge University Press, 2001. 730 pages. $120.00.

Stern, Sacha, *Calendar and Community: A History of the Jewish Calendar Second Century BCE—Tenth Century CE.* Oxford University Press, 2001. 306 pages. $72.00.

Stevens, Keith G., *Chinese Mythological Gods.* Oxford University Press, 2001. 82 pages. $12.95.

Talbot, Cynthia, *Precolonial India in Practice: Society, Region, and Identity in Medieval Andhra.* Oxford University Press, 2001. 305 pages. $49.95.

Taylor, Mark C., *The Moment of Complexity: Emerging Network Culture.* University of Chicago Press, 2001. 340 pages. $32.00.

Thiede, Carsten Peter, *The Dead Sea Scrolls and the Jewish Origins of Christianity.* Palgrave, 2001. 256 pages. $27.95.

Trumbower, Jeffrey A., *Rescue for the Dead: The Posthumous Salvation of Non-Christians in Early Christianity.* Oxford University Press, 2001. 206 pages. $45.00.

Urban, Hugh B., *The Economics of Ecstasy: Tantra, Secrecy, and Power in Colonial Bengal.* Oxford University Press, 2001. 286 pages. $55.00.

Verhey, Allen, *Remembering Jesus: Christian Community, Scripture, and the Moral Life.* William B. Eerdmans, 2002. 526 pages. $35.00.

Vincent, Nicholas, *The Holy Blood: King Henry III and the Westminster Blood Relic.* Cambridge University Press, 2001. 254 pages. $50.00.

Ward, Graham, ed., *The Blackwell Companion to Postmodern Theology.* Blackwell Publishers, 2001. 530 pages. $124.95.

Weaver, Jace, *Other Words: American Indian Literature, Law, and Culture.* University of Oklahoma Press, 2001. 381 pages. $34.95.

Witherington, Ben, *New Testament History: A Narrative Account.* Baker Academic, 2001. 430 pages. $26.99.

Work, Telford, *Living and Active: Scripture in the Economy of Salvation.* William B. Eerdmans, 2002. 343 pages. $35.00.

Younger, Paul, *Playing Host to Deity: Festival Religion in the South Indian Tradition.* Oxford University Press, 2002. 189 pages. $49.95.

PAPER

Alexandrakis, Aphrodite, ed., *Neoplatonism and Western Aesthetics.* Edited by Nicholas J. Moutafakis. State University of New York Press, 2002. 254 pages. $23.95.

Allen, Prudence, *The Concept of Woman, Vol. 2: The Early Humanist Reformation, 1250–1500.* William B. Eerdmans, 2002. 1,161 pages. $70.00.

Bainbridge, William Sims, *The Endtime Family: Children of God.* State University of New York Press, 2002. 204 pages. $23.95.

Banks, Robert, *Redeeming the Routines: Bringing Theology to Life.* Baker Academic, 2001 (reprint; original edition, Victor Books, 1993). 187 pages. $16.99.

Bayes, Jane H., and Nayereh Tohidi, eds., *Globalization, Gender, and Religion: The Politics of Women's Rights in Catholic and Muslim Contexts.* Palgrave, 2001. 280 pages. $18.95.

Beeck, Frans Jozef van, *God Encountered: A Contemporary Catholic Systematic Theology. Vol. 2: The Revelation of the Glory. Part 4B: The Genealogy of Depravity: Living Alive to the Living God.* Liturgical Press, 2001. 425 pages. $24.95.

Bell, Daniel M., Jr., *Liberation Theology after the End of History: The Refusal to Cease Suffering.* Routledge, 2001. 208 pages. $25.95.

Bendroth, Margaret Lamberts, *Growing Up Protestant: Parents, Children, and Mainline Churches.* Rutgers University Press, 2002. 195 pages. $20.00.

Bendroth, Margaret Lamberts, and Virginia Lieson Brereton, eds., *Women and Twentieth-Century Protestantism.* University of Illinois Press, 2002. 350 pages. $19.95.

Benor, Daniel J., *Spiritual Healing: Scientific Validation of a Healing Revolution.* Vision Publications, 2001. 597 pages. $28.00.

Berquist, Jon L., *Controlling Corporeality: The Body and the Household in Ancient Israel.* Rutgers University Press, 2002. 238 pages. $22.00.

Biallas, Leonard J., *Pilgrim: A Spirituality of Travel.* Franciscan Press, 2002. 341 pages. $19.95.

Boccaccini, Gabriele, *Roots of Rabbinic Judaism: An Intellectual History, from Ezekiel to Daniel.* William B. Eerdmans, 2002. 230 pages. $24.00.

Boethius, *Consolation of Philosophy.* Translated by Joel C. Relihan. Hackett Publishing, 2001. 216 pages. $9.95.

Bradstock, Andrew, and Christopher Rowland, eds., *Radical Christian Writings: A Reader.* Blackwell Publishers, 2002. 349 pages. $29.95.

Braude, Ann, *Radical Spirits: Spiritualism and Women's Rights in Nineteenth-Century America.* 2d ed. Indiana University Press, 2001. 268 pages. $19.95.

Brettler, Mark Zvi, *The Book of Judges.* Routledge, 2002. 144 pages. $25.95.

Brown, Delwin, Sheila Greeve Davaney, and Kathryn Tanner, eds., *Converging on Culture: Theologians in Dialogue with Cultural Analysis and Criticism.* Oxford University Press, 2001. 202 pages. $18.95.

Broyles, Craig C., *Interpreting the Old Testament: A Guide for Exegesis.* Baker Academic, 2001. 272 pages. $19.99.

Bulgakov, Sergius, *The Bride of the Lamb.* Translated by Boris Jakim. William B. Eerdmans, 2002. 531 pages. $40.00.

Bulkeley, Kelly, ed., *Dreams: A Reader on the Religious, Cultural, and Psychological Dimensions of Dreaming.* Palgrave, 2001. 392 pages. $24.95.

Bushman, Claudia Lauper, and Richard Lyman Bushman, *Building the Kingdom: A History of Mormons in America.* Oxford University Press, 2001. 123 pages. $9.95.

Callen, Barry L., *Authentic Spirituality: Moving beyond Mere Religion.* Baker Academic, 2001. 271 pages. $18.99.

Carson, D. A., Peter T. O'Brien, and Mark A. Seifrid, eds., *Justification and Variegated Nomism, Vol. 1: The Complexities of Second Temple Judaism.* Baker Academic, 2001. 619 pages. $44.95.

Chidester, David, *Christianity: A Global Perspective.* HarperSanFrancisco, 2001. 627 pages. $21.00.

Culbertson, Philip L., ed., *The Spirituality of Men: Sixteen Christians Write about Their Faith*. Fortress Press, 2002. 282 pages. $25.00.

Davis, Derek H., ed., *Church–State Relations and Religious Liberty in Mexico: Historical and Contemporary Perspectives*. J. M. Dawson Institute of Church–State Studies, 2002. 250 pages. $15.95.

Docherty, Jayne Seminare, *Learning Lessons from Waco: When the Parties Bring Their Gods to the Negotiation Table*. Syracuse University Press, 2001. 351 pages. $24.95.

Esposito, John L., Darrell J. Fasching, and Todd Lewis, eds., *World Religions Today*. Oxford University Press, 2002. 562 pages. $45.00.

Faubion, James D., *The Shadows and Lights of Waco: Millennialism Today*. Princeton University Press, 2001. 242 pages. $22.50.

Fine, Lawrence, ed., *Judaism in Practice: From the Middle Ages through the Early Modern Period*. Princeton University Press, 2001. 537 pages. $22.95.

Formicola, Jo Renee, *Pope John Paul II: Prophetic Politician*. Georgetown University Press, 2002. 264 pages. $19.95.

Freinkel, Lisa, *Reading Shakespeare's Will: The Theology of Figure from Augustine to the Sonnets*. Columbia University Press, 2002. 384 pages. $20.00.

Garfield, Jay L., *Empty Words: Buddhist Philosophy and Cross-Cultural Interpretation*. Oxford University Press, 2002. 306 pages. $24.95.

Goldberg, Harvey E., ed., *The Life of Judaism*. University of California Press, 2001. 258 pages. $18.95.

Goldin, Paul Rakita, *The Culture of Sex in Ancient China*. University of Hawaii Press, 2002. 231 pages. $24.95.

Gorringe, T. J., *The Education of the Desire: Towards a Theology of the Senses*. Trinity Press International, 2001. 144 pages. $16.00.

Gregorios, Paulos Mar, ed., *Neoplatonism and Indian Philosophy*. State University of New York Press, 2002. 275 pages. $23.95.

Gundry, Robert H., *Jesus the Word according to John the Sectarian: A Paleo-fundamentalist Manifesto for Contemporary Evangelicalism, Especially Its Elite, in North America*. William B. Eerdmans, 2002. 137 pages. $14.00.

Hardy, Friedhelm, *Viraha-Bhakti: The Early History of Kṛṣṇa Devotion in South India*. Oxford University Press, 2001 (reprint; original edition, 1983). 692 pages. $29.95.

Harris, R. Baine, ed., *Neoplatonism and Contemporary Thought, Part 1*. State University of New York Press, 2002. 407 pages. $26.95.

Harris, R. Baine, ed., *Neoplatonism and Contemporary Thought, Part 2.* State University of New York Press, 2002. 406 pages. $25.95.

Helmick, Raymond G., and Rodney L. Petersen, eds., *Forgiveness and Reconciliation: Religion, Public Policy, and Conflict Transformation.* Templeton Foundation Press, 2001. 450 pages. $22.95.

Hodges, Graham Russell, ed., *Black Itinerants of the Gospel: The Narratives of John Jea and George White.* Palgrave, 2002. 200 pages. $19.95.

Hollywood, Amy, *Sensible Ecstasy: Mysticism, Sexual Difference, and the Demands of History.* University of Chicago Press, 2002. 371 pages. $19.00.

Homerin, Th. Emil, *From Arab Poet to Muslim Saint: Ibn al-Fāriḍ, His Verse, and His Shrine.* American University in Cairo Press, 2001. 162 pages. $19.95.

Horsley, Richard A., and Neil Asher Silberman, *The Message and the Kingdom: How Jesus and Paul Ignited a Revolution and Transformed the Ancient World.* Fortress Press, 2002 (reprint; original edition, Grosset/ Putnam, 1997). 290 pages. $18.00.

Hull, John M., *In the Beginning There Was Darkness: A Blind Person's Conversations with the Bible.* Trinity Press International, 2001. 176 pages. $18.00.

Hunt, Stephen J., *Religion in Western Society.* Palgrave, 2002. 235 pages. $22.95.

Jones, L. Gregory, and Stephanie Paulsell, eds., *The Scope of Our Art: The Vocation of the Theological Teacher.* William B. Eerdmans, 2002. 263 pages. $20.00.

Jonte-Pace, Diane, *Speaking the Unspeakable: Religion, Misogyny, and the Uncanny Mother in Freud's Cultural Texts.* University of California Press, 2001. 190 pages. $17.95.

Kane, Robert, ed., *Free Will.* Blackwell Publishers, 2002. 310 pages. $24.95.

Kelly, Thomas M., *Theology at the Void: The Retrieval of Experience.* University of Notre Dame Press, 2002. 203 pages. $20.00.

Klassen, Randy, *What Does the Bible Really Say about Hell?: Wrestling with the Traditional View.* Pandora Press, 2001. 144 pages. $13.95.

Kripal, Jeffrey J., *Roads of Excess, Palaces of Wisdom: Eroticism and Reflexivity in the Study of Mysticism.* University of Chicago Press, 2001. 412 pages. $21.00.

Lambek, Michael, ed., *A Reader in the Anthropology of Religion.* Blackwell Publishers, 2002. 620 pages. $39.95.

Langford, Michael J., *A Liberal Theology for the Twenty-first Century: A Passion for Reason.* Ashgate, 2001. 259 pages. $29.95.

Larson, Gerald James, ed., *Religion and Personal Law in Secular India: A Call to Judgment.* Indiana University Press, 2001. 362 pages. $22.95.

Lipner, Julius J., *Brahmabandhab Upadhyay: The Life and Thought of a Revolutionary.* Oxford University Press, 2001 (reprint; original edition, 1999). 409 pages. $21.95.

Livingston, David J., *Healing Violent Men: A Model for Christian Communities.* Fortress Press, 2002. 129 pages. $17.00.

Llewelyn, John, *Appositions of Jacques Derrida and Emmanuel Levinas.* Indiana University Press, 2002. 255 pages. $24.95.

Long, D. Stephen, *The Goodness of God: Theology, the Church, and Social Order.* Brazos Press, 2001. 336 pages. $22.99.

Loy, David R., *A Buddhist History of the West: A Study in Lack.* State University of New York Press, 2002. 244 pages. $19.95.

Lund, Eric, ed., *Documents from the History of Lutheranism, 1517–1750.* Fortress Press, 2002. 330 pages. $30.00.

Maddox, Marion, *For God and Country: Religious Dynamics in Australian Federal Politics.* Parliament of Australia, 2001. 299 pages. N.P.

Madsen, Richard, William M. Sullivan, Ann Swidler, and Steven M. Tipton, eds., *Meaning and Modernity: Religion, Polity, and Self.* University of California Press, 2002. 345 pages. $24.95.

Magid, Shaul, ed., *God's Voice from the Void: Old and New Studies in Bratslav Hasidism.* State University of New York Press, 2002. 298 pages. $22.95.

Marshall, John W., *Parables of War: Reading John's Jewish Apocalypse.* Wilfrid Laurier University Press, 2001. 258 pages. $29.95.

Martin, David, *Pentecostalism: The World Their Parish.* Blackwell Publishers, 2002. 197 pages. $24.95.

McDannell, Colleen, ed., *Religions of the United States in Practice, Vol. 1.* Princeton University Press, 2001. 512 pages. $21.95.

McDannell, Colleen, ed., *Religions of the United States in Practice, Vol. 2.* Princeton University Press, 2001. 472 pages. $21.95.

Miller, David, and Sohail H. Hashmi, eds., *Boundaries and Justice: Diverse Ethical Perspectives.* Princeton University Press, 2001. 367 pages. $19.95.

Mitchell, Donald W., *Buddhism: Introducing the Buddhist Experience.* Oxford University Press, 2002. 368 pages. $24.95.

Moore, Stephen D., *God's Beauty Parlor: And Other Queer Spaces in and around the Bible.* Stanford University Press, 2001. 344 pages. $22.95.

Nanos, Mark D., *The Irony of Galatians: Paul's Letter in First-Century Context.* Fortress Press, 2002. 376 pages. $26.00.

Nelson, Kristina, *The Art of Reciting the Qur'an.* American University in Cairo Press, 2001. 246 pages. $24.50.

Noll, Mark A., *The Old Religion in a New World: The History of North American Christianity.* William B. Eerdmans, 2002. 340 pages. $24.00.

Noll, Mark A., *God and Mammon: Protestants, Money, and the Market, 1790–1860.* Oxford University Press, 2001. 313 pages. $21.95.

O'Connor, Kathleen M., *Lamentations and the Tears of the World.* Orbis Books, 2002. 156 pages. $20.00.

O'Regan, Cyril, *Gnostic Apocalypse: Jacob Boehme's Haunted Narrative.* State University of New York Press, 2002. 300 pages. $20.95.

Pennock, Robert T., ed., *Intelligent Design Creationism and Its Critics: Philosophical, Theological, and Scientific Perspectives.* MIT Press, 2001. 805 pages. $45.00.

Porter, Andrew P., *Elementary Monotheism, Vol. 1: Exposure, Limitation, and Need.* University Press of America, 2001. 282 pages. $71.00 (set price).

Porter, Andrew P., *Elementary Monotheism, Vol. 2: Action and Language in Historical Religion.* University Press of America, 2001. 257 pages. $71.00 (set price).

Promey, Sally M., *Painting Religion in Public: John Singer Sargent's "Triumph of Religion" at the Boston Public Library.* Princeton University Press, 2001. 365 pages. $24.95.

Ranft, Patricia, *A Woman's Way: The Forgotten History of Women Spiritual Directors.* Palgrave, 2001. 254 pages. $19.95.

Reagan, Michael, ed., *The Hand of God: Thoughts and Images Reflecting the Spirit of the Universe.* Templeton Foundation Press, 2001. 160 pages. $15.95.

Robbins, Jill, ed., *Is It Righteous to Be?: Interviews with Emmanuel Levinas.* Stanford University Press, 2001. 305 pages. $24.95.

Robinson, James M., ed., *The Sayings of Jesus: The Sayings Gospel Q in English.* Fortress Press, 2002. 35 pages. $6.00.

Rogers, Eugene F., Jr., ed., *Theology and Sexuality: Classic and Contemporary Readings.* Blackwell Publishers, 2002. 422 pages. $29.95.

Rosemont, Henry, Jr., *Rationality and Religious Experience: The Continuing Relevance of the World's Spiritual Traditions.* Open Court, 2001. 111 pages. $17.95.

Rothstein, Mikael, ed., *New Age Religion and Globalization.* David Brown Book Company, 2001. 178 pages. $23.00.

Ruether, Rosemary Radford, *Visionary Women: Three Medieval Mystics.* Fortress Press, 2002. 81 pages. $6.00.

Russell, Neil, *Can I Still Kiss You?: Answering Your Children's Questions about Cancer.* Health Communications, Inc., 2001. 125 pages. $8.95.

Sharma, Arvind, *Classical Hindu Thought: An Introduction.* Oxford University Press, 2001. 221 pages. $16.95.

Sharma, Arvind, *Hinduism for Our Times.* Oxford University Press, 2001 (reprint; original edition, 1996). 116 pages. $8.95.

Silva, Moisés, *Interpreting Galatians: Explorations in Exegetical Method.* 2d ed. Baker Academic, 2001. 256 pages. $17.99.

Smith, D. Moody, *John among the Gospels.* 2d ed. University of South Carolina Press, 2001. 262 pages. $14.95.

Somerville, Margaret, *Death Talk: The Case against Euthanasia and Physician-Assisted Suicide.* McGill-Queen's University Press, 2001. 433 pages. $24.95.

Spickard, James V., J. Shawn Landres, and Meredith B. McGuire, eds., *Personal Knowledge and Beyond: Reshaping the Ethnography of Religion.* New York University Press, 2002. 284 pages. $19.50.

Srinivas, Smriti, *Landscapes of Urban Ministry: The Sacred and the Civic in India's High-Tech City.* University of Minnesota Press, 2001. 329 pages. $22.95.

Steck, Christopher William, *The Ethical Thought of Hans Urs von Balthasar.* Crossroad, 2001. 226 pages. $35.00.

Stein, Edith, *Edith Stein: Essential Writings.* Selected by John Sullivan. Orbis Books, 2002. 158 pages. $15.00.

Steiner, Rudolf, *According to Luke: The Gospel of Compassion and Love Revealed.* Translated by Caterine E. Creeger. Anthroposophic Press, 2001. 258 pages. $16.95.

Steiner, Rudolf, and Friedrich Benesch, *Reverse Ritual: Spiritual Knowledge Is True Communion.* Anthroposophic Press, 2001. 288 pages. $19.95.

Thurman, Suzanne R., *"O Sisters Ain't You Happy?": Gender, Family, and Community among the Harvard and Shirley Shakers, 1781–1918.* Syracuse University Press, 2002. 262 pages. $19.95.

Tripolitis, Antonía, *Religions of the Hellenistic-Roman Age.* William B. Eerdmans, 2002. 165 pages. $16.00.

Urban, Hugh B., *Songs of Ecstasy: Tantric and Devotional Songs from Colonial Bengal.* Oxford University Press, 2001. 187 pages. $19.95.

Vahanian, Gabriel, *Anonymous God: An Essay on Not Dreading Words.* Davies Group, 2002. 149 pages. $16.95.

Villafane, Eldin, Bruce W. Jackson, Robert A. Evans, and Alice Frazer

Evans, eds., *Transforming the City: Reframing Education for Urban Ministry.* William B. Eerdmans, 2002. 206 pages. $24.00.

Volf, Miroslav, and Dorothy C. Bass, eds., *Practicing Theology: Beliefs and Practices in Christian Life.* William B. Eerdmans, 2002. 265 pages. $18.00.

Vries, Hent de, and Samuel Weber, eds., *Religion and Media.* Stanford University Press, 2001. 649 pages. $29.95.

Vysheslavtsev, Boris P., *The Eternal in Russian Philosophy.* Translated by Penelope V. Burt. William B. Eerdmans, 2002. 202 pages. $26.00.

Wagner, Michael F., ed., *Neoplatonism and Nature: Studies in Plotinus' Enneads.* State University of New York Press, 2002. 338 pages. $24.95.

Webb, Stephen H., *Good Eating.* Brazos Press, 2001. 272 pages. $21.99.

Yamaguchi, Satoko, *Mary and Martha: Women in the World of Jesus.* Orbis Books, 2002. 204 pages. $24.00.

OTHER

Pelikan, Jaroslav, and Helmut T. Lehmann, eds., *Luther's Works on CD-ROM.* Fortress Press, 2001. $249.00.

JOIN THE
AMERICAN ACADEMY OF RELIGION

AAR

Benefits of AAR Membership include:

- **Communication and Collegiality among Religion Scholars**
  Belong to the largest and most inclusive association of
  religion scholars – over 9,000 strong.

- **The World's Largest Annual Meeting in Religion**
  Obtain greatly discounted rates to attend the AAR/SBL
  Annual Meeting each November. Receive the Call for Papers
  and Program Book every year.

- **Journal of the American Academy of Religion**
  Receive the flagship journal in religion quarterly.

- **Religious Studies News – AAR Edition**
  Keep up-to-date with the newspaper of record for the field,
  including Spotlight on Teaching.

- **AAR Membership Directory**
  Access contact information for colleagues; the directory is
  the world's most complete listing of religion scholars.

- **Annual Regional Meetings**
  Attend the AAR's scholarly meeting in your region.

- **Employment Information Services**
  Connect with potential employers or job candidates
  through the EIS interview center and the Openings monthly
  job-listing service.

- **Research Grant Programs**
  Apply for research grants open only to members.

- **Publications for Scholars in Religion**
  Stay on top of the field with some of the best religion
  scholarship in five AAR/Oxford University Press series.

- **Website**
  Visit AAR's comprehensive website and gain access to
  Members Only sections.

- **Enhancing the Study of Religion**
  Support the field by joining the AAR and its advocacy on
  behalf of religion and theology in higher education.

Contact the AAR at 1•404•727•7920 or visit us on-line at aarweb.org

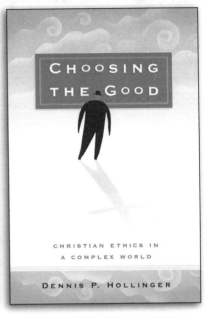

JPS Bible Commentary:
HAFTAROT
Michael Fishbane

From one of the foremost Hebrew Bible scholars in the world comes the first extensive modern commentary on all the prophetic readings recited on Sabbaths and Festivals. Fishbane provides an introduction to the history of these readings, called *haftarot*, and detailed discussions on the history, language, themes, and theology of each text. The relations between the Torah portions and propetic readings are fully explored. Fishbane's textual notes incorporate ancient Near Eastern literature, ancient and medieval rabbinic sources, and modern discussions. This volume is the latest in the acclaimed *JPS Bible Commentary* series.

700 pages, Cloth, ISBN 0-8276-0691-5, $75
Study Guide: 116 pages, Paper
ISBN 0-8276-0718-0, $14.95

Chanting the Hebrew Bible
The Art of Cantillation
Joshua R. Jacobson

Cantillation, the public reading of a passage of Scripture, is an essential element of the Jewish worship service. This encyclopedia text is the most comprehensive guidebook available on this ancient tradition. Jacobson provides a fine history of biblical chanting and a unique explanation of the sense of cantillation, as well as an extensive guide to the modern pronunciation of biblical Hebrew.
This book will be invaluable to cantors and cantorial students who wish to improve their technique, and to readers interested in acquiring a new skill. It is destined to become the definitive work on the subject.

1,000 pages, 8 1/2 x 11, Casebound
ISBN 0-8276-0693-1, $75
CD included

To Do the Right and the Good
A Jewish Approach to Modern Social Ethics
Elliot N. Dorff

In his compelling new book Dorff, one of the most respected leaders in the field of Jewish ethics, esamines Judaism's commitment to social equality. He brings the discussion of social justice, a central principle in the Jewish tradition, to the present day, covering many current issues concerning poverty, war, intrafaith and interfaith relations, family, and privacy. He also explains how Jewish social ethics relate to and contrast with today's Christian and American belief systems. Dorff shows how Jewish sources, when properly applied to modern-day realities, can provide guidance for Jews looking "to do the right and the good" in their lives.

423 pages, 6 x 9, Cloth
ISBN 0-8276-0715-6
$34.95

THE JEWISH PUBLICATION SOCIETY
2100 ARCH STREET, 2ND FLOOR, PHILADELPHIA, PA 19103
Fax: 215-568-2017 * E-mail: jewishbook@jewishpub.org
Order at www.jewishpub.org or 800-234-3151

What to read next.

'Our Place in al-Andalus'
Kabbalah, Philosophy, Literature in Arab Jewish Letters

GIL ANIDJAR

"This is an original and extraordinarily refined work. . . . The author handles with equal ease the range of sources, both modern and medieval. His extremely elegant organization of the material reflects, at a very advanced level, a sense of style commensurate with the sophistication of his thinking."
—Maria Rosa Menocal, Yale University

This book offers a reading of Andalusi, Jewish, and Arabic texts that represent the 12th and 13th centuries as the end of el-Andalus (Islamic Spain).
$24.95 paper $55.00 cloth

Glimpses of Glory
John Bunyan and English Dissent

RICHARD L. GREAVES

"The culmination of a lifetime of scholarly work, this book is essential reading for anyone pursuing serious work on Bunyan and on the religious history of the Restoration to 1688. It will probably stand as the definitive study on Bunyan for a generation."
—Paul S. Seaver, Stanford University
$75.00 cloth

God, Death, and Time

EMMANUEL LEVINAS
TRANSLATED BY BETTINA BERGO
Foreword and Afterword
by Jacques Rolland

This book consists of transcripts from two lecture courses on ethical relation Levinas delivered at the Sorbonne. In seeking to explain his thought to students, he utilizes a clarity and an intensity altogether different from his other writings.
$19.95 paper $55.00 cloth

I Am the Truth
Toward a Philosophy of Christianity

MICHEL HENRY

"Defiant, moving, and vastly challenging, this book contains intellectual drama of the highest order." —Douglas Collins, University of Washington

A part of the "return to religion" now evident in European philosophy, this book represents the culmination of the career of a leading phenomenologist who investigates the multiple kinds of truth associated with Christianity.
$21.95 paper $55.00 cloth

NOW IN PAPERBACK
Between Mecca and Beijing
Modernization and Consumption Among Urban Chinese Muslims

MARIS BOYD GILLETTE

"For Muslims in China, eating is a political act, and this book, the most detailed and comprehensive study of a Muslim community in China to date, explains why. In a society that views pork and secularism as the norm, to be a Muslim can be a challenging if not impossible endeavor. The book shows how a small minority can survive and maintain its values in the face of frequent intolerance by the dominant culture."
—Dru C. Gladney, University of Hawaii
$18.95 paper $49.50 cloth

Belief

GIANNI VATTIMO
Translated by Luca D'Isanto
and David Webb

In this highly personal book, one of Europe's foremost contemporary philosophers confronts the theme of faith and religion.
$13.95 paper $40.50 cloth

Stanford University Press

800·621·2736 | www·sup·org

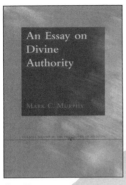

An Essay on Divine Authority

MARK C. MURPHY

For Mark C. Murphy, divine authority is a contingent matter: while created rational beings have decisive reason to subject themselves to the divine rule, they are under divine authority only insofar as they have chosen to allow God's decisions to take the place of their own in their practical reasoning. The author formulates and defends his arguments for this view, and notes its implications for understanding the distinctiveness of Christian ethics.

"Mark C. Murphy's [book] is religiously serious, thoroughly informed by the relevant historical and contemporary literature, philosophically rigorous, and full of intellectual imagination of a very high order."—Nicholas Wolterstorff, Yale University. Cornell Studies in the Philosophy of Religion. $39.95

Choosing Character

Responsibility for Virtue and Vice

JONATHAN JACOBS

"In defending a notion of 'ethical disability' Jonathan Jacobs has much to contribute to current debates on moral responsibility, on the possibility of revision of character, and on the metaethical issues that undergird virtue theory."—Daniel Frank, University of Kentucky. $29.95

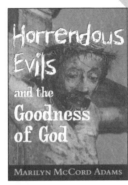

Horrendous Evils and the Goodness of God

MARILYN MCCORD ADAMS

"[Adams] proposes an entirely different approach. Instead of seeking reasons why a good God might permit evil, philosophy should seek an explanation of how God might 'make good' on evil."
—*New York Times*.
Cornell Studies in the Philosophy of Religion. $17.95 paper

Naturalism Defeated?

Essays on Plantinga's Evolutionary Argument against Naturalism

EDITED BY
JAMES BEILBY

Almost a decade ago, Alvin Plantinga articulated his bold and controversial evolutionary argument against naturalism. This intriguing line of argument raises issues of importance to epistemologists and to philosophers of mind, of religion, and of science. In this, the first book to address the ongoing debate, Plantinga presents his influential thesis and responds to critiques by distinguished philosophers from a variety of subfields. $45.00 cloth, $19.95 paper

Reenchantment without Supernaturalism

A Process Philosophy of Religion

DAVID RAY GRIFFIN

"This is both a clear and accurate introduction to the metaphysical philosophy of A.N. Whitehead, using much of his self-devised technical language, and an examination of all the questions of philosophical theology from that viewpoint."—*Theology*. Cornell Studies in the Philosophy of Religion. $57.50 cloth, $24.95 paper

Only In America

RUTGERS *University Press*

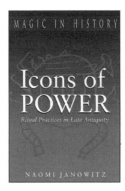

ICONS OF POWER

RITUAL PRACTICES IN LATE ANTIQUITY

Naomi Janowitz

"*Icons of Power* will interest anyone who wants to understand the role that ritual played in the Late Antique world. Crossing sectarian boundaries and examining texts from Jewish, Christian, and pagan sources, Janowitz succeeds in outlining the hidden syntax underlying ritual practices in a wide variety of religious communities."
—Gregory Shaw, Stonehill College

In *Icons of Power*, Naomi Janowitz recovers a lost world of religious expression that has been clouded by misinterpretation for many centuries. In the process, Icons of Power makes an important contribution to our understanding of society in Late Antiquity.

176 pages • $45.00 cloth
Magic in History Series

CARING FOR BODY AND SOUL

BURIAL AND THE AFTERLIFE IN THE MEROVINGIAN WORLD

Bonnie Effros

"A very thorough and up-to-date study of death and burial in early medieval society."
—Guy Halsall, Birkbeck College, University of London

The relationship between the living and the dead was especially significant in defining community identity in the early medieval world. For clerics and laypersons alike, funerals and burial sites were important means for establishing power over rivals. In *Caring for Body and Soul,* Bonnie Effros reveals the social significance of burial rites in early medieval Europe during the time of the Merovingian, or so-called "Long-Haired" Kings.

208 pages • 11 illustrations/4maps
$45.00 cloth

RETHINKING HUMANITARIAN INTERVENTION

A FRESH LEGAL APPROACH BASED ON FUNDAMENTAL ETHICAL PRINCIPLES IN INTERNATIONAL LAW AND WORLD RELIGIONS

Brian D. Lepard

"Brian Lepard brings a massive research effort to bear in support of his fresh approach to humanitarian intervention. By relying on a blend of ethics, religion, and law, this study challenges the validity of both realism and liberalism as the basis for policy and interpretation in international relations. An excellent book that deserves a wide readership and much discussion."
—Richard Falk, Princeton University

516 pages • 6 illustrations
$55.00 cloth

penn state press

820 N. University Drive, USB 1, Suite C • University Park, PA 16802 • fax 1-877-PSU-BOOK • www.psupress.org
AVAILABLE IN BOOKSTORES, OR ORDER TOLL FREE 1-800-326-9180